Fodor's Thailand

SECOND New EDITION

RAU

D1623013

Fodor's Travel Publications, Inc.
New York and London

Fodor's Thailand

Editor: Amanda B. Jacobs
Contributors: Nigel Fisher, Robert Halliday, Marcy Pritchard
Art Director: Fabrizio LaRocca
Cartographer: David Lindroth
Illustrator: Karl Tanner
Cover Photograph: M. Freeman / Viesti Associates

Design: Vignelli Associates

Special Sales

Contents

Foreword

While every care has been taken to ensure the accuracy of the information in this guide, the passage of time will always bring change, and consequently the publisher cannot accept responsibility for errors that may occur.

All prices and opening times quoted here are based on information supplied to us at press time. Hours and admission fees may change, however, and the prudent traveler will avoid inconvenience by calling ahead.

Fodor's wants to hear about your travel experiences, both pleasant and unpleasant. When a hotel or restaurant fails to live up to its billing, let us know and we will investigate the complaint and revise our entries where the facts warrant it.

Send your letters to the editors of Fodor's Travel Publications, 201 E. 50th St., New York, NY 10022.

Highlights '92 and Fodor's Choice

Highlights '92

No other country in Southeast Asia can compare with Thailand in its headlong rush in becoming a newly industrialized country while at the same time treasuring its heritage and independence. Contrasts are everywhere: New factories spring up on the Eastern Seaboard, but the government increases spending tenfold to restore ancient temples. Overseas investment is sought, but the new immigration and alien act does not permit foreigners to own property outright in Thailand. More and more women are holding executive positions in the workforce, but the accepted practice of husbands having an unofficial second wife continues. In resorts, hotels and holiday condominiums are built with abandon, but national parks are sometimes closed to the public to give nature a rest. These and other contradictions form the magnet that makes Thailand so fascinating. A dynamic economy and an energetic people whose traditions are rooted in centuries of culture make Thailand the fulcrum of Southeast Asia.

Thailand continues to draw increasing numbers of visitors. Tourism was expected to be Thailand's top income earner in 1991, with a projected 6 million visitors—a number that is forecast to increase by 10% every year for the next five years, with an especially large increase for 1992, promoted as the "Visit ASEAN Year."

Traveling to Thailand should become easier. Thai International Airways has increased the number of flights from Toronto and is opening up a Los Angeles gateway. For North Americans living on the East Coast, Swissair is actively promoting flights to Bangkok through Zurich, and Finnair is doing the same with flights through Helsinki.

The tourist infrastructure can barely keep up—finding a hotel room in Bangkok during peak season can be impossible. The staffing of hotels also has become a problem. While educational institutes train only 3,000 people a year, hotels seek 10,000 qualified service employees. Hotels now engage in bitter head-hunting, luring experienced staff from other hotels. Thailand's reputation for fine hotel service is likely to suffer.

Hopefully the shortage of hotel rooms in Bangkok will be alleviated by a dozen or more hotels scheduled to open within the next three years. The 450-room **Grand Hyatt Erawan** has already opened as has the **Holiday Inn Crowne Plaza.** The latter, like many new hotels, suffers from the pangs of ill-trained staff.

Outside of Bangkok, other tourist destinations are constructing hotels and holiday condominiums. Pattaya, already over-crowded with hotels, has sprawled over into neighboring Jontien Beach where, among other high-rise resorts, the **Ambassador City hotel,** when completed, will have 5,000 rooms. Vacationers in search of untarnished, idyllic beaches must travel farther along the coast to Ko Cheung near the Kampuchea border.

On the western shore of the Gulf of Siam, the Dusit Thani hotel group, which owns some of Thailand's finest hotel properties, has recently opened a resort in Cha' Am. The Sheraton Corporation is building in Hua Hin, and farther south on Ko Samui, the 100-room **Palm Reef Hotel** opened on Chaweng Beach. Also on Ko Samui, the Imperial Hotel Group has opened their third property, the **Boat House Hotel;** it consists of 36 renovated rice barges and a regular U-shaped hotel.

In Thailand's north, Chiang Mai is becoming a mini-Bangkok: sprawling and congested. New hotels are opening all the time, and, like the new Empress Hotel, they are finding it difficult to find trained, capable staff. By the end of 1991, a new Dusit Thani will have opened and could rival the Chiang Mai Orchid hotel as offering the most deluxe accommodation in Thailand's northern capital. These two hotels will have their premier positions challenged when the Shangri-La opens its new hotel planned for 1993.

Farther north at Chiang Rai, a city that was a quiet, provincial capital a few years ago, there are now three large, ultramodern resorts of which the most dramatic is the **Dusit Thani,** sitting on an island in the middle of the Mae Kok River. Nearby in the Golden Triangle, once a place where only drug smugglers did business, two luxury resorts overlook the Mae Khong River and Burma and Laos beyond. More disquieting is the construction of a casino situated on a point of land jutting into the Mae Khong. Even the countryside northwest of Thailand, along the Burman border and long off the beaten path, now has a **Holiday Inn** at Mae Hae Son.

Thailand's last tourist frontier is the northeast. This has always been the country's poorer region left to the mercy of the monsoons. To appease environmentalists, the Thai government created many national parks and built rustic cabins for hikers and nature lovers. Realizing the area's potential, hoteliers are moving in. The first resort, **Juldis Khao Yai** in Patchong, Nakornratchashima, has already opened. Next year, The Sima Thani group will be opening a 330-room hotel to be managed by the Sheraton Corporation.

A note of caution: Tourists should be aware that Thailand has some great con artists. Visitors are wise to be skeptical—the best cons are incredibly convincing and their scams brilliant—so be on guard, especially when approached with an offer that seems too good to refuse.

Fodor's Choice

No two people will agree on what makes a perfect vacation, but it's fun to know what others think. We hope you'll have a chance to experience some of Fodor's Choices yourself while visiting Thailand. For more information about each entry, refer to the appropriate chapters within this guidebook.

Special Moments

Scuba diving off the Similan Islands
Sunset at Nai Harn Bay, Phuket
Early morning mist on the Mae Khong
Speaking a phrase in Thai and being understood

Dining

Le Normandie, Bangkok *(Very Expensive)*
Amanpuri, Phuket *(Expensive)*
Royal Kitchen, Bangkok *(Expensive)*
Sala Rim Naam, Bangkok *(Expensive)*
Baen Suan, Chiang Mai *(Moderate)*

Lodging

Amanpuri, Phuket *(Very Expensive)*
Oriental, Bangkok *(Very Expensive)*
Shangri-La, Bangkok *(Very Expensive)*
Dusit Island Resort, Chiang Rai *(Expensive)*
Golden Triangle Resort, Chiang Rai *(Expensive)*
The Regent, Cha' Am *(Expensive)*
River View Lodge, Chiang Mai *(Inexpensive)*

Museums

National Museum, Bangkok
Pin Buranaket Folklore Museum, Phitsanulok

Temples and Buildings

Phra Buddha Chinaraj, Phitsanulok
Suan Pakkard Palace, Bangkok
Wat Benjamabopit—Marble Temple, Bangkok
Wat Chaimongkol, Chiang Mai
Wat Phanan Choeng, Ayutthaya
Wat Phra Keo—Temple of the Emerald Buddha, Bangkok
Wat Sra Sri, Sukhothai
Wat Traimitr—Temple of the Golden Buddha, Bangkok

Sights

Erawan Waterfall, Kanchanaburi
Floating Market, Damnoen Saduak
Golden Triangle, northern Thailand
Phang Nga Bay, off Phuket
Thai classical dancing

Beaches

Pansea Beach, Phuket
Nai Harn, Phuket
Ao Phrang Bay, Krabi
Ko Samui
Ko Samet

Shopping

Pottery from Chiang Mai and Lamphun
Sapphires and rubies in Bangkok
Silver and crafts from northern hill tribes
Thai silk in Chiang Mai and Bangkok

Thailand

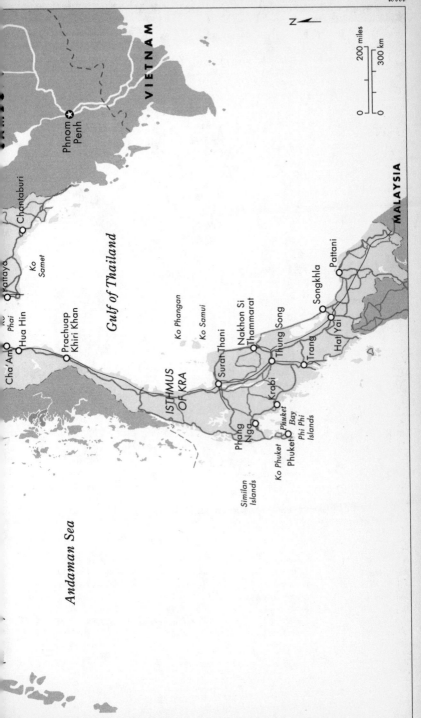

World Time Zones

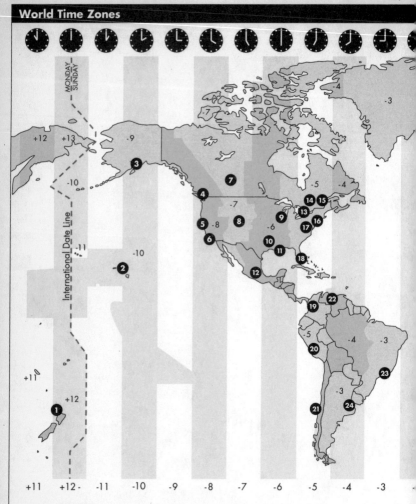

Numbers below vertical bands relate each zone to Greenwich Mean Time (0 hrs.).
Local times frequently differ from these general indications,
as indicated by light-face numbers on map.

Introduction

by Nigel Fisher

A frequent contributor to Fodor's, Nigel Fisher is the editor of a monthly travel publication Voyager International. *He has lived and worked in Thailand.*

Thailand is unique among Southeast Asian nations in having developed its culture independently of Western colonialism, and the Thais are proud of their history. The kingdom's Buddhism is the purest in the region. Its language is like no other, and it is enormously rich, with an extraordinary capacity for exact expression of the finest nuances of human relationships, a sign of the importance Thais place on dealing with one another peaceably and with dignity. Contrasts abound in the country, both geographically and socially. In a land the size of France, beach resorts run the gamut from sleazy Pattaya to dignified Hua Hin. Idyllic island hideaways of virgin beaches sheltered by palm groves and lapped by gentle waters contrast with the frenetic capital.

Bangkok is a sensory kaleidoscope in which temples and palaces of amazing beauty stand alongside ramshackle homes on the banks of evil-smelling *klongs* (canals); appetizing odors of exotic street food mix with the earthy pungency of open drains; and graceful classical dancers perform on stages next door to bars where go-go girls gyrate in clinical nakedness. BMWs stall in traffic jams while *tuk-tuks* (three-wheel cabs) scoot between them; deluxe hotels share the same block with tin-roof stalls; and designer boutiques compete with street vendors hawking knockoff Pierre Cardin shirts.

Chiang Mai, Thailand's second-largest city, is situated in the mountainous north of the country. Older than Bangkok—in fact, older than the Thai kingdom—Chiang Mai has a cultural heritage that reflects those of its neighbors, Burma and Laos, as much as it does Thailand's. The surrounding hills are dotted with small villages of a people collectively known as the hill tribes, whose way of life has, until the last two decades, remained independent from Thailand's national development and the 20th century. To the northeast is the Golden Triangle, once notorious for opium trafficking and still famous for its mountainous scenery spreading over three countries—Thailand, Burma, and Laos.

The small, sleepy market towns of Sukhothai and Ayutthaya contain restored ruins that bear witness to their mighty pasts as the capitals of the Thai kingdom.

Away from the towns are no fewer than 50 national parks. Phu Kradung in the northeast, for example, is 60 square miles of tableland covered with pine trees and tropical flora. Just south of Bangkok is the province of Kanchanaburi, filled with breathtakingly lush forests and cascades.

Forest cover, though, is declining in Thailand, down from 57% in 1961 to 30% today. The mighty elephant, which used to work the great teak forests, has joined the ranks of the unemployed. What work he picks up nowadays is performing for tourists a charade euphemistically called "Elephants at Work."

Just as tourism has given elephants a new lease on life, so has it created alternative opportunities for a population that is 70% agrarian. More than 4 million visitors flock to Thailand each year to seek a quick fix of the exotic at bargain prices. Their demands and willingness to pay top dollar for their pleasures have changed the Thai view of the foreigner. No longer a guest, the visitor is something akin to a one-armed bandit: If the Thai can jerk the tourist just right, he will hit the jackpot. Because the Thai does this with a smile, the foreigner keeps coming back for more. This is not the Thai heritage. In the past, making money for its own sake was frowned upon. Important to the Thai was social harmony and the simple goal of enough "fish in the rivers and rice in the fields" for everybody—an idyllic state associated with the 13th-century founding of the kingdom.

Thailand's origins may reach as far back as 5,600 years to the world's oldest Bronze Age civilization. Much later, from the 6th to the 13th centuries, known as the Dvaravati period, people from the southern Chinese province of Yunnan moved into the fertile basin of the Chao Phraya River.

The Sukhothai period began when two Siamese chieftains banded together, captured the Khmer outpost of Sukhothai, and established the first Thai kingdom in 1238. Early in the Sukhothai period, Thailand's first great king, Ramkhamhoeng, came to power. Not only was he an outstanding warrior, but he made two lasting and significant contributions to Thai culture. He revised and adapted the Khmer alphabet to the requirements of the Thai language, and he invited Ceylonese monks to purify the Khmer-corrupted Theravada (sometimes called Hinayana) Buddhism and establish the religion in a form that is, for the most part, still practiced today.

By 1350, Sukhothai's strength had waned sufficiently for the rising and dynamic young state of Ayutthaya to usurp the reins of power. For four centuries and 33 kings, Ayutthaya was the heart and brain of Thailand. In the 1650s, the city's population exceeded that of London and—according to many foreign travelers—with its golden spires, waterways, and roads, it was the most glorious capital not just in Asia, but in all the world.

In 1768, the Burmese attacked the city. After a 15-month siege, they finally captured Ayutthaya and plundered it. Golden Buddhas were melted down, treasuries ransacked, and buildings burned. Thais who were unable to escape were killed or sent into slavery; by the time the Burmese left, Ayutthaya's population had dropped from 1 million to 10,000.

Under General Taksin, the Thais regrouped, established a capital on the Chao Phraya River at Thonburi (opposite present-day Bangkok), and set about successfully expelling the Burmese from Thailand. In 1782, Chao P'ya Chakri, a supporter of General Taksin, who had briefly been crowned king, became the first king of the current Chakri dynasty. (The present monarch, King Bhumibol Adulyadej, is the ninth in the line.) One of the first acts of P'ya Chakri, or Rama I (all kings of the Chakri dynasty are given the title Rama), was to move the Thai capital to Bangkok.

During the past 200 years, Thailand has had two prime concerns: staving off foreign encroachment on its sovereignty and restructuring its society to meet the demands of modern industrialism.

Western powers were first welcomed when they arrived in 1512, but the French (from whom the Thai word *farang*, meaning foreigner, is derived) tried to overthrow the legitimate government and install a puppet regime. The result was that the Thais not only threw out the French, but also closed their doors to all outsiders until the middle of the 19th century. When the West again threatened Thailand's sovereignty, King Mongkut (Rama IV, 1851–1868), kept the colonial forces at bay through a series of adroit treaties. His efforts were continued by King Chulalongkorn (Rama V, 1868–1910). Thai independence was eventually secured by the cession to the British of a little of what is now Malaysia and to the French of a little of what is now Kampuchea.

Thailand's other concern was adapting to modern social pressures. Under King Chulalongkorn, slavery was abolished, hospitals and schools were established, and some upper-class Thais received a European education so they could replace Western advisers. Under King Prajadhipok (Rama VII, reigned 1925–1935), the world's economic depression brought its share of discontent to Thailand. The pressure for sweeping reform ended in 1932 with the military demanding the establishment of a constitutional monarchy on lines similar to that of Great Britain. Since then, quasimilitary governments and a strong bureaucracy have administered the country. Changes in government have been by coup as often as by election. Despite such occasional upheavals, the nation's policies have been remarkably consistent in fostering the expansion of the industrial economy.

Up to now, the Thais' strong belief in Buddhism (except in the south, where most of Thailand's 2 million Muslims live) has accounted for their tolerant attitude, which can be summed up by their expression *mai pen rai* ("never mind, it does not matter"). The Thais' respect and deference for the monarchy (it is an indictable offense to slander the monarchy) has fostered an acceptance of political authority, and a coup is treated with the attitude of mai pen rai. Whether the resilience of the Thai culture can withstand the pressures of the late 20th century is the current question.

Thailand's attraction rests with the people. Proud of their independence, the Thais believe in accommodation rather than confrontation. Thais believe there is, or at least should be, a way to resolve differences politely and amicably. Demands, displays of anger, and any behavior that upsets harmony are frowned upon. The Thais communicate by smiles, which have many meanings, some of which we are probably better off not knowing.

1 Essential Information

Before You Go

Government Tourist Offices

Call or write the following organizations for free brochures; listings of hotels, restaurants, sights, and shops; and up-to-date calendars of events. The **Pacific Asia Travel Association** (1 Montgomery St., San Francisco, CA 94104, tel. 415/986–4646) can answer some general questions about the area. It also sells a Pacific Asia Information Offices brochure (with tourist board locations for 34 countries) for $3.

In the United States **Tourism Authority of Thailand** (5 World Trade Center, Suite 3443, New York, NY 10048, tel. 212/432–0433; 3440 Wilshire Blvd., Los Angeles, CA 90010, tel. 213/382–2353).

In Canada Thailand currently has no tourist office in Canada. For information, write to any U.S. office.

In the United Kingdom **Thailand Tourist Office** (49 Albemarle St., London W1X 3FE, tel. 071/499–7679).

Tour Groups

Package tours are a good idea if you are willing to trade independence for a guide who knows the language, a fairly solid guarantee that you will see the highlights, and some savings on airfare, hotels, and ground transportation. Listed below is a select sampling of tour operators serving Thailand, and of the tours they offer. Often you can customize existing tours to suit your preferences. If you'd like to keep group travel to a minimum, look for tours with plenty of free or optional days.

When considering a tour, be sure to find out (1) exactly what expenses are included in the price, particularly tips, taxes, side trips, meals, and entertainment; (2) ratings of all hotels on the itinerary and the facilities they offer; (3) cancellation policies for both you and the tour operator; (4) the number of travelers in your group; and (5), if you are traveling alone, the cost of the single supplement. Most tour operators request that bookings be made through a travel agent, and in most cases, there is no additional charge for doing so.

General-Interest Tours *Multicountry* Deluxe-tour packager **Abercrombie & Kent International** (1420 Kensington Rd., Oak Brook, IL 60521, tel. 708/954–2944 or 800/323–7308) offers an "Oriental Capitals" tour of Singapore, Hong Kong, Tokyo, and Bangkok, plus the exotic "Borneo and Beyond" trip to Bangkok, Kuala Lumpur, Borneo, and Hong Kong. An eight-day "Glimpse of Thailand" is also available. **Globus-Gateway** (9525 Queens Blvd., Rego Park, NY 11374, tel. 718/268–1700 or 800/221–0090 from eastern U.S.) teams Singapore, Bangkok, and Hong Kong in an 11-day package or Tokyo, Hong Kong, Seoul, Bangkok, Kuala Lumpur, Singapore, and Bali in its 16-day "Exotic Orient" tour. The 14-day "Orient Adventure" from **Maupintour** (Box 807, Lawrence, KS 66044, tel. 913/843–1211 or 800/255–4266) includes Hong Kong, Bangkok, Bali, and Singapore.

InterPacific Tours International (111 E. 15th St., New York, NY 10003, tel. 212/953–6010 or 800/221–3594) has a base of operations in Hong Kong and a wide range of Orient packages (and prices) as a result. **American Express Vacations** (Box 5014,

Atlanta, GA 30302, tel. 800/241–1700 or 800/282–0800 in GA) is another supermarket of Orient packages. **Pacific Delight Tours** (132 Madison Ave., New York, NY 10016, tel. 212/684–7707 or 800/221–7179) offers single-country packages to Singapore, Thailand, or Hong Kong, as well as mixed Orient tours. **Cultural Tours** (9920 La Cienega Blvd., Suite 715, Englewood, CA 90301, tel. 213/216–1332, 800/282–8898, or in CA, 800/282–8899) offers a 15-day "Orient Shangri-La" tour to Hong Kong, Bangkok, Singapore, and Bali, as well as a 21-day tour of Hong Kong, Bangkok, Chiang Rai, Chiang Mai, Kuala Lumpur, Singapore, Jakarta, and Bali.

Single-Country **Odyssey Tours** (10935 Camarillo St., North Hollywood, CA 91602, tel. 818/769–9212 or 800/456–7436) and **Travel Plans International** (1200 Harger Rd., Oak Brook, IL 60521, tel. 708/573–1400 or 800/323–7600) offer trips just to Thailand.

U.K.-based **Bales Tours Ltd.** (Bales House, Junction Rd., Dorking, Surrey
Operators RH4 3HB, tel. 0306/885991) specializes in escorted tours, such as 10 days in northern Thailand or an 18-day overland tour from Bangkok to Singapore.

Kuoni Travel Ltd. (Kuoni House, Dorking, Surrey RH5 4AZ, tel. 0306/740888) offers numerous packages to Thailand, including holidays in Bangkok with stays in Hong Kong, Singapore, and Thai beaches; excursion packages; and a 16-day Thailand Discovery tour.

Speedbird Holidays (Pacific House, Hazelwick Ave., Three Bridges, Crawley, West Sussex RH10 1NP, tel. 0293/611611) offers a variety of holidays in Bangkok and Thai beach resorts, as well as excursion packages to Northern Thailand, the up-country jungle, and Burma.

Tradewinds Faraway Holidays (Station House, 81-83 Fulham High St., London SW6 3JP, tel. 071/731–8000) offers packages of five nights or more to Bangkok and Thai beach resorts, with optional inland excursions.

Special-Interest **Sobek Expeditions** (Box 1089, Angels Camp, CA 95222, tel. 209/
Tours 736–4524 or 800/777–7939) offers several adventure outings to
Adventure Thailand, including sailing and hiking. **Mountain Travel** (6420 Fairmount Ave., El Cerrito, CA 94530, tel. 800/227–2384), a specialist in adventure travel, has a 16-day "Thai Elephant Safari" tour during which you visit remote hill tribes and stay in simple village houses.

Business **Mindful Journeys** (1242 24th St., Santa Monica, CA 90404, tel. 213/828–5443 or 800/654–7975), in addition to air and first-class accommodations, provides such services as bilingual business cards, letters of introduction in Thai, a list of business contacts, and pretrip counseling on local business practices.

Natural History "Thailand and Malaysia" is a 23-day nature-and-culture tour from **Questers Worldwide Nature Tours** (257 Park Ave. S, New York, NY 10010, tel. 212/673–3120). The group will follow wild elephant tracks, looking for gibbons and tropical birds; boat down the Kok River; and take in a wealth of temples and shrines.

Cruises **Pearl Cruises** (1510 S.E. 17th St., Fort Lauderdale, FL 33316, tel. 800/426–3588) offers a 20-day "Great Cities of Asia" land-sea "Cruise Tour" to Bangkok, Singapore, Malaysia, Brunei, Manila, Canton, and Hong Kong. The 19-day "Spice Islands" tour calls at Singapore, Penang, Phuket, and several Indonesian islands.

Package Deals for Independent Travelers

Most packages include air transportation, accommodations, and transfers to and from your hotel. Some add on meals and sightseeing and make local representatives available to answer questions and offer advice. The travel section of a local newspaper and a good travel agent are your best sources for shopping around. The airlines also provide individualized service for the independent traveler. For example, **Thai Airways International** offers "Royal Orchid Holiday Discover Tours" flight/hotel packages. These cover not only Thailand, but also other countries in Southeast Asia.

Japan & Orient Tours (3131 Camino del Rio N, Suite 1080, San Diego, CA 92108, tel. 619/282–3131 or 800/877–8777) offers flexible packages that allow you to design your own itinerary with options for hotels, air and ground transportation, and sightseeing. **InterPacific Tours International** (*see* Tour Groups, above) has three-day "Pacific à la Carte" packages. **Tourcrafters** (30 S. Michigan Ave., Chicago, IL 60603, tel. 312/726–3886 or 800/621–2259) has two-day (or longer) "Short Stay" packages offering hotels in all ranges. Other good sources of independent packages are **Abercrombie & Kent International** (*see* Tour Groups, above), **American Express** (*see* Tour Groups, above) and **United Airlines** (800/328–6877).

When to Go

Thailand has two climatic regions: tropical savannah in the northern regions and tropical rain forest in the south. Three seasons run from hot (March to May) to rainy (June to September) and cool (October to February). Humidity is high all year, especially during the hot season. The cool season is pleasantly warm in the south, but in the north, especially in the hills around Chiang Mai, it can become quite chilly. The cool season is the peak season. Prices are often twice as high then as in the low seasons, yet hotels are often fully booked.

Climate The following are average daily maximum and minimum temperatures for Bangkok. The north will generally be a degree or two cooler.

Jan.	89F	32C	May	93F	34C	Sept.	89F	32C
	68	20		77	25		75	24
Feb.	91F	33C	June	91F	33C	Oct.	88F	31C
	72	22		75	24		75	24
Mar.	93F	34C	July	89F	32C	Nov.	88F	31C
	75	24		75	24		72	22
Apr.	95F	35C	Aug.	89F	32C	Dec.	88F	31C
	77	25		75	24		68	20

Current weather information on more than 750 cities around the world may be obtained by calling the WeatherTrak information service at 900/370–8728. Dialing this number will connect you to a computer, with which you can communicate by touch tone—at a cost of 95¢ per minute. A taped message will tell you to dial a three-digit access code for the destination in which you're interested. The code is either the area code (in the

United States) or the first three letters of the foreign city. For a list of all access codes, send a stamped, addressed envelope to Cities, 9B Terrace Way, Greensboro, NC 27403. For further information, phone 800/247–3282.

What to Pack

Pack light, because porters can be hard to find and baggage restrictions are tight on international flights—be sure to check on your airline's policies before you pack. And either leave room in your suitcase or bring expandable totes for all your bargains.

Clothing If you'll be traveling through several different types of climate, your wardrobe will have to reflect this. (For weather information on your particular destinations, *see* When to Go, above.) Light cotton or other natural-fiber clothing is appropriate for Thailand; drip-dry is an especially good idea, because the tropical sun and high humidity encourage frequent changes of clothing. Avoid exotic fabrics because you may have difficulty getting them laundered.

Thailand is generally informal: A sweater, shawl, or lightweight linen jacket will be sufficient for dining and evening wear, except for top international restaurants, where men will still be most comfortable in (and may in fact be required to wear) a jacket and tie. A sweater is also a good idea for cool evenings or overly air-conditioned restaurants.

Toiletries It might be wise to bring your favorite toilet articles (in plastic containers to avoid breakage and reduce the weight of luggage)—make sure that bottles containing liquids are tightly capped to prevent leakage.

Footwear The paths leading to temples can be rough; in any case, a pair of sturdy and comfortable walking shoes is always appropriate when traveling. Slip-ons are preferable to lace-up shoes, as they must be removed before you enter shrines and temples.

Miscellaneous Prepare for the tropical sun by bringing along a hat and sunscreen. Mosquito repellent is a good idea, and toilet paper is not always supplied in public places.

Electricity Thailand operates on 220-volt electrical current, so if you plan to use a hair dryer, razor, travel iron, or other compact electric appliance, be sure to bring a convertor along. (The United States operates on 120-volt electric current.)

Taking Money Abroad

Traveler's checks and major U.S. credit cards—particularly Visa—are accepted in larger cities and resorts. In smaller towns and rural areas, you'll need cash. Small restaurants and shops in the cities also tend to operate on a cash basis. It is not necessary to obtain foreign currency before you arrive. Thailand has exchange booths at large airports and in major towns. Also, the rate of exchange is considerably better than what you would receive in North America or Britain. Still, if you do wish to have some baht before you arrive, try your nearest major bank. If it can't provide this service, you can exchange money through Thomas Cook Currency Services. To find the office nearest you, contact the company at 29 Broadway, New York, NY 10009 (tel. 212/757–6915). Because Thailand does not permit the export of large sums of cash, you may find baht hard to obtain from abroad.

For safety and convenience, it's always best to take traveler's checks. The most recognized are American Express, Barclay's, Thomas Cook, and those issued through major commercial banks, such as Citibank and Bank of America. Some banks will issue the checks free to established customers, but most charge a 1% commission fee. Buy some of the checks in small denominations to cash toward the end of your trip. This will save you from having to cash a large check and ending up with more baht than you need. Remember to take the addresses of offices where you can get refunds for lost or stolen traveler's checks. Banks and government-approved exchange houses give the best rates; hotels will also change currency, but generally at lower rates.

Getting Money from Home

There are at least three ways to get money from home:

(1) Have it sent through a large commercial bank with a branch in the city or town where you're staying. The drawback is that you must have an account with the bank; if not, you'll have to go through your own bank, and the process will be slower and more expensive.

(2) Have it sent through American Express. If you are a cardholder, you can cash a personal check or a counter check at an American Express office for up to $1,000; $200 will be in cash and $800 in traveler's checks. There is a 1% commission. Through the American Express MoneyGram service, you can receive up to $10,000 in cash. It works this way: You call home and ask someone to go to an American Express office or a MoneyGram agent located in a retail outlet and to fill out a MoneyGram. It can be paid for with cash or any major credit card. The person making the payment is given a reference number and telephones you with that number. The MoneyGram agent calls an 800 number and authorizes the transfer of funds to an American Express office or participating agency in the town where you're staying. In most cases, the money is available immediately on a 24-hour basis. You pick it up by showing identification and giving the reference number. Fees vary according to the amount of money sent. For sending $300, the fee is $30; for $5,000, $195. For the American Express MoneyGram location nearest your home, and to find out where the service is available overseas, call 800/543–4080. You do not have to be a cardholder to use this service.

(3) Have it sent through Western Union (tel. 800/325–6000). If you have a MasterCard or Visa, you can have money sent for any amount up to your credit limit. If not, have someone take cash or a certified cashier's check to a Western Union office. The money will be delivered in two business days to a bank near where you're staying. Fees vary with the amount of money sent and where it's being sent. For $1,000, the fee is about $70; for $500, about $60.

Cash Machines

Virtually all U.S. banks now belong to a network of Automatic Teller Machines (ATMs) that dispense cash 24 hours a day. The largest of the major networks—Cirrus, owned by MasterCard, and Plus, affiliated with Visa—have now begun providing access to ATMs abroad, mostly in cities that attract large numbers of tourists and business travelers. Each network has a toll-free number you can call to find out whether it provides service in a given city and to locate its machines in that city. (Cirrus: 800/424–7787. Plus: 800/843–7587.) Note that these "cash cards" are not issued automatically; they must be requested at your specific branch.

Cards issued by Visa, American Express, and MasterCard can also be used in the ATMs, but the fees are usually higher than the fees on bank cards (and there is a daily interest charge on the "loan"). All three companies issue directories listing the national and international outlets that accept their cards. You can pick up a Visa or MasterCard directory at your local bank. For an American Express directory, call 800/CASH–NOW (this number can also be used for general inquiries). Contact your bank for information on fees and the amount of cash you can withdraw on any given day. Although each bank individually charges for taking money with the card, using your American Express, Visa, or MasterCard at an ATM can be cheaper than exchanging money in a bank because of variations in exchange rates.

Passports and Visas

All Americans, Canadians, and Britons must have a valid passport to enter Thailand. Visas are not required for stays of up to 15 days for Americans, Canadians, and Britons, providing visitors can show proof of onward travel arrangements.

Extended-stay visas can be obtained by contacting the Embassy of Thailand, 2300 Kalorama Rd. NW, Washington, DC 20008, tel. 202/483–7200.

Also, if you have recently visited areas infected with yellow fever, cholera, or smallpox, you will need a certificate of vaccination in order to be allowed into Thailand.

Americans. Applications for a new passport must be made in person; renewals can be obtained in person or by mail (*see* below). First-time applicants should apply to one of the 13 U.S. Passport Agency offices well in advance of their departure date. In addition, local county courthouses, many state and probate courts, and some post offices accept passport applications. Necessary documents include: (1) a completed passport application (Form DSP-11); (2) proof of citizenship (birth certificate with raised seal or naturalization papers); (3) proof of identity (unexpired driver's license, employee ID card, or any other document with your photograph and signature); (4) two recent, identical, 2-inch-square photographs (black-and-white or color); (5) $42 application fee for a 10-year passport (those under 18 pay $27 for a five-year passport). Passports are mailed to you within about 10 working days.

To renew your passport by mail, you'll need a completed Form DSP-82; two recent, identical passport photographs; a passport less than 12 years old; and a check or money order for $35.

Canadians. Send a completed application (available at any post office or passport office) to the Bureau of Passports, Suite 215, West Tower, Guy Favreau Complex, 200 René Lévesque Blvd.

W, Montreal, Quebec H2Z 1X4. Include $25, two photographs, a guarantor, and proof of Canadian citizenship. Applications can be made in person at the regional passport offices in Calgary, Edmonton, Halifax, Montreal, Toronto, St. John's (Newfoundland), Vancouver, Victoria, or Winnipeg. Passports are valid for five years and are nonrenewable.

Britons. Applications are available from travel agencies or a main post office, or the Passport Office (Clive House, 70 Petty France, London SW1H 9HD, tel. 071/279–3434 for recorded information, or 071/279–4000). Send the completed form to a regional Passport Office. The application must be countersigned by your bank manager, or by a solicitor, barrister, doctor, clergyman, or Justice of the Peace who knows you personally. In addition, you'll need two photographs and the £15 fee.

Customs and Duties

On Arrival If you are bringing any foreign-made equipment from home, such as cameras, it is wise to carry the original receipt with you or register it with U.S. Customs before you leave (Form 4457). Otherwise, you may end up paying duty on your return.

One quart of wine or liquor, 200 cigarettes or 250 grams of smoking tobacco, and all personal effects may be brought into Thailand duty-free. Visitors may bring in any amount of foreign currency; amounts taken out may not exceed those declared upon entry. Narcotic drugs, pornographic materials, and firearms are strictly prohibited.

On Departure Visitors may not export more than 500 baht per person or 1,000 baht per family passport.

U.S. Residents U.S. residents may bring home duty-free up to $400 worth of foreign goods, so long as they have been out of the country for at least 48 hours, and they haven't claimed this exemption in the past 30 days. Each member of the family is entitled to the same exemption, regardless of age, and exemptions can be pooled. For the next $1,000 worth of goods, a flat 10% rate is assessed; above $1,400, duties vary with the merchandise. Included for travelers 21 or older are one liter of alcohol, 100 cigars (non-Cuban), and 200 cigarettes. Only one bottle of perfume trademarked in the United States may be brought in. However, there is no duty on antiques or art more than 100 years old. Anything exceeding these limits will be taxed at the port of entry and may be taxed additionally in the traveler's home state. Gifts valued at less than $50 may be mailed to friends or relatives at home duty-free, but must not exceed one package per day to any one addressee and must not include perfumes costing more than $5, tobacco, or liquor.

Canadian Residents Canadian residents have an exemption ranging from $20 to $300, depending on the length of stay out of the country. For the $300 exemption, you must be out of the country for at least one week. Residents are allowed one $300 exemption per year. Residents may also bring in duty-free: (1) up to 50 cigars, 200 cigarettes, and 2 pounds of tobacco; and (2) 40 ounces of liquor, provided these are declared in writing to customs on arrival and accompany the traveler in hand or checked-through baggage. Personal gifts should be mailed as "Unsolicited Gift— Value under $40." Request the Canadian Customs brochure, *I Declare*, for further details.

U.K. Residents Returning to the United Kingdom, those 17 or older may take home: (1) 200 cigarettes or 100 cigarillos or 50 cigars or 250 grams of tobacco; (2) two liters of table wine and (a) one liter of alcohol over 22% by volume (most spirits), or (b) two liters of alcohol under 22% by volume (fortified or sparkling wine), or (c) an additional two liters of table wine; (3) 60 milliliters of perfume and 250 milliliters of toilet water; and (4) other goods up to a value of £32, but not more than 50 liters of beer or 25 mechanical lighters.

Traveling with Film

If your camera is new, shoot and develop a few rolls before leaving home. Pack some lens tissue and an extra battery for your built-in light meter. Invest about $10 in a skylight filter, and screw it onto the front of your lens. It will protect the lens and also reduce haze.

Film doesn't like hot weather. If you're driving in the heat, don't store film in the glove compartment or on the shelf under the rear window. Put it behind the front seat on the floor, on the side opposite the exhaust pipe.

On a plane trip, never pack unprocessed film in check-in luggage; if your bags are X-rayed, say good-bye to your pictures. Always carry undeveloped film with you through security, and ask to have it inspected by hand. (It helps to isolate your film in a plastic bag, ready for quick inspection.) Inspectors at American airports are required by law to honor requests for hand inspection; abroad, you'll have to depend on the kindness of strangers.

The old airport scanning machines—still in use in some countries—use heavy doses of radiation that can turn a family portrait into an early morning fog. The newer models—used in all U.S. airports—are safe for anything from five to 500 scans, depending on the speed of your film. The effects are cumulative; you can put the same roll of film through several scans without worry. After five scans, though, you're asking for trouble.

If your film gets fogged and you want an explanation, send it to the National Association of Photographic Manufacturers (550 Mamaroneck Ave., Harrison, NY 10528). They will try to determine what went wrong. The service is free.

Staying Healthy

Shots and Although Thailand does not require or suggest vaccinations be-
Medications fore traveling, the United States Centers for Disease Control offer the following recommendations:

Tetanus and polio vaccinations should be up-to-date, and you should be immunized against (or immune to) measles, mumps, and rubella. If you plan to visit rural areas, where there's questionable sanitation, you'll need a gamma globulin vaccination as protection against hepatitis A. If you are staying for longer than three weeks, and traveling into rural areas, antimalaria pills and typhoid vaccination are recommended. If staying for six months or more, you should be vaccinated against hepatitis B, rabies, and Japanese encephalitis. For news on current outbreaks of infectious diseases, ask your physician and check with your state or local department of health.

Precautions To minimize the risk of digestive-tract infections, never drink tap water unless it has been boiled; order bottled water and make sure that the seal has not been broken. Hot tea or coffee is never a problem, but be wary of ice; some international hotels now make their ice from distilled/purified water. Avoid eating salads that have not been washed in purified water, and always peel fruit. Dengue fever is on the rise in Southeast Asia, and malaria is always a threat; so be careful; remain in well-screened areas, wear clothing that covers your arms and legs, and bring plenty of mosquito repellent. Both Ko Samet and northern Thailand are known to have malarial mosquitoes; so take extra precautions if you visit these areas.

Doctors Many Thai hotels have physicians on call 24 hours a day. Also, the **International Association for Medical Assistance to Travelers (IAMAT;** 417 Center St., Lewiston, NY 14092, tel. 716/754–4883; 40 Regal Rd., Guelph, Ont. N1K 1B5, Canada; 57 Voirets, 1212 Grand-Lancy, Geneva, Switzerland) offers a list of approved English-speaking doctors abroad whose training meets British and American standards. Membership is free.

Insurance

Travelers may seek insurance coverage in three areas: health and accident, lost luggage, and trip cancellation. Your first step is to review your existing health and home-owner policies. Some health-insurance plans cover health expenses incurred while traveling, some home-owner policies cover luggage theft, and some major medical plans cover emergency transportation.

Companies offering comprehensive travel insurance packages that cover personal accident, trip cancellation, lost luggage, and sometimes default and bankruptcy include **Access America, Inc.,** a subsidiary of Blue Cross/Blue Shield (Box 11188, Richmond, VA 23230, tel. 800/334–7525 or 800/284–8300); **Near Services** (450 Prairie Ave., Suite 101, Calumet City, IL 60409, tel. 708/868–6700 or 800/654–6700); **Carefree Travel Insurance** (Box 310, 120 Mineola Blvd., Mineola, NY 11501, tel. 516/294–0220 or 800/343–3149); and **Travel Guard International,** underwritten by Transamerica Occidental Life Companies (1145 Clark St., Stevens Point, WI 54481, tel. 715/345–0505 or 800/782–5151).

Health and Accident Several companies offer coverage designed to supplement existing health insurance for travelers:

The **Association of British Insurers** (Aldermary House, 10–15 Queen St., London EC4N 1TT, tel. 071/248–4477) gives free general advice on all aspects of holiday insurance.

Carefree Travel Insurance (*see* above) provides coverage for emergency medical evacuation and accidental death and dismemberment. It also offers 24-hour medical advice by phone.

Europ Assistance (252 High St., Croydon, Surrey CR0 1NF, tel. 081/680–1234) is a proven leader in the holiday-insurance field.

International SOS Assistance (Box 11568, Philadelphia, PA 19116, tel. 215/244–1500 or 800/523–8930), a medical assistance company, provides emergency evacuation services, worldwide medical referrals, and optional medical insurance.

Travel Guard International (*see* above) offers emergency evacuation services and reimbursement for medical expenses with no deductibles or daily limits.

Wallach and Company, Inc. (243 Church St. NW, Suite 100D, Vienna, VA 22180, tel. 703/281–9500 or 800/237–6615) offers comprehensive medical coverage, including emergency evacuation services worldwide.

Luggage Airlines are responsible for lost or damaged property only up to $1,250 per passenger on domestic flights, and $9.07 per pound ($20 per kilo) for checked baggage on international flights, and up to $400 per passenger for unchecked baggage on international flights. If you're carrying valuables, either take them with you on the airplane or purchase additional insurance for lost luggage. Some airlines will issue additional insurance when you check in, but many do not. Rates are $1 for every $100 valuation, with a maximum of $25,000 valuation per passenger. Hand luggage is not included.

Insurance for lost, damaged, or stolen luggage is available through travel agents or directly through various insurance companies. Two companies that issue luggage insurance are **Tele-Trip** (Box 31685, 3201 Farnam St., Omaha, NE 68131, tel. 800/228–9792), a subsidiary of Mutual of Omaha, and **The Travelers Corporation** (Ticket and Travel Dept., 1 Tower Sq., Hartford, CT 06183–5040, tel. 203/277–0111 or 800/243–3174). Tele-Trip, which operates sales booths at airports and also issues policies through travel agents, insures checked luggage for up to 180 days; rates vary according to the length of the trip. The Travelers Corp. insures checked or hand luggage for $500–$2,000 valuation per person, also for a maximum of 180 days. Rates for up to five days for $500 valuation are $10; for 180 days, $85. Both companies offer the same rates on domestic and international flights. Check the travel pages of your local newspaper for the names of other companies that insure luggage.

Before you go, itemize the contents of each bag in case you need to file an insurance claim. Be certain to put your home address on each piece of luggage, including carry-on bags. If your luggage is stolen and later recovered, the airline will deliver the luggage to your home free of charge.

Trip Cancellation Flight insurance is often included in the price of a ticket when paid for with an American Express, Visa, or other major credit or charge card. It is usually included in combination travel insurance packages available from most tour operators, travel agents, and insurance agents.

Student and Youth Travel

The **International Student Identity Card (ISIC)** entitles students to special fares on local transportation and discounts at museums, theaters, sports events, and many other attractions, though few, in fact, in Thailand. If purchased in the United States, the $14 ISIC also includes $3,000 in emergency medical insurance, plus $100 a day for up to 60 days of hospital coverage, as well as a collect phone number to call in case of an emergency. Apply to the **Council on International Educational Exchange** (CIEE; 205 E. 42nd St., New York, NY 10017, tel. 212/661–1450). In Canada, the ISIC is available for Can$12 from **Travel Cuts** (187 College St., Toronto, Ont. M5T 1P7, tel. 416/979–2406).

Council Travel, a CIEE subsidiary, is the foremost U.S. student travel agency, specializing in low-cost charters and serving as the exclusive U.S. agent for many student airfare bargains and student tours. (CIEE's 80-page *Student Travel Catalog* and "Council Charter" brochure are available free from any Council Travel office in the United States; enclose $1 postage if ordering by mail.) In addition to the CIEE headquarters at 205 East 42nd Street and a branch office at 35 West 8th Street in New York City (tel. 212/254–2525), there are Council Travel offices throughout the United States. Check with the New York City office for the one nearest you.

The **Educational Travel Center** (438 N. Frances St., Madison, WI 55703, tel. 608/256–5551) is another student-travel specialist with information on tours, bargain fares, and bookings.

Students who would like to work abroad should contact CIEE's **Work Abroad Department** (205 E. 42nd St., New York, NY 10017, tel. 212/661–1414, ext. 1130). The council arranges various types of paid and voluntary work experiences overseas for up to six months. CIEE also sponsors study programs in Latin America and Asia and publishes many books of interest to the student traveler, including *Work, Study, Travel Abroad: The Whole World Handbook* ($10.95 plus $1 book-rate postage or $2.50 first-class postage) and *Volunteer! The Comprehensive Guide to Voluntary Service in the U.S. and Abroad* ($6.95 plus $1 book-rate postage or $2.50 first-class postage).

The Information Center at the **Institute of International Education** (IIE, 809 UN Plaza, New York, NY 10017, tel. 212/984–5413) has reference books, foreign-university catalogues, study-abroad brochures, and other materials that may be consulted by students and nonstudents alike, free of charge. Open weekdays 10–4.

IIE administers a variety of grant and study programs offered by U.S. and foreign organizations and publishes a well-known annual series of study-abroad guides, including *Academic Year Abroad*, *Vacation Study Abroad*, and *Management Study Abroad*. The institute also publishes *Teaching Abroad*, listing employment and study opportunities overseas for U.S. teachers. For a current list of IIE publications, prices, and ordering information, write to Institute of International Education Books (809 UN Plaza, New York, NY 10017). Books must be purchased by mail or in person; telephone orders are not accepted. General information on IIE programs and services is available from the institute's regional offices in Atlanta, Chicago, Denver, Houston, San Francisco, and Washington, DC.

An **International Youth Hostel Federation** (IYHF) membership card can be used in inexpensive, dormitory-style hostels in Thailand. Hostels provide separate sleeping quarters for men and women at rates ranging from $7 to $20 a night per person, and are situated in a variety of buildings, including converted farmhouses and specially constructed modern buildings. There are more than 5,000 hostel locations in 68 countries around the world. IYHF memberships, which are valid for 12 months from the time of purchase, are available in the United States through **American Youth Hostels** (AYH, Box 37613, Washington, DC 20013, tel. 202/783–6161). The cost for a first-year membership is $25 for adults 18–54. Renewal thereafter is $15. For youths (under 18), the rate is $10, and for senior citizens (55 and older), the rate is $15. Family membership is available for $35. Every national hostel association arranges special reductions for members visiting its country, such as discounted rail fare or free bus travel; so be sure to ask for an international concessions list when you buy your membership.

Economical bicycle tours for small groups of adventurous, energetic students are another popular AYH student travel service. For information on these and other AYH services and publications, contact the AYH at the address above.

For a list of hostels, write to the tourist authorities (*see* Tourist Information, above) of Thailand.

YMCAs can be found in Thailand. For a listing of Y's worldwide, send a stamped, addressed envelope to "Y's Way," 356 W. 34th St., New York, NY 10001, tel. 212/760–5856. The organization can also make reservations.

Traveling with Children

The American Institute for Foreign Study (AIFS; 102 Greenwich Ave., Greenwich, CT 06830, tel. 203/869–9090) offers programs for college-age children and interested adults. For information on programs for high-school children and their families, contact the **Educational Travel Division,** American Council for International Studies, 19 Bay State Rd., Boston, MA 02215, tel. 617/236–2015 or 800/825–AIFS.

Rascals in Paradise (Adventure Express Travel, 650 5th Ave., Suite 505, San Francisco, CA 94107, tel. 415/442–0799) specializes in organizing family tours to exotic destinations. Escorted tours provide children's activities, a babysitter for each family, and teacher programs.

Publications   *Family Travel Times* is an eight- to 12-page newsletter published 10 times a year by TWYCH (Travel with Your Children, 80 8th Ave., New York, NY 10011, tel. 212/206–0688). The $35 subscription includes access to back issues and twice-weekly opportunities to call in for specific information. Send $1 for a sample issue.

Great Vacations with Your Kids, by Dorothy Jordan (founder of TWYCH) and Marjorie Cohen, offers complete advice on planning a trip with children (toddlers to teens). If unavailable at your local bookstore, write to E.P. Dutton (375 Hudson St., New York, NY 10014, tel. 212/366–2000).

Kids and Teens in Flight is a brochure developed by the U.S. Department of Transportation on children traveling alone. To order a free copy, call 202/366–2220.

Family Travel Guides (Carousel Press, Box 6061, Albany, CA 94706, tel. 415/527–5849) is a catalog of guidebooks, games, and magazine articles geared to traveling with children. Send $1 for postage and handling.

Getting There   All children, including infants, must have a passport for foreign travel; family passports are no longer issued.

On international flights, children under 2 not occupying a seat pay 10% of adult fare. Various discounts apply to children 2–12 years of age. Regulations regarding infant travel on airplanes are in the process of being changed. Until they do, however, you must buy a separate ticket and bring your own infant car seat if you want to be sure that your infant is secure and travels in his or her own safety seat. (Check with the airline in advance; certain seats aren't allowed.) Some airlines allow babies to travel in their own car seats at no charge if there's a spare seat available; otherwise, safety seats are stored and the child has to be held by a parent. (For the booklet "Child/Infant Safety Seats Acceptable for Use in Aircraft," write to the Federal Aviation Administration, APA-200, 800 Independence Ave. SW, Washington DC 20591, tel. 202/267–3479.) If you opt to hold your baby on your lap, do so with the infant outside the seat belt so he or she won't be crushed in case of a sudden stop.

See TWYCH's Airline Guide, published in the February 1990 issue of *Family Travel Times* (and again in February 1992) for more information about children's services offered by 46 airlines.

Hotels Baby-sitting services are available at almost all of the better hotels, including Hilton, Inter-Continental, Marriott, and Ramada Inn, and at most YMCAs. At many hotels, children can stay free in their parents' room.

Hints for Disabled Travelers

Organizations The **Information Center for Individuals with Disabilities** (Fort Point Place, 1st floor, 27–43 Wormwood St., Boston, MA 02210, tel. 617/727–5540, TDD 617/727–5236) offers useful problem-solving assistance, including lists of travel agents who specialize in tours for the disabled.

Mobility International USA (Box 3551, Eugene, OR 97403, tel. 503/343–1284) is an internationally affiliated organization with 500 members. For a $20 annual fee, it coordinates exchange programs for disabled people around the world and offers information on accommodations and organized study programs.

The **Society for the Advancement of Travel for the Handicapped** (26 Court St., Penthouse Suite, Brooklyn, NY 11242, tel. 718/ 858–5483) offers access information. Annual membership costs $45, $25 for senior travelers and students. Send $1 and a stamped, addressed envelope for information on a specific country.

Travel Industry and Disabled Exchange (TIDE, 5435 Donna Ave., Tarzana, CA 91356, tel. 818/368–5648) is an industry-based organization with a $15-per-person annual membership fee. Members receive a quarterly newsletter and information on travel agencies and tours.

Evergreen Travel Service (19505L 44th Ave. W, Lynnwood, WA 98036, tel. 206/776–1184 or 800/435–2288) has been specializing in unique tours for the disabled for 33 years. Its 1992 Southeast Asia itineraries will include visits to China, Hong Kong, Bangkok, Singapore, and Bali.

Publications *The Itinerary* (Box 2012, Bayonne, NJ 07002, tel. 201/858– 3400) is a bimonthly travel magazine for the disabled. Call for a subscription ($10 for one year, $20 for two); it's not available in stores.

Access to the World: A Travel Guide for the Handicapped, by Louise Weiss, is available from Henry Holt & Co. for $12.95

plus $2 shipping (tel. 800/247–3912; the order number is 0805 001417).

Twin Peaks Press (Box 129, Vancouver, WA 98666, tel. 206/694–2462 or 800/637–2256 for orders only) specializes in books for the disabled. *Travel for the Disabled* offers helpful hints, as well as a comprehensive list of guidebooks and facilities geared to the disabled. *Directory of Travel Agencies for the Disabled* lists more than 350 agencies throughout the world. The press also offer a "Traveling Nurse's Network," which provides registered nurses trained in all medical areas to accompany and assist disabled travelers. Add $2 shipping per book; $1 for each additional book.

Hints for Older Travelers

Organizations The **American Association of Retired Persons** (AARP; 1909 K St. NW, Washington, DC 20049, tel. 202/662–4850) has a program for independent travelers called the Purchase Privilege Program, which offers discounts on hotels, airfare, car rentals, and sightseeing. The AARP arranges group tours through **AARP Travel Experience from American Express** (Box 5850, Norcross, GA 30091, tel. 800/927–0111). AARP members must be at least 50 years old. Annual dues are $5 per person or per couple.

If you're planning to use an AARP or other senior-citizen identification card to obtain a reduced hotel rate, mention it at the time you make your reservation rather than when you check out. At participating restaurants, show your card to the maître d' before you're seated; discounts may be limited to certain set menus, days, or hours. Your AARP card will identify you as a retired person, but will not ensure a discount in all hotels and restaurants. For a free list of hotels and restaurants that offer discounts, call or write the AARP and ask for the "Purchase Privilege" brochure or call the AARP Travel Service. When renting a car, remember that economy cars, priced at promotional rates, may cost less than the cars that are available with your ID card.

National Council of Senior Citizens (925 15th St. NW, Washington, DC 20005, tel. 202/347–8800) is a nonprofit advocacy group with some 5,000 local clubs across the country. Annual membership is $12 per person or per couple. Members receive a monthly newspaper with travel information and an ID for reduced rates on hotels and car rentals.

Mature Outlook (6001 N. Clarke St., Chicago, IL 60660, tel. 800/336–6330), a subsidiary of Sears, Roebuck & Co., is a travel club for U.S. residents over 50 years of age, offering Holiday Inn discounts and a bimonthly newsletter. Annual membership is $9.95 per person or couple.

Vantage Travel Service (111 Cypress St., Brookline, MA 02146, tel. 800/322–6677) offers land/cruise tours geared toward senior citizens. The itinerary includes visits to Bangkok, Bali, Hong Kong, and Singapore. Nonsenior, adult companions are welcome.

Publications *The International Health Guide for Senior Citizen Travelers,* by W. Robert Lange, M.D., is available for $4.95 plus $1 for shipping from Pilot Books (103 Cooper St., Babylon, NY 11702, tel. 516/422–2225).

The Discount Guide for Travelers over 55, by Caroline and Walter Weintz, lists helpful addresses, package tours, reduced-rate car rentals, etc., in the United States and abroad. If unavailable from your local bookseller, send $7.95 plus $1.50 shipping and handling to NAL/Cash Sales (Bergenfield Order Dept., 120 Woodbine St., Bergenfield, NJ 07621, tel. 800/526–0275).

Further Reading

Sources *Good Books for the Curious Traveler: Asia and the South Pacific* provides synopses of 35 texts on Southeast Asian countries in the categories of fiction, archaeology, history, nature, the performing arts, and folktales.

Southeast Asia *The Travelers' Guide to Asian Customs and Manners,* by Kevin Chambers, advises on how to dine, tip, dress, make friends, do business, bargain, and do just about everything else in Asia, Australia, and New Zealand. *Shopping in Exotic Places,* by Ronald L. Krannich, Jo Reimer, and Carl Rae Krannich, discusses all major shopping districts and tells how to pick a tailor, how to bargain, how to pack. For full reservation information with detailed descriptions of lodgings in 16 countries, read Jerome E. Klein's *Best Places to Stay in Asia.* Also, *Video Night in Kathmandu,* by Pico Iyer, is a delightful collection of essays on the *Time* correspondent's recent travels through Southeast Asia.

History Three highly recommended works on Southeast Asian history are *Southeast Asia,* 3rd edition, by M. Osborne; *Southeast Asia: A History* by Lea E. Williams; and *In Search of Southeast Asia: A Modern History,* edited by David J. Steinberg.

Religion Taufik Abdullah and Sharon Siddique's *Islam and Society in Southeast Asia.*

Fiction Southeast Asia has been an inspiration for much of Joseph Conrad's work, including the novels *An Outcast of the Islands, Lord Jim, The Shadow-Line, Victory, Almayer's Folly,* and *The Rescue* and the short stories "Karain," "The Lagoon," "Youth," "The End of the Tether," "Typhoon," "Flak," "The Secret Sharer," and "Freya of the Seven Isles."

Thailand *Monsoon Country* is a contemporary novel by Pira Sudham, who portrays life in the northeast of Thailand. For insights into Thai culture and everyday life, read Denis Segaller's *Thai Ways* and *More Thai Ways.* For a humerous account of an expatriate's life in Thailand in the 1950s, read *Mai Pen Rai* by Carol Iollinger. An excellent account of life in northern Thailand is provided by Gordon Young in *The Hill Tribes of Northern Thailand.*

Arriving and Departing

From North America by Plane

The Airlines **Thai Airways International** (tel. 800/426–5204), known for its exceptional service, offers flights from Seattle to Bangkok via Tokyo. Six times a week these Thai Airways International flights originate in Toronto; flights originating in Los Angeles are planned to begin service in July 1991. **United Airlines** (tel.

800/538–2929) offers direct, one-stop flights from San Francisco and Seattle to Bangkok. Flying time is 16 hours from Seattle, 20 hours from Chicago, and 22 hours from New York. East Coast travelers departing from New York should consider using **Finnair** via Helsinki for flights to Bangkok; the flying time is only 17 hours, the fare is slightly cheaper than the Pacific route, and the service is excellent. **Swissair** is another airline that promotes this route with good connecting times through Zurich. Also, Swissair is linked with United Airlines, which means that you could choose the "Round the World Ticket" and cross the Pacific with United on either the outbound or inbound flight.

Stopovers For independent travelers, most airlines, including **United** and **Thai Airways International,** offer special "Circle Pacific" fares. These allow four stopovers at no extra charge, but the tickets must be purchased 14–30 days in advance and they carry cancellation penalties. You usually can add on extra stopovers, including Australian and South Pacific destinations, for a nominal charge (about $50).

Several airlines work together to offer "Around the World" fares, but you must follow a specific routing itinerary and you cannot backtrack. "Around the World" itineraries usually include several Southeast Asian destinations before continuing through Asia and Europe.

Discount Flights Because of the great number of air miles covered, fares are expensive, but it is possible to save some money off regular coach tickets. The key is to start with a flexible schedule and to make your reservations as far in advance as possible. Discounted, advance-purchase seats are limited and tend to sell out quickly. Compared with full economy fare, travel is cheaper through a tour operator.

If you are not already participating in the airline's frequent-flyer program, join. Membership is free, and all it takes is a simple application. Traveling halfway around the world will add about 22,586 km (14,000 mi) to your account. Many programs will give you additional bonus miles if you travel within a certain time period following your application submission.

Flights Most of the major airlines offer a range of tickets, the price of which can vary by more than 300%, depending on the day of purchase. As a rule, the further in advance you buy the ticket, the less expensive it is, but the greater the penalty (up to 100%) for canceling. Check with airlines for details.

The best buy is not necessarily an APEX (advance purchase) ticket on one of the major airlines. APEX tickets carry certain restrictions: They must be bought in advance (usually 21 days); they restrict your travel, usually with a minimum stay of seven days and a maximum of 90; and they penalize you for changes— voluntary or not—in your travel plans. But if you can work around these drawbacks (and most can), they are among the best-value fares available.

Charter flights offer the lowest fares, but often depart only on certain days and seldom on time. Though you may be able to arrive at one city and return from another, you may lose all or most of your money if you cancel your trip. Travel agents can make bookings, though they won't encourage you, since commissions are lower than on scheduled flights. Checks should, as a rule, be made out to the bank and specific escrow account for your flight. Don't sign up for a charter flight unless you've checked with a travel agency about the reputation of the packager. It's particularly important to know the packager's policy concerning refunds should a flight be canceled. Charter companies advertise in Sunday travel sections of newspapers.

Somewhat more expensive—but up to 50% below the cost of APEX fares—are tickets purchased through companies known as consolidators, who buy blocks of tickets on scheduled airlines and sell them at wholesale prices. Here again, you may lose all or most of your money if you change plans, but at least you will be on a regularly scheduled flight with less risk of cancellation than a charter. Once you've made your reservation, call the airline to make sure you're confirmed. Among the best known consolidators are **UniTravel** (Box 12485, St. Louis, MO 63132, tel. 314/569–2501 or 800/325–2222) and **Access International** (101 W. 31st St., Suite 1104, New York, NY 10001, tel. 212/465–0707 or 800/825–3633). Others advertise in the Sunday travel sections of newspapers as well.

A third option is to join a travel club that offers special discounts to its members. Three such organizations are **Moment's Notice** (425 Madison Ave., New York, NY 10017, tel. 212/486–0503), **Discount Travel International** (114 Forrest Ave., Narberth, PA 19072, tel. 215/668–7184), and **Worldwide Discount Travel Club** (1674 Meridian Ave., Miami Beach, FL 33139, tel. 305/534–2082). These cut-rate tickets should be compared with APEX tickets on the major airlines.

Enjoying the Flight Flights to Thailand are long and trying. Because of the time difference, jet lag and fatigue are nearly inevitable. The air on a plane is dry, and so it helps, while flying, to drink a lot of nonalcoholic liquids; drinking alcohol contributes to jet lag. Feet swell at high altitudes, so it's a good idea to remove your shoes while in flight. Sleepers usually prefer window seats to curl up against; those who like to move about the cabin should ask for aisle seats. Bulkhead seats (located in the front row of each cabin) have more legroom, but seat trays are attached to the arms of your seat rather than to the back of the seat in front.

Smoking You can request a nonsmoking seat during check-in or when you book your ticket. If a U.S. airline tells you there are no seats available in the nonsmoking section, insist on one: Department of Transportation regulations require U.S. carriers to find seats for all nonsmokers on the day of the flight, provided they meet check-in time restrictions.

Luggage
Labeling Luggage Put your home address on each piece of luggage, including hand baggage. If your luggage is lost and then found, the airline will deliver it to your home, at no charge to you.

Insurance *See* Insurance in Before You Go, above.

Luggage Regulations Luggage allowances vary slightly from airline to airline. Many carriers allow three checked pieces; some allow only two. Check before you go. In all cases, check-in luggage cannot weigh more than 70 pounds per piece or be larger than 62 inches (length + width + height).

Passengers on U.S. airlines are generally limited to two carry-on bags. For a bag you wish to store under the seat, the maximum dimensions are 9″ × 14″ × 22″; for bags to be hung in a closet or on a luggage rack, 4″ × 23″ × 45″; for bags to be stored in an overhead bin, 10″ × 14″ × 36″. Any item that exceeds the specified dimensions may be rejected as a carryon and taken as checked baggage. Keep in mind that an airline can adapt the rules to circumstances; so on an especially crowded flight don't be surprised if you are allowed only one carryon.

In addition to the two carryons, you may bring aboard a handbag (pocketbook or purse); an overcoat or wrap; an umbrella; a camera; a reasonable amount of reading material; an infant bag; and crutches, a cane, braces, or other prosthetic device. Infant/child-safety seats can also be brought aboard if parents have purchased a ticket for the child or if there is space in the cabin.

Foreign airlines have slightly different policies. They generally allow only one piece of carry-on luggage in tourist class, in addition to handbags and bags filled with duty-free goods. Passengers in first and business class are also allowed to carry on one garment bag. It is best to call your airline to find out its current policy.

From the United Kingdom by Plane

British Airways and **Thai Airways International** fly to Bangkok from London. Check *Time Out* and the Sunday papers for charters. Thomas Cook Ltd. can often book you on inexpensive flights; call the branch nearest you and ask to be put through to the "Airfare Warehouse."

From North America by Ship

Some cruise lines, including **Cunard** (tel. 800/221–4770) and **Royal Viking** (tel. 800/426–0821), call at major Southeast Asian ports as part of their around-the-world itineraries. Plan on spending at least four weeks cruising from the West Coast of the United States to Southeast Asia, as these ships usually visit ports in the Pacific and Australia along the way.

Staying in Thailand

Getting Around

By Plane The major domestic carrier is **Thai Airways International.** Its planes connect Bangkok with all major cities and tourist areas in Thailand with one exception. The closest Thai Airways flies to Ko Samui is Surat Thani, a two-hour bus-and-ferry ride from the island. For direct flights to Ko Samui, call **Bangkok Airways** (tel. 02/253–4014), which has three scheduled daily flights between Bangkok and Ko Samui using 40-seater planes. Bangkok Airways also has two daily flights to Phuket and one to Hat Yai. Thai Airways offers a travel package called **The Discover Thailand Pass.** For $199, you can take four flights to any of the airline's Thailand destinations. You must purchase the pass outside Thailand. Virtually all planes go through Bangkok, though Thai Airways has recently initiated daily nonstop service between Chiang Mai and Phuket. On popular tourist routes during peak holiday times, flights are often fully booked. Make sure you have reservations, and make them well in advance of your travel date. Flights should be reconfirmed when you arrive in Thailand. Arrive at the airport well before departure time. Recently, the airlines have started to give away the reserved seats of late passengers to standby-ticket holders. Thai Airways has a good record for keeping to schedule. During the rainy season, however, you may experience delays due to the weather.

By Train The State Railway of Thailand has three lines, all of which terminate in Bangkok. The Northern Line connects Bangkok with Chiang Mai, passing through Ayutthaya and Phitsanulok; the Northeastern Line travels up to Udorn Thani near the Laotian border; and the Southern Line goes all the way south through Surat Thani—the stop for Ko Samui—to the Malaysian border and on to Kuala Lumpur and Singapore, a journey that takes 37 hours. (There is no train to Phuket, though you can go as far as Surat Thani and change onto a scheduled bus service.)

Most trains offer second- or third-class tickets, but the overnight trains to the north (Chiang Mai) and to the south offer first-class sleeping cabins. Couchettes, with sheets and curtains for privacy, are available in second class. Do not leave valuables unguarded on these overnight trains, as professional thieves have been known to board the train and take what they fancy.

Tickets may be bought at the railway stations. Travel agencies can also sell tickets for the overnight trains. Reservations are strongly advised for all long-distance trains. Train schedules in English are available from travel agents and from major railway stations. The State Railway of Thailand offers two types of rail passes. Both are valid for 20 days of unlimited travel on all trains in either second or third class. The **Blue Pass** costs B1,500 (children B750) and does not include supplementary charges such as air-conditioning and berths; for B3,000 (children B1,500), the **Red Pass** does. For more information, call **Bangkok Railway Station** (tel. 02/223-7010.)

Fares are reasonable. An air-conditioned, second-class couchette, for example, for the 14-hour journey from Bangkok to Chiang Mai is B530; first class is B980.

By Bus Long-distance buses are cheaper and faster than trains, and there are buses into every corner of the country. A typical fare for the nine-hour trip between Chiang Mai and Bangkok is B230. The level of comfort depends on the bus company. Air-conditioned buses are superior, but the air-conditioning is always turned on full blast, and so you may want to take along an extra sweater. The most comfortable long-distance buses are operated by private travel/tour companies. For the most part, these private buses serve only resort destinations. Travel agents have the bus schedules and can make reservations and issue tickets.

By Car Cars are available for rent in Bangkok and in major tourist destinations. An international driving license is required. Driving is on the left; speed limits are 60 kph (37 mph) in cities and 90 kph (56 mph) outside. It is advisable to hire a driver. The additional cost is small, and the peace of mind great. If a foreigner is involved in an automobile accident, he—not the Thai—is likely to be judged at fault.

In Chiang Mai, Ko Samui, Pattaya, and Phuket, hiring a jeep or motorcycle is a popular and convenient way to get around. Be aware that many rentals, especially those from small companies, are not covered by insurance, and you are liable for any damage to the vehicle, regardless of who is at fault. **Avis** (16/23 N. Sathorn Rd., Bangkok, tel. 02/233–0397) and **Hertz** (1620 Petchburi Rd., Bangkok, tel. 02/252–4903) rental companies are more expensive, but tend to offer better insurance coverage.

Also be aware that motorcycles skid easily on gravel roads or on gravel patches on the pavement. In Ko Samui, a sign posts the year's count of foreigners who never made it home from their vacation!

The major roads in Thailand tend to be very congested and street signs are often in Thai only. But the limited number of roads and, with the exception of Bangkok, the straightforward layout of cities combine to make navigation relatively easy. Driving at night in rural areas, especially north and west of Chiang Mai and in the south beyond Surat Thani is not advised, as highway robberies have been reported.

By Taxi Taxis do not have meters; fares are negotiated. Taxis waiting at hotels are more expensive than those flagged down while cruising. Never enter the taxi until the price has been established. Most taxi drivers do not speak English, but all understand the finger count. One finger means B10, two is for B20 and so on. Ask at your hotel what the appropriate fare should be. Never pay more than what the hotel quotes, as they will have given you the high price. If in doubt, accept 65%–75% of the cabbie's quote.

With any form of private travel, never change your initial agreement on destination and price unless you clearly establish a new "contract." Moreover, if you agree to the driver's offer to wait for you at your destination and be available for your onward or return journey, you will be charged for waiting time, and, unless you have fixed the price, the return fare can be double the outbound fare.

By Samlor Often called tuk-tuks for their spluttering sound, these three-wheel cabs are slightly less expensive than a taxi and, because of their maneuverability, the most rapid form of travel through congested traffic. All tuk-tuk operators drive as if your ride will be their last, but, in fact, they are remarkably safe. Tuk-tuks are not very comfortable, though, and are best used for short journeys.

By Songthaew Songthaews seat passengers on side bench seats and can serve as minibuses or as private taxis. If they travel as a minibus, they will follow a fixed route and the fare is set. If they are used as a taxi, the fare must be negotiated.

By Bicycle Rickshaws For short trips, bicycle rickshaws are a popular, inexpensive form of transport. They become expensive for long trips. Fares are negotiated. It is imperative to be very clear with these drivers about what price is agreed upon. They have a tendency to create a misunderstanding leading to a nasty scene at the end of the trip.

Telephones

Public telephones are available in most towns and villages and take B1 coins or both B1 and B5 pieces. Long-distance calls can only be made on phones that accept both B1 and B5 coins. For a long-distance call in Thailand, dial the area code and then the number. When telephoning Thailand from overseas, the "0" at the beginning of the area code is omitted. To make overseas calls, you are advised to use either your hotel switchboard—Chiang Mai and Bangkok have direct dialing—or the overseas telephone facilities at the central post office and telecommunications building. You'll find one in all towns. In Bangkok, the overseas telephone center, next to the general post office, is open 24 hours; up-country, the facilities' hours may vary, but they usually open at 8 AM and some stay open until 10 PM. Some locations in Bangkok, including the telecommunications building next to the general post office, have **AT&T USADirect** phones. These phones place you in direct contact with an AT&T operator, who will accept your AT&T credit card or place the call collect. If you wish to receive assistance for an overseas call, dial 100/233–2771. For local telephone inquiries, dial 100/183, but you will need to speak Thai. In Bangkok, you can dial 13 for an English-speaking operator.

Mail

Thailand's mail service is reliable and efficient. Major hotels provide basic postal services. Bangkok's central general post office on Charoen Krung (New Road) is open weekdays 8–6, weekends and public holidays 9–1. Up-country post offices close at 4:30 PM.

Airmail postcard rates to the United States are B9; B8 to the United Kingdom. The minimum rate for airmail letters is B12 to the United States and B10 to the United Kingdom. Allow about two weeks for your mail to arrive at its overseas destination. If you want to speed that process, major post offices offer overseas express mail (EMS) services, where the minimum rate (200 g or 8 oz) is B230.

You may have mail sent to you "poste restante." Usually, there is a B1 charge for each piece collected. Thais write their last name first; so be sure to have your last name written in capital letters and underlined.

Currency

The basic unit of currency is the baht. There are 100 satang to one baht. There are five different bills, each a different color: B10, brown; B20, green; B50, blue; B100, red; and B500, purple. Coins in use are 25 satang, 50 satang, B1, B5, and the recently introduced B10. One-baht coins are smaller than B5 coins; both come in three different sizes—get the feel of them quickly. The new B10 coin has a gold-colored center surrounded by silver.

The baht is considered a stable currency. All hotels will convert traveler's checks and major currencies into baht, though exchange rates are better at banks and authorized money changers. The rate tends to be better in Bangkok than up-country. Major international credit cards are accepted at most tourist shops and hotels.

At press time, B25 = US $1.

What It Will Cost

The cost of visiting Thailand is very much up to you. It is possible to live and travel quite inexpensively if you do as Thais do—eat in local restaurants, use buses, and stay at nonair-conditioned hotels. Once you start enjoying a little luxury, prices jump drastically. For example, crossing Bangkok by bus is a 10¢ ride, but by taxi the fare may run to $10. Prices are typically higher in resort areas catering to foreign tourists, and Bangkok is more expensive than other Thai cities. Anything purchased in a luxury hotel is considerably more expensive than it would be if purchased elsewhere. Imported items are heavily taxed.

Sample Prices Continental breakfast at a hotel, $8; large bottle of beer at a hotel, $3; dinner at a good restaurant, $15; 1-mile taxi ride, $1.50; double room, $20–$40 inexpensive, $40–$80 moderate, $80–$120 expensive.

Language

Thai is the country's national language. As it uses the Khmer script and is spoken tonally, it is confusing to most foreigners. What may sound to a foreigner as "krai kai kai kai" will mean to a Thai, said with the appropriate pitch, "who sells chicken eggs?" However, it is easy to speak a few words, such as "sawahdee krap" (good day) and "khop khun krap" (thank you). Women end greetings or questions with "ka" instead of "krap." With the exception of taxi drivers, Thais working with travelers in the resort and tourist areas in Bangkok generally speak sufficient English to permit basic communication.

Some words that may be useful to know in Thailand are:

Bot: The main chapel of a wat (*see* below), where ordinations occur and the chief image of the Lord Buddha is kept.
Chedi: A pagoda built in Thai style with a bell-shaped dome tapering to a pointed spire, often where holy relics are kept.
Farang: Foreigner.
Klong: Canal.
Ko (often written *Koh*): Island.
Nam: Water, often used to mean river.
Prang: A chedi built in the old Khmer style with an elliptical spire.
Soi: Small street, or lane, often assigned a number and described in conjunction with the abutting main street.
Stupa: Another word for chedi.
Viharn: The large hall in a wat where priests perform religious duties.
Wat: The complex of buildings of a Buddhist religious site (monastery), or a temple.

Opening and Closing Times

Thai and foreign **banks** are open weekdays 8:30–3:30, except for public holidays. Most **commercial concerns** in Bangkok operate on a five-day week and are open 8–5. **Government offices** are generally open 8:30–4:30 with a noon–1 lunch break. Many **stores** are open daily 8–8.

National Holidays

The following are national holidays: New Year's Day, January 1; Chinese New Year, February 15; Magha Puja, February, on the full moon of the third lunar month; Chakri Day, April 6; Songkran, mid-April; Coronation Day, May 5; Visakha Puja, May, on the full moon of the sixth lunar month; Queen's Birthday, August 12; King's Birthday, December 5. Government offices, banks, commercial concerns, and department stores are usually closed on these days, but smaller shops stay open.

Festivals and Seasonal Events

The festivals listed below are national and occur throughout the country unless otherwise noted. Many events follow the lunar calendar, so dates vary from year to year.

Dec. 31–Jan. 2: New Year celebrations are usually at their best around temples. In Bangkok, special ceremonies at Pramanae Ground include Thai dances.

Feb.: Magha Puja commemorates the day when 1,250 disciples spontaneously heard Lord Buddha preach the cardinal doctrine on the full moon of the third lunar month.

Feb.–Apr.: Kite-flying contests are held (in Bangkok, see them at the Pramanae Ground). Barbs attached to kite strings are used to destroy the other contestants' kites.

Apr. 6: Chakri Day. This day commemorates the enthronement of King Rama I, founder of the present dynasty, in 1782.

Mid-Apr.: Songkran. This marks the Thai New Year and is an occasion for setting caged birds and fish free, visiting family, dancing, and water-throwing where everyone splashes everyone else in good-natured merriment. The festival is at its best in Chiang Mai with parades, dancing in the streets, and a beauty contest.

May: Plowing Ceremony. At the Pramanae Ground in Bangkok, Thailand's king and queen take part in a traditional ritual that serves to open the rice-planting season.

May 5: Coronation Day: The king and queen take part in a procession to the Royal Chapel to preside over ceremonies commemorating the anniversary of their coronation.

May: Visakha Puja: On the full moon of the sixth lunar month, the nation celebrates the holiest of Buddhist days—Lord Buddha's birth, enlightenment, and death. Monks lead the laity in candle-lit processions around their temples.

Aug. 12: Queen's Birthday. Queen Sirikit's birthday is celebrated with religious ceremonies at Chitralda Palace.

Nov.: Loi Krathong Festival. Held on the full moon of the 12th lunar month, this is the loveliest of Thai festivals. After sunset, people throughout Thailand make their way to a body of water and launch small lotus-shaped banana-leaf floats bearing lighted candles. The aim is to honor the water spirits and wash away one's sins of the past year.

Nov.: Golden Mount Festival. Of all the fairs and festivals in Bangkok, this one at the Golden Mount is the most spectacular, with sideshows, food stalls, bazaars, and crowds celebrating.

Nov.: Elephant Roundup. Held at Surin in the northeast, this is a stirring display of 100 noble animals' skills as traditional beasts of war, as bulldozers, and even soccer players.

Dec. 5: King's Birthday. A trooping of the colors is performed in Bangkok by Thailand's elite Royal Guards.

Tipping

In Thailand, tips are generally given for good service, except when a price has been negotiated in advance. A **taxi driver** is not tipped unless hired as a private driver for an excursion. **Hotel porters** expect at least a B20 tip, and **hotel staff** who have given good personal service are usually tipped. A 10% tip is appreciated at a **restaurant** when no service charge has been added to the bill.

Shopping

Thailand offers some of the world's best shopping, and Bangkok and Chiang Mai are the best shopping cities. The critical factor in successful shopping is to know the product, especially if it is a precious stone or an antique. Another requirement for a successful buy is bargaining. It's a process that takes time, but it saves you money and wins respect from the vendor.

Thailand produces several specialties to tempt shoppers:

Antiques The Thai government has very strict regulations on the export of antiques and religious art. Images of the Lord Buddha are not permitted to be exported. By law, no antique may leave the country, and even reproductions not sold as antiques may need an export permit issued by the Fine Arts Department. A reputable dealer can obtain these permits in about one week.

Bronzeware Uniquely handcrafted bronzeware can be bought in complete table services, coffee-and-creamer and bar sets, letter openers, bowls, tankards, trays, and candlesticks. Lately, the designs have become modern and simple. Traditional methods are still used, but a silicone coat is added to prevent tarnishing. Chiang Mai is a good source for this product.

Carved Wood Teakwood carvings, in the form of boxes, trays, or figures, are popular. Beware, there is a very convincing technique that makes carvings into instant antiques! You'll find wood carving all over Thailand, but Chiang Mai is its main center.

Dolls The more expensive dolls come dressed in Thai silk and represent classical Thai dancers or mythological characters.

Lacquerware Lacquerware, which is usually made into small tables or boxes, is lightweight and commonly comes in a gold-and-black color scheme. You'll find the better pieces are made in Chiang Mai.

Nielloware This special kind of silver with its inlaid design, which looks black when held against the light at an angle and white when looked at straight on, is also available with color inlays. Nielloware comes as cufflinks, lights, jewelry, ashtrays, creamer sets, and a host of other articles. Bangkok or the southern province of Nakhon Si Thammarat are good places to buy it.

Precious Stones Rubies and sapphires are associated with Thailand. These can be bought loose or in jewelry. Unless you are a gemologist, you may wish to make your purchases from a Tourism Authority of Thailand-approved store. You should also get a guarantee and receipt written in English.

Thai Celadon The ancient art of making this type of pottery has been revived, and the ware can be found mostly around Chiang Mai, though some can be purchased in Bangkok. Also made in the Chiang

Mai area is Sukhothai stoneware. Near Bangkok, the kilns produce a very fine blue-and-white porcelain.

Thai Silk Through the efforts of Jim Thompson, Thai silk has become a
much sought-after luxury fabric. The prices are fairly high, but
they are much less than what you would pay at home. Be aware
that the weights and quality do differ. Most yardage comes 40
inches wide and may be bought by the yard or as ready-made
goods. Rivaling Thai silk is the handwoven cotton made in the
Chiang Mai area.

Aside from traditional crafts, Thailand offers a host of other
good buys, ranging from local handicrafts to ready-made
clothes to designer knockoffs. There are also knockoff watches
with designer names. A "Rolex" can be purchased for $20,
though the emblem may be a little crooked. Pirated cassettes
are another phenomenally inexpensive item. However, be
aware that it is illegal to import pirated goods into the United
States. Beauty is a big business in Thailand, and walk-in beauty parlors are ubiquitous. For 40¢ to $2, you can have a mani-
cure or pedicure; facials, permanents, and massages can be had
at correspondingly low prices.

Prices are fixed in department stores. In fashion boutiques,
there is no harm in asking for a small discount. In stores selling
artifacts, price is open to negotiation, and in bazaars and
street-side stalls, bargaining is essential.

Sports

Spectator Sports With so many rivers, Thailand has many kinds of boat racing.
Boat Racing Teams from various towns or provinces vie for honors in color-
ful paddle-powered boats. Annual races are held in Bangkok,
Pichit, Ayutthaya, and Nan.

Horse Racing Races are held at tracks in Bangkok (*see* Spectator Sports in
Chapter 3).

Kite-fighting This sport dates back hundreds of years. Elaborate kites
armed with barbs, designated *pakpao* (female) or *chula* (male),
struggle for dominance, trying to ensnare or cut the opponent's
line. A good place to watch this is at Bangkok's Pramanae
Ground near the Royal Palace, particularly in March and April.

Motorcycle Racing With the opening of the Bira Pattaya Circuit, on Route 36 between Pattaya and Rayong, international motorcycle events
are held regularly.

Takro This sport involves passing a small rattan ball back and forth as
long as possible before it falls to the ground. All parts of the
body may be used. The more complicated the pass, the better it
is judged. Other forms of takro require a hoop or net.

Thai Boxing Thai boxing, known locally as *muay Thai*, allows boxers to use
their feet, knees, thighs, and elbows, as well as their gloved
fists, to hit an opponent. Moreover, all parts of the opponent's
body can be struck, and points are awarded for any blow. Thai
boxing requires years of training, and prior to each bout, boxers indulge in ritual praying that involves complicated maneu-
vers designed to limber up the body.

Participant Sports Some 50 excellent golf courses are spread around the kingdom,
Golf though the majority are in the Bangkok region. Three of the
best are Navatanee golf course, site of the 1975 World Cup

tournament, the Rose Garden course, and the Krung Thep
Kreta course.

Hiking and Trekking   Hiking is especially popular in the north, where groups go in search of hill-tribe villages and wildlife. The main center for northern treks is Chiang Mai. But with dozens of national parks around the country, you may hike in tropical jungles and isolated highlands alike. Contact the Tourism Authority of Thailand for information on bungalow-style accommodations in the national parks.

Horseback Riding   Though some of the beach resorts may have horses, only Pattaya has a permanent stable, where horse treks into the countryside are available to the public.

Water Sports   With its long coastline and warm waters, Thailand offers splendid opportunities for all sorts of water sports, including waterskiing, surfing, windsurfing, and parasailing. It is possible to rent power boats, water scooters, and sailboats. Scuba diving and snorkeling in the clear waters are also available, especially in Ko Samui and Phuket, where rentals, instruction, and trips to uninhabited islands may be arranged. Big-game fishing is a feature at Bang Saray, near Pattaya.

Beaches

The beaches of Thailand, both on the Gulf of Siam (the south and east coasts) and on the Andaman Sea (the southwest coast) are popular with Europeans. Full-scale resort areas have been developed on both coasts—Pattaya, Hua Hin and Cha' Am on the Gulf, Phuket on the Andaman Sea. New resort areas are developing all the time. Ko Samui on the Gulf is becoming increasingly crowded, as is Ko Phi Phi off Phuket. For those who like idyllic havens of beaches and no people, the area around Krabi facing the Andaman Sea is paradise, and Ko Samet on the Gulf (near Pattaya) has a number of small beaches and bungalows for rent. The waters around Bangkok are tropical, warm, and inviting, but do check on two factors before you plunge in: the undertow and the presence of stinging jellyfish. Sand tends to be golden in color and slightly coarse. Scuba diving and snorkeling are best off Ko Samui and among the Similan Islands off Phuket.

Dining

Thai cuisine is distinctive, often hot and spicy, and perfumed with herbs, especially lemon grass and coriander. It is influenced by the cooking styles of China, India, Java, Malaysia, and Portugal. Rice, boiled or fried, forms the basis for most Thai meals, though noodles can also play this role. Meats, poultry, and seafood are highly seasoned with herbs and chilies. Soups are also important in Thai cuisine and are usually spiced with lemongrass and chilies. All courses of a Thai meal are served at the same time.

Each region has its own specialties. The northeast favors sticky rice served with barbecued chicken and shredded green papaya mixed with shrimp, lemon juice, fish sauce, garlic, and chilies. In the north, a local sausage, *naem*, is popular, while in the South there is an abundance of fresh seafood. Dessert is usually exotic fresh fruit or sweets made of rice flour, coconut milk, palm sugar, and sticky rice. Singha beer and Mekong whiskey (made from rice) are the usual beverages. Western food is available in most hotels and at many restaurants in resort areas.

Among the myths that just won't die is that all Thai food is hot. There are plenty of pungent dishes, of course, but most Thai recipes are not especially aggressive. Indeed, many Thais do not care for very spicy food and tend to avoid it. A normal Thai meal is composed of several dishes, including a hot and spicy one—a curry, perhaps, or a hot stir-fried dish—that is balanced with a bland soup, a salad, and a vegetable dish or stuffed omelet.

Thai food is eaten with a fork and tablespoon, with the spoon held in the right hand and the bottom of the fork used like a plow to push food into the spoon. Chopsticks are used only for Chinese dishes, such as noodle recipes. After you have finished eating, place your fork and spoon on the plate at the 5:25 position; otherwise the server will assume you would like another helping.

Because the English translations, when they are provided at all, can be bizarre, it is not a bad idea to be armed with a few food-related words in Thai when you take to the streets in search of an authentic meal. This short list will give you a head start.

jued ("jood," sounding like "good")—bland. A *kaeng jued* is a clear soup without chili, often with clear vermicelli noodles and wood-ear mushrooms added for texture.
kaeng (pronounced "gang")—curry, although the term covers many thin, clear, souplike dishes that are very different from what most Westerners think of as curry.
kaeng khio waan ("gang khee-yo wahn")—a rich curry made with coconut cream and a complicated mixture of spices and other flavorings as well as eggplant and meat or fish (chicken, beef, shrimp, and a fish ball called *luuk cheen plaa krai* are the most common) pounded into a paste. The Thai name means "green, sweet curry," but it is very rarely sweet. "Green, hot curry" is more like it.
nam plaa ("nahm plah")—fish sauce used instead of salt in Thai cooking.
phad ("pot")—stir-fried.
phad bai kaphrao ("pot by ka-*prow*")—stir-fried with fresh basil, hot chili, garlic, and other seasonings.
phad phed ("pot pet")—popular dishes in which meat or fish is stir-fried with hot chili, sweet basil, onion, garlic, and other seasonings. They can be *very* phed; so watch it.
phed or **phet** ("pet")—spicy hot.
phrik ("prik")—any hot chili pepper. The notorious, nuclear-strength bird chilies are called *phrik kee noo*, and you can always find them on the table in a Thai restaurant, cut into pieces and steeping in *nam plaa* (*see* above). They should be approached with respect.
thawd ("taught")—deep-fried.
tom khaa ("tome khah")—a rich soup made with coconut cream, lime, hot chilies, *khah* (a root spice related to ginger), and chicken (or, less commonly, shrimp).
tom yam ("tome yom")—a semiclear hot-and-sour soup based on lime juice and small hot chilies, with lemongrass, mushrooms, and fresh coriander. Popular versions are made with shrimp, chicken, or fish.

yam ("yom")—a hot-and-sour saladlike dish, served cold and flavored with hot chilies, lime juice, and onions.

Highly recommended restaurants are indicated by a star ★.

Except in the Bangkok Dining section, the following dining price categories apply throughout this book:

Category	Cost*
Very Expensive	over B500 ($20)
Expensive	B250–B500 ($10–$20)
Moderate	B100–B250 ($4–$10)
Inexpensive	under B100 ($4)

per person, including service charge

An 8.25% government tax is added to restaurant bills.

Lodging

Every town of reasonable size offers accommodations. In the smaller towns, the hotels may be fairly simple, but they will usually be clean and certainly inexpensive. In major cities or resort areas, there are hotels to fit all price categories. At the high end, the luxury hotels can compete with the best in the world. Service is generally superb—polite and efficient—and most of the staff usually speak English. At the other end of the scale, the lodging is simple and basic—a room with little more than a bed. The least expensive places may have Asian toilets (squat type with no seat) and a fan rather than air-conditioning.

All except the budget hotels have restaurants and offer room service throughout most of the day and night. Most will also be happy to make local travel arrangements for you—for which they receive commissions. All hotels advise that you use their safe-deposit boxes.

During the peak tourist season, October–March, hotels are often fully booked and charge peak rates. At special times, such as December 30–January 2 and Chinese New Year, rates climb even higher, and hotel reservations are difficult to obtain. Weekday rates at some resorts are often lower, and during the off-season, it is possible to negotiate a reduced rate. Breakfast is never included in the room tariff.

An 11% government tax is sometimes included in the base rate, but more often now it is tacked on at the end. In addition, deluxe hotels often add 10%–15% service charge.

Highly recommended lodgings are recommended by a star ★.

Throughout this book the following lodging price categories apply:

Category	Cost*
Very Expensive	over B4,000 (over $160)
Expensive	B2,000–B4,000 ($80–$160)
Moderate	B1,000–B2,000 ($40–$80)

Inexpensive	B500–B1,000 ($20–$40)
Budget	under B500 ($20)

per double room, including service and tax

2 Portrait of Thailand

Love in a Duty-free Zone

by Pico Iyer

Educated at Oxford and Harvard, Pico Iyer was a correspondent for Time *magazine for four years. This piece is an abridged version of a chapter in his book,* Video Night in Kathmandu, and Other Reports from the Not-So-Far East, *first published in 1988.*

I had long been wary of big bad Bangkok. It was a city, they said, whose main industry was recreation and whose main business was pleasure. Wickedness, by all accounts, was an art form here. For not only were all the seven vices, and quite a few others, embellished, expanded and refined in Bangkok, but they were also coupled with all the seven graces. In free-and-easy Bangkok, so legend had it, half the women were pros and half the men were cons. Everywhere in Asia, the Thai capital was spoken of in whispers, with the fascinated horror that attends a shadow Saigon. It was, by common consent, the best place around for procuring anything and everything illicit—smuggled goods, fake Rolexes, pirated cassettes, hard drugs, forged passports and IDs. And the Thais were famous for their gentleness and grace.

"Ah, such a charming people," mused Alan, a kindly 69-year-old British photographer-eccentric I met in Bali, "and yet the streets of Bangkok are really so terribly wicked." Once, he said, he had been approached on the sidewalk by a man offering Number One king prawns; when he accepted, the man led him down a shady side street and into a dark café, served him the promised prawns, and then presented him with a bill for $100. ("I must say, though, the prawns were awfully good.") Another time, he reported, a monk took him out for a drink and then asked him pointedly whether he was sleeping alone, adding, "I am very nice man!" "Imagine that!" cried Alan with an innocence only strengthened by his knowledge of the world. "And he a monk! But still, you know, the Thais are really such a charming people."

Of all the unlikely resources husbanded in Bangkok, however, the most famous were potential wives. Two days after meeting Alan, I ran into another Brit, who was, by profession, "how shall I put it—a smuggler." No stranger to the blackest of markets, this character assured me that along the roads of northern Thailand $35 would buy a boy for life, and $50 a girl. I had also read that at village auctions virgins were the pièce de résistance. And it was common knowledge that the principal crops grown in certain parts of the country were young girls sent by their families to the bars of Bangkok to make fortunes they could plow back into the community as soon as they resumed their rustic lives. Indeed, said one Thai gentleman, talent scouts roamed the northern villages, offering families $150 for every prospective B-girl. "Here," he reported happily, "everything is for sale. Even human life."

The government itself seemed hardly bashful about advertising the skin trade. The yellow pages alone listed 100 massage parlors, and 350 bars, in every corner of the capital. Brochures circulated around the world, enticing packs of male visitors from Japan and Germany and the Gulf on special sex-tour vacations with the assurance that in Bangkok "you can pick up girls as easily as a pack of cigarettes" (those who found even that too onerous could select their companions from photo booklets before leaving home). In the city itself, accredited tourist agencies organized expeditions around Bangkok's most breathtaking natural wonders—its pretty shopgirls. By now, in fact, an estimated 60% of all the country's visitors came only for the dirt-cheap sex, and more than a million girls were waiting to oblige them. And since their international reputation—not to mention their gross national product—depended on the mass production of pleasure, the authorities made sure that the fantasy business was the best-run industry in town: well organized, fastidiously tended, and lavishly displayed. All the playboys of the Western world made for Bangkok, and Bangkok was increasingly made for them.

Of late, of course, a terrible shadow had fallen over the business: Crowded with bar-girls, heroin addicts, and men who were gay just for money, Bangkok had the perfect conditions for an epidemic of AIDS. By the spring of 1986, six people had already died of the syndrome, and four of them were foreigners. Yet where countries like Japan had responded to the threat with a panic-stricken decisiveness and talk of testing all who entered the country, many Thais seemed content just to shrug off the danger. The public health minister himself had requested agencies to exercise discretion about publicizing AIDS statistics so as not to damage the tourist trade.

And indeed, the minute I entered my Bangkok hotel, I found myself surrounded by consumers of the Bangkok Dream. Simon, from Durham University in Britain, had first visited Thailand a couple of months ago and had now returned, he said, with a sly smile, for no reason at all really, and for how long, he didn't know. An Indian who was entwined in the snack bar with a couple of local ladies told me, rather shyly, that he had collected photos and tapes of almost a thousand Bangkok girls as souvenirs of his annual visits. A black man from the South Bronx explained that he was here on an extended R and R break from the pro basketball league in Australia. "People come here for different things," explained a male nurse from San Francisco. "Some people come for the temples. Some people come for the deals. Some people come for the sex." He pronounced this last with such disgust that I was moved to ask what he had come for. "Girls," he said, hardly pausing. "Fourteen-, 15-year-old girls. I've already been to Sri Lanka and Korea, but this is the best place to find them: The girls are real fresh here, straight from the hills." Noting my look of bemusement, he went on to explain himself.

"Look," he began earnestly, "I'm 42 years old. I'm losing some hair. I could lose a little weight here and there. I'm not getting any younger. But I don't want no 35-year-old woman. I want to marry a girl who's 22, 23 at the most. In America, none of them girls are gonna look at me. But here—here it's different."

No less typical of the city's supplicants was 21-year-old Dave, who had arrived three months ago on vacation from the University of British Columbia. By now his tertiary education was a thing of the distant past, his ownership of a local bar a prospect for the perpetual future. Bright with ingenuous good nature, Dave had somehow managed to bring sincerity even to Sin City. Not long after we sat down to dinner, he leaned over in my direction. "Just look at these beauties," he whispered, gesturing toward the waitresses. "And you know something? They aren't even working girls." His own girlfriend, he confessed, was "out at work" tonight.

As soon as we finished eating, Dave volunteered to serve as my Virgil through the inner circles of Bangkok's inferno. The best introduction to the city, he declared, was a pilgrimage to the heart of the Patpong Road, a mess of more than 50 look-alike bars set along two narrow lanes, designed with nothing in mind but the bodily pleasure of foreigners. We could try the Honey Bar, or the Pink Panther, or the Adam and Eve—they were all the same. But we might as well go to the Superstar.

And so we did. At the door, a scantily clad young sylph flashed me a soft smile, led me by the hand to a bar stool, pressed her body lightly against mine, urged me to order a drink. As soon as I did so, she threaded long and languid arms around me, brushed lustrous, sweet-smelling hair against my face, inclined my straw into my mouth, tickled her lips with her tongue, and whispered sweet nothings that could not have been sweeter or more full of nothing. Then, gradually, gently, all sidelong glances, kittenish giggles and seraphic smiles, she glided through a cross-questioning as ritualized and precise as those delivered by immigration officers deliberating whether to allow one entry. "Where you from? Where you live in Bangkok? How long you stay?" Give the right answers, I quickly discovered, and the response was immediate.

"Where you live?" asked a bewitching, orange-bikinied houri.

"Metro Hotel."

"Oh," she said, "sexy eyes."

All my reservations confirmed, I had, I felt, been transported back to some B-movie image of Saigon, 1968. Behind me, a jukebox with a throbbing bass pounded out "Do It to Me" and "Slow Hand" and "Da Ya Think I'm Sexy." A

psychedelic light show on the wall fuzzily gave off a deli-
quescent blur of naked bodies mixing and mingling. On a
platform behind the bar, a handful of beauties went through
the motions of excitement in body language that needed no
translation. Their reflections kept them company in mirrors behind them, above them, and in front of them. And
distractedly gawking up at the dancers from their bar
stools were rows upon rows of burly men in white bush
shirts and crumpled trousers, Australians and Germans
and Americans. As they looked on, every one of them
bounced a giggly girl up and down on his lap, pawing soft
limbs, stroking spare parts, slurring endearments. For
purposes of identification, every handmaiden had a number
on her breast.

Though Bangkok was famous for its narcotic properties, I
did not sleep well that evening. All night long, from outside
my room came the sounds of giggles and slamming doors,
heavy feet padding after light ones down the corridor. And
sometime before sunrise, I was abruptly awoken by a call
from a hotel employee. "I miss you," she purred. This was
strange, I thought, since I had not yet had the pleasure of
her acquaintance. "I see you last night," she moaned. "I
love you very much. You no remember me—the one with
black hair and brown skin?"

She was indeed no different from all the others.
Everywhere, at every time, it was the same: intimacy on the grand scale. Wherever I looked in this huge
and hazy city, scattered harum-scarum along its main
roads, were hundreds upon hundreds of short-time hotels,
girlie bars, sex shows, massage parlors, "no hands" restaurants, pickup coffee shops, brothels, escort agencies,
discos, and—following as surely as the day the night—VD
clinics. At one end of town gleamed the showy crystal palaces of the Patpong Road, at the other their tarted-up country cousins on a street known as Soi Cowboy. Between
them, around them, and on every side there seemed to be
bars with videos, bars with shows, bars with dance floors,
Swiss and American and German bars and special Japa-
nese-language bars where businessmen from Tokyo could
pay a flat $110 for a full night of entertainment, no holds
barred, no strings attached. And in and out and all around
were massage parlors, small massage parlors, back-alley
massage parlors, massage parlors that were three-story
pleasure domes as luxurious as Las Vegas casinos, each one
equipped with one-way mirrors through which its customers could watch, unwatched, up to 400 masseuses seated in
a huge glass tank, knitting, filing their nails, or turning
their deadened gaze to a TV screen. For the sake of convenience, these girls too had numbers on their breasts.

As a young, unattached foreign male, I found myself caught
in a swarm of propositions. When I entered a taxi, the driver offered me "a private girl" (to which I was tempted to re-

ply that I was a private man). When I stopped at a street corner, in the midst of a monsoony downpour, a shabby young man thrust upon me a soggy Polaroid of the girl he owned. When I peered into a barbershop, I was asked— nudge, nudge—whether I would like a private room. And everywhere I went, I heard from the shadows a busy, steady buzz of "Sex show. Sex show. Sex show" as ceaseless as the song of cicadas in Japan.

Nowhere, it seemed, was I safe. I checked into a tourist hotel and found that it was a "knock-knock" place, which provided girls, along with Cokes and pay phones, in the lobby. Many of these houses of good repute, I later discovered, took the liberty of sending spare girls, uninvited, up to the rooms at night. Even first-class hotels posted notices observing, with all regretful courtesy, that guests in single rooms would have to pay double since it was assumed that they would not, could not, be sleeping alone.

What else did Bangkok have to offer? I turned to the official government tourist magazine, *This Week in Bangkok*. Four pages were devoted to such agencies as the Darling Escort Services (which provided "educated ladies who come in many different languages to help you get around or get down"), a smattering of cocktail lounges ("Welcome to our real paradise," offered Madonna), and a bevy of massage parlors ("Experience unique courtesy only Thai girls can offer"). The next page featured a list of VD clinics, and the next a group of barbershops and beauty salons ("Guarantee full satisfaction," "Expert lady barbers for men"). The following page listed eight more escort agencies ("For lonely visitors to find the most beautiful, sensuous or sexy partner," cooed Eve. "So easy. Just call us"). Most of the rest of the tourist magazine was given over to a five-page listing of bars and clubs, and to such specialty clubs—Bangkok was nothing if not an equal opportunity employer—as Gentlemen (providing "gentle boys for gentlemen"). One entire page contained nothing but photographs of "special friends."

The magazine did, however, reserve a little space for mention of the Rotary Club's annual fund-raising extravaganza, which it acclaimed as a must for the entire family and extolled in the tones generally reserved for folkloric spectacles. This traditional event came with the blessing of the city's mayor and of a spokesman from the Prime Minister's office. Ah, I thought, a celebration of some of the country's distinctive customs.

Indeed it was. The charity affair was held in the Patpong Road. It featured an elaborate outdoor beauty contest involving a gaggle of lovelies from the area's bars, undressed to kill. The bars themselves were thrown open to the daylight so that any pedestrian could peep inside, where a harem's worth of damsels were wiggling and writhing on cue. The booths that lined the streets offered drinks with girls, dances with girls, or girls with girls. I could, I thought, be only in Bangkok.

The city, in fact, made me decidedly squeamish. Just to be exposed to such a society was, I thought, to contract a kind of social disease; just to be here was to be guilty. Not for nothing, I told myself, did "Thailand" mean "Land of the Free." Taken in by Bangkok's willingness to take one in, I felt myself outraged; Bangkok was dangerously easy, was my dangerously easy conclusion.

Thailand offered a good deal more, of course, than just the sex trade. My first week in the country, I took a night train to the north, watched darkness fall over the rice paddies, felt a hot tropical breeze against my face, saw great sheets of lightning break across the land. Next day, at dawn, I followed a vaulting, cross-eyed hill tribesman up steep hills and through a butterflied jungle, and that night, in an animist village, I watched, by the light of a single candle, as the local headman, reclining on pillows, filled himself with opium, then played a weird kind of bagpipes, while jigging his way through a discombobulated dance in the guttering light of the shadows. Never had I felt myself so close to mystery.

Yet even then, I could not help recalling the Dutchman I had met in Corsica the year before. When he trekked into the Thai jungle, he told me with pleasure, the hill tribesmen, though conversant with no dialect but their own, had greeted his group by spelling out "Welcome" with the tops of Coke bottles. And in nearby Chiang Mai, a quiet center of tribal handicrafts, there was little doubt that the West was coming through loud and clear. Teenage girls sat on the hoods of muscle cars on the town's main drag, while Nike-shod jocks revved up their Yamahas. Singers in hot pants were lip-synching Top 40 tunes on screens in the Video 83 store, and across the street from Burger House, a neon sign advertised a bowling alley. A local Christian girl invited me to dinner, then sat at the table reading Maupassant. And early one evening, as dusk began to fall, a lazy-eyed rickshaw driver gave me a guided tour of his hometown. "Ah," he said as we bounced past a fallen hut where a wanton was combing her thick black hair, "no good place. Suzie Wong."

In the capital, of course, the Western influence was even more pronounced. Like every tourist, I was fascinated by the city's famous weekend market, a spicy department store of the subconscious that offered such niceties as rabbits for sale, and iridescent fish, crunchy grasshopper snacks and an evil-smelling wizard's brew of delicacies whipped up, so it seemed, from a recipe in the Wyrd Sisters' Cookbook. But the locals who were crowding the narrow aisles had no time for such common-or-garden fare. They had come to savor the real exotica: bright orange toy guitars; a bowling shirt that read "Rick's Carpet Center, Granada Hills"; and posters, fluttering along the sides of ramshackle stalls, of Jennifer Beals and Phoebe Cates—the newly canonized goddesses of the Orient—sitting in Mustangs, showing off UCLA letter jackets or simply carrying themselves as embodiments of the Promised Land. The largest crowd of all congregated around a craftsman who was meticulously brass-rubbing Maidenform ads onto T-shirts.

Bangkok, in fact, had a glamour and a sparkle that far outshone those of Bombay, Casablanca, even Athens; smartly done up in art nouveau restaurants and chandeliered super-luxury hotels, it glittered with a fast and flashy style that would not have been out of place in Paris or San Francisco. Yet more than anywhere else, Bangkok reminded me of L.A. Not just because its 900,000 cars were forever deadlocked, or because its balmy skies were perpetually smoggy and sullen with exhaust fumes. Not even because it was, both literally and metaphorically, spaced out and strung out, sprawling and recumbent and horizontal (where New York and Hong Kong, its true opposites, were thrustingly, busily, ambitiously vertical). Mostly, the "City of Angels" reminded me of Los Angeles because it was so laid-back (in topography and mood) as to seem a kind of dreamy suburban Elysium, abundantly supplied with flashy homes and smart-fronted boutiques, streamlined Jaguars and Mexican cafés, fancy patisseries, and even a wood-and-fern vegetarian restaurant (complete with classical guitarist and James Bond on the video). Down every puddle-glutted lane in Bangkok lay pizzas, pizzazz, and all the glitzy razzmatazz of the American Dream, California style: video rental stores, Pizza Hut and Robinson's, pretty young things looking for sugar daddies, and trendy watering holes with Redskins decals on the window and tapes of "This Week in the NFL" inside. In an inspired Freudian slip, one dingy hole-in-the-wall even promised "VDO."

It was during the Vietnam War, I reminded myself, that Bangkok first became celebrated in the West as a factory of dreams, a cathedral of sex and drugs and rock 'n' roll. So why should I be surprised that much of what remained resembled the bastard child of America and Indochina, a sad and shaming reminder of a difficult liaison? "My whorehouse," says Paul Theroux's Saint Jack, "was a scale model of the imperial dream."

The skin trade did indeed seem to underwrite the metaphor. For although the Patpong Road and the Grace Hotel were not exactly offering Love American Style, they were tricked up, even more than every other hopeful business, in all the hard and made-up finery of America. The bar girls were clad in Lee jeans and K-Mart tops; the songs on the jukebox were American, and so were the shows on the video. This was not, like the Philippines, a former American colony. Yet on any given day, the flashdancers of Bangkok

Duke Barbershop, then move from the Manhattan Hi-Tech Store to the Club Manhattan to the Manhattan Hotel (or the Florida, the Atlanta, the Reno, the Niagara, the Impala, or the Miami). And on any given night, I could travel from the Don Juan Cocktail Lounge to the Honey Hotel, and thence, by way of the Lolita Nightclub and Disco Duck, to the Je T'Aime Guest House.

My first reaction to Bangkok was shock; my second was to know that shock was not right, but I didn't know what was. "Those who go beneath the surface do so at their own peril," wrote Wilde, and the more I looked at the bar scene, the more my vision blurred.

The system of kept women was no import, an English-educated Thai lady indignantly assured me; it was an honored tradition for men here to relieve their wives of certain pressures by spending a few nights now and then with concubines. Many husbands, in fact, participated in a kind of "scholarship" system whereby they paid a young lady's way through college in exchange for her occasional services.

Nor was the system new. Well before the war in Vietnam, Ian Fleming had noted that while tourists in Bangkok were courting trouble by escorting Thai girls in the streets, the problem was that they didn't understand the right procedure: If they went to the nearest police station, an officer on duty would gladly provide them with suitable names and addresses. Nor did the system pander exclusively to the West: A recent American guidebook, choosing its verbs carefully, pointed out that by 1983 "Asian [single male] visitors to Thailand outstripped American." Besides, the girls of Bangkok always insisted, nothing could be more exciting than a boyfriend from abroad ("Thai men no good" was their constant refrain). Queen Sirikit herself once told a friend of mine that the word for foreigner, *farang*, was synonymous with all that was wondrously exotic.

Before very long, in fact, I began to discover that the ubiquitous couple of Bangkok—the pudgy foreigner with the exquisite girleen—was not quite the buyer and seller, the subject and object, I had imagined. In many cases, I was told, the girls did not simply make their bodies available to all while they looked at their watches and counted their money; they chose to offer their admirers their time, their thought, even their lives. The couple would sometimes stay together for two weeks, or three, or thirty. They would travel together and live together and think of themselves as lovers. She would show him her country, cook him local delicacies, mend his clothes, even introduce him to her parents and her friends. He would protect her from some parts of the world, teach her about others. For the girl, her Western suitor might prove the mature and sophisticated companion she had always lacked; for the man, his Eastern consort could be the attentive, demure, and sumptuously compliant goddess of his dreams. He would obviously provide material comforts and she physical; but sometimes—in subtler ways—their positions were reversed. And as the months passed, sensations sometimes developed into emotions, passions settled down into feelings. Often, in the end, they would go through a traditional marriage in her village.

Thus my tidy paradigm of West exploiting East began to crumble. Bangkok wasn't dealing only in the clear-cut trade of bodies; it was trafficking also in the altogether murkier exchange of hearts. The East, as Singapore Airlines knows full well, has always been a marketplace for romance. But Thailand was dispensing it on a personal scale, and in heavy doses. It offered love in a duty-free zone: a context in which boy meets girl without having to worry about commitments, obligations, even identities. Love, that is, or something like it.

Bangkok's intricate blend of dynamism and languor had long intrigued me. But as I spent more time in the country, Thailand began to betray other combinations I found more difficult to square. For savagery and grace were so cunningly interwoven here that beauty often seemed brutal and brutality itself quite beautiful. At official performances of Thai classical dance, sketches that featured lissome girls making supple turns were juxtaposed with others that showed off bruising, but no less sinuous, displays of sword fighting. Meanwhile, bouts of Thai boxing resembled nothing so much as ritualized ballets, in which two agile boys bowed their heads before the spirit of the ring, then pounded each other to the accompaniment of weird pipes, ominous drums, and a steady chanting.

Late one evening, as I wandered through the streets of Chiang Mai, I came upon groups of men flinging themselves through a game of volleyball played entirely with head and feet. Their suppleness was a marvel. They somersaulted and pirouetted, making corkscrew pivots in the air; they lunged and twisted high above the ground; they dazzled with their slinky acrobatics. Yet all the while, feet kicked faces, heads banged nastily together. And all around the dusty floodlit square hung a cockfight air of menace.

The Thais, wrote le Carré, are the world's swiftest and most efficient killers. Yet executioners would shoot their victims through gauze so as not to offend the Buddha, and monks would strain their water through their teeth so as not, by chance, to harm a single insect.

But at least, I thought, there was one clear-cut division here, in the Manichean setup of Bangkok. The city's two most common and appealing sights, after all, were its holy men, in spotless saffron robes, and its scarlet ladies. By day, the monks evoked a vision of purity, of hallowed groves filled with golden novitiates; by night, the whole grimy city felt polished, renewed, and transformed as sequined girls sang the body electric. At least, so I thought, this day-and-night division would ensure that good was good, and evil evil, and never the twain would meet.

But no. For after a while, I began to notice that, as the whores were engagingly girlish, the monks seemed endearingly boyish. I saw them poring over Walkmans in electronics stores with shopping bags slung over their shoulders, puffing ruminatively on cigarettes, playing tag with their friends in temple courtyards. Once, on venturing inside a monastery on a drowsy afternoon, I chanced upon a group of monks, with beautiful faces, huddled, in the cool shadows, before a TV set that was blasting out cartoons. Then I registered a deeper confusion: Some monks, I gathered, were criminals on the lam, while others scattered blessings each night upon the go-go bars; many bar girls, for their part, paid regular visits to Buddhist temples, joined palms together whenever they passed a shrine, and knelt in prayer before undertaking their bump and daily grind. Finally, quite flummoxed, I was coming to see the girls as something close to martyrs ("72 prostitutes rescued," proclaimed *The Nation),* and the holy men as something close to con men (the Bangkok *Post* told how five monks had killed one of their fellows with axes and knives because he dared to criticize them for shooting another monk during a party).

Thus the real sorcery of this dizzying place was that, before one knew it, it could work on one not just a physical but a moral seduction. For here was decadence so decorous that it disarmed the criticism it invited; a morality expressed with the delicacy of a ballerina's nod. And amid such a guiltless marketing of love, righteous indignation could only bounce off the mirrors and the shadows. Slowly, I saw, the city would unbutton your beliefs; gently, it would unbuckle your scruples; coolly, it would let your defenses slither to the floor. Buddhism did not forbid pleasure, the Thais kept saying—just the infliction of pain. So why find shame in enjoyment, and why take enjoyment in shame? What is so harmful or unnatural in love? Must sweetness be seen as a kind of laxness? Why not see sex as an act of communion? *"Mai pen rai"* ran their constant refrain. No matter. No sweat. Never mind.

And for all my unease in Bangkok, I could not deny that it was quite the most invigorating, and accommodating, city I had ever seen—more lazily seductive than even Rio or Havana. For elegance here was seasoned with funkiness, and efficiency was set off by mystery. Sugar was blended with spice. On Sunday mornings, I often went early to the Temple of the Dawn, and spent several noiseless hours there, surrounded by Buddhas and gazing at the gilded temples that lay across the river like slumberous lions; the minute I grew hungry, however, I could jump into a ten-cent local bus and savor a delectable lunch of watermelon juice and spicy chicken while watching Eurhythmics videos in a spotless air-conditioned café. In the evenings, I would sip

Twining's tea from porcelain cups in an exquisite teak-tabled restaurant, soothed by the sound of George Winston, then saunter outside to find the wind blowing around the sleeping canals and three-wheel tuk-tuks puttering through the tropical night.

Bangkok was the heart of the Orient, of course. But it was also every Westerner's synthetic, five-star version of what the Orient should be: all the exoticism of the East served up amidst all the conveniences of the West ("It seems to combine," a fascinated S. J. Perelman once wrote, "the Hannibal, Missouri, of Mark Twain's boyhood with Beverly Hills, the Low Countries and Chinatown"). And all the country's variegated Western influences seemed, finally, nothing more than decorative strands that could be woven at will into the beautiful and ornamental tapestry of the country's own inalienable texture ("We provide attractive Thai, Australian, Japanese, Chinese, Swedish, Dutch, Danish, Belgian, Austrian, and French girls," offered one escort agency. "Also handsome and nice boys [gay] entirely at your service"). The Thais, moreover, seemed to know exactly what their assets were—melting smiles, whispering faces, a beseeching frailty, a luxurious grace—and exactly how to turn those virtues into commodities that the West would covet. The carnal marketplace known as the Grace Hotel was, to that extent, aptly named. "Experience unique courtesy only Thai girls can offer."

I n the end, then, the lovely doubleness with which the bar scene enthralled its foreign votaries seemed scarcely different from the way in which the stealthy East had often disarmed its visitors from abroad. For had not the Buddha himself said that all that we see is illusion?

Ultimately, then, it began to seem no coincidence that Thailand, the most open and most complaisant of all Asian nations, was also the only one that had never been conquered or colonized. The one woman who *never* gives herself away, D. H. Lawrence once wrote, is the free woman who always gives herself up. Just so with Thailand, a place, quite literally, more ravishing than ravished. For though it was known as the "Land of Smiles," the smiles here really gave nothing away; Thai eyes often seemed to laugh, and Thai smiles shone with the light of all that was left unsaid. Many years ago, some Americans tried to unravel the mystery by calling the Thais "the nicest people money can buy." But even that seemed too simple a summary of the country's opacities. And even now, the Thais, with a gentle smile, continued to confound their visitors from abroad. A Westerner was not exactly in the dark here; just always in the shadows.

3 Bangkok

Introduction

by Nigel Fisher

A foreigner's reaction to Bangkok is often as confused as the city's geography. Bangkok has no downtown, and the streets, like the traffic, seem to veer off in every direction. The oldest quarter clusters around the eastern bank of the Chao Phraya River. The river winds between two cities, Thailand's current capital and Thonburi, where the Thais first established their capital after the fall of Ayutthaya in 1767.

Even Bangkok's name is disconcerting. Foreigners call the city Bangkok, but Thais refer to their capital as Krung Thep, the City of Angels. When Thailand's capital was Ayutthaya, to the north of present-day Bangkok, foreign vessels would reach there by the Chao Phraya. After the fall of Ayutthaya, King Rama I decided in 1782 to move his capital from Thonburi to a new site across the river. Foreigners looked at their navigational charts and understood the capital to be where the village of Bangkok was marked.

In the last 20 years, the face of Bangkok has changed. Before the Vietnam War, and before Bangkok became the R & R destination for American servicemen, the city had a population of 1.5 million. Then, the flaunting of U.S. dollars attracted the rural poor to the city. Within two decades, it grew to 6 million, 40 times the size of any other city in Thailand. Space in which to live and breathe is inadequate. Air pollution is the worst in the world. Traffic jams the streets from morning to evening, and no cure is in sight. Use the pedestrian crosswalks—the traffic will stop if you insist—or use the pedestrian flyovers.

Yet, while hurtling headlong into the world of modern commercialism and technology, Bangkok strangely gives a sense of history and timelessness, even though it is only 200 years old. This is perhaps because King Rama I was determined to build a city as beautiful as the old capital of Ayutthaya had been before the Burmese ransacked it. Bangkok requires an adjustment on our part, but we soon come to appreciate the gentle nature of the Thai people and their respect for others.

Essential Information

Arriving and Departing by Plane

Airports and Airlines
Bangkok's Don Muang Airport's new international terminal, adjacent to what is now the domestic terminal, has relieved passenger congestion and presents international passengers with modern efficiency on arrival. As you exit customs, you'll find an array of information desks where you can make arrangements for taxis into Bangkok and transport to other destinations; a reservation desk for Bangkok hotels (no fee); and a TAT (Tourist Authority of Thailand) desk that has a large selection of free brochures and maps. Both terminals have luggage-checking facilities (tel. 02/535–1250).

There is a tax of B200 for international departures and B20 for domestic departures.

Don Muang is 25 km (15 mi) from the city center. The road is often congested with traffic. Be prepared for a 90-minute journey by taxi, though there are times when it can take less than 40 minutes.

Thai Airways International is the national airline, and most of its flights come in and out of Don Muang. Thai International has direct flights from the West Coast of the United States and from Toronto in Canada. The airline also has daily flights to Hong Kong, Singapore, Taiwan, and Japan, and direct flights from London.

United Airlines is the major U.S. carrier with service to Bangkok. There are direct flights from the West Coast, and connecting flights from the East Coast with one change of planes at San Francisco, Tokyo, or Hong Kong. **Singapore Airlines** flies in from Singapore, and **British Airways** flies in from London. In total, 35 airline companies have flights to and from Bangkok, and more are seeking landing rights. From the East Coast of North America, flying time is less heading east across the Atlantic than going west over the Pacific (17 hours versus 22). **Finnair** actively promotes this route out of New York via Helsinki, permitting a stopover in Helsinki to visit Finland.

The only other airline to promote this route is **Swissair** through Zurich to Bangkok and continuing on to other Southeast Asian destinations. Swissair also flies through Bombay enroute to Bangkok, permitting a stopover in India.

Between the Airport and Center City
By Taxi Obtain a taxi reservation at the counter (at either terminal) and a driver will lead you to the taxi. The fare for any Bangkok destination is B300 from the international terminal and B200 from the domestic. Taxis to the airport from downtown Bangkok are, with negotiation, approximately B130.

By Minibus Thai Airways has a minibus service between the airport and Bangkok's major hotels. The minibuses depart when they are full. Cost: B100.

By Bus Bus No. 4 goes to Rama Garden Hotel, Indra Regent, Erawan, Hyatt, and Dusit Thani hotels, and down Silom Road. (The last bus comes at 8 PM.) Bus No. 10 goes to Rama Garden Hotel, the Northern Bus Terminal, the Victory Monument, and the Southern Bus Terminal. (Last bus at 8:30 PM.) Bus No. 13 goes to the Northern Bus Terminal, Victory Monument, and down Sukhumvit Road to the Eastern Bus Terminal. (Last bus at 8 PM.) Bus No. 29 goes to the Northern Bus Terminal, Victory Monument, Siam Square, and Bangkok's main railway station, Hualamphong. (Last bus at 8:30 PM.) Buses are air-conditioned. Cost: B15.

By Train Trains into Bangkok's central railway station run approximately every 30 minutes from 5:30 AM to 9 PM. The fare is B5 for a local train, B13 for an express.

Arriving by Train and Bus

By Train **Hualamphong Railway Station** (Rama IV Rd., tel. 02/223–7461) is the city's main station and serves most long-distance trains. There is also **Bangkok Noi** (Arun Amarin Rd., tel. 02/411–3102) on the Thonburi side of the Chao Phraya River, used by local trains to Hua Hin and Kanchanaburi.

By Bus Bangkok has three main bus terminals. **Northern/Northeast Bus Terminal** (Phaholyothin Rd., tel. 02/279–4484 for air-conditioned buses, tel. 02/279–6222 for nonair-conditioned buses)

is for Chiang Mai and the north. **Southern Bus Terminal**
(Charansanitwong Rd., tel. 02/411–4978 for air-conditioned
buses, tel. 02/511–0511 for nonair-conditioned buses), on the
Thonburi side of the river, is for Hua Hin, Ko Samui, Phuket,
and points south. **Eastern Bus Terminal** (Sukhumvit Rd., Soi
40, tel. 02/391–3310 for air-conditioned buses, tel. 02/392–2391
for nonair-conditioned buses), often simply referred to as
Ekkimae, is for Pattaya and points southeast.

Getting Around

There is no subway, and road traffic is horrendous. Allow twice
the normal travel time during rush hours, 7–10 AM and 4–7 PM.

By Bus Though buses can be very crowded, they are convenient and inexpensive for getting around. For a fare of only B2, B3 for the
blue buses, and B5 for the less frequent air-conditioned buses,
you can travel virtually anywhere in the city. Buses operate
from 5 AM to around 11 PM. The routes are confusing, but usually someone at the bus stop will know the number of the bus you
need to catch. It is even simpler if you pick up a route map.
These are available at most bookstalls for B35. Be aware of
purse snatchers on the buses.

By Taxi Taxis are not metered, and bargaining is essential before
climbing into the taxi. As a rough guide to price, a taxi fare
from the Hilton to the Grand Palace may run B70 ($2.80); from
the Hilton to the Oriental Hotel, about B50 ($2).

By Samlor Tuk-tuks are slightly cheaper than taxis and best used for short
trips in congested traffic.

By Boat Water taxis and express (ferry) boats ply the Chao Phraya River. For the express boats, the fare is based on zones, but B5 will
cover most trips that you are likely to take. You'll also have to
pay a B1 jetty fee. The jetty adjacent to the Oriental Hotel is a
useful stop. In about 10 minutes, you can travel up the river,
making half a dozen stops, to the Grand Palace, or farther up to
the other side of Krungthon Bridge in about 15 minutes. It is
often the quickest way to travel in a north–south direction.

Long-tailed (so called for the extra-long propeller shaft that extends behind the stern) boats may be hired for about B250 an
hour.

Important Addresses and Numbers

Tourist The **Thailand Tourist Authority** (TAT; Ratchadamnoen Rd., tel.
Information 02/282–1143) tends to have more in the way of colorful brochures than hard information. The staff does try to be helpful,
and you may want to drop in when you are near the Democracy
Monument in the northern part of the city, but you can probably get all the brochures you want from the TAT branch at the
airport (tel. 02/523–8973).

Thai International Airways has an office at 485 Silom Road (tel.
02/233–3810).

Telephone information from an English-speaking operator is
available by dialing 13.

Immigration Division (Soi Suan Sathorn Tai Rd., tel. 02/286–
9176) is the place to go for a visa extension. Visas are not required for many nationalities, but tourists are permitted to

stay only 15 days in the country without an extension. If you go beyond your specified stay by a few days, don't worry. You can simply pay a B100 per diem fine as you exit through emigration at Bangkok's airport.

Embassies Most nations maintain diplomatic relations with Thailand and have embassies in Bangkok. Should you need to apply for a visa to another country, the consulate hours are usually 8–noon: **Australian Embassy** (37 Sathorn Tai Rd., tel. 02/287–2680); **British Embassy** (1031 Wireless Rd., tel. 02/253–0191); **United States Embassy** (95 Wireless Rd., tel. 02/252–5040).

Emergencies **Tourist Police** (509 Vorachak Rd., tel. 02/221–6209), with headquarter post located opposite the Dusit Thani hotel in Lumpini Park, are available daily 8 AM–midnight. You're advised to contact the Tourist Police rather than the local police in an emergency.

Police, tel. 195; **fire,** tel. 199; **ambulance,** tel. 02/246–0199.

Hospitals **Chulalongkorn Hospital** (Rama I Rd., tel. 02/252–8181).

English-Language Bookstores The English-language dailies, the *Bangkok Post* and *The Nation*, are available at newsstands.

Asia Books (221 Sukhumvit Rd., Soi 15, tel. 02/252–7277) has a wide selection, as does DK Books or, more properly, **Duang Kamol Bookshop** (244–6 Siam Sq., tel. 02/251–6335).

Pharmacies There is no shortage of pharmacies in Bangkok. Compared to the United States, fewer drugs require prescriptions, but should you need them, you must have a prescription written in Thai. Be aware that over-the-counter drugs are not necessarily of the same chemical composition as those in the United States.

Travel Agencies In virtually every major hotel, a travel desk books tours in and around Bangkok. Smaller travel agencies sometimes do not live up to their promises, and so for significant purchases and arrangements, you may want to select a larger and more established agency, such as **Diethelm** (544 Phoenchit Rd., tel. 02/252–4041) or **World Travel Service** (1053 New Charoen Krung Rd., tel. 02/233–5900).

Bangkok used to be the world's leading center for discounted airline tickets. The prices are not as competitive as they used to be, but agencies still offer some good prices, usually on lesser-known airlines. Be sure that you read the restrictions on the ticket carefully before you part with any money. You are safer buying open tickets rather than those naming a specific flight and time.

Guided Tours

Numerous tours cover Bangkok and its environs. Each tour operator offers some slight variation, but, in general, they cover the following itineraries.

Floating Market Tour. This half-day tour is a boat ride on the Chao Phraya and into the *klongs* (small canals), former site of a lively floating market with vendors selling vegetables, fruits, meats, and other fare from their sampans. Most of these vendors have long since disappeared, and the visual splendor has gone. Recommended, instead, is a tour to the floating market at Damnoen Saduak, south of Bangkok.

Grand Palace and Emerald Buddha Tour. Because you can easily reach the palace by taxi or public transport and hire a guide on the spot, you may want to visit these sights independently.

City and Temples Tour. In half a day, you can visit some of Bangkok's most famous temples: Wat Po with the reclining Buddha; Wat Benjamabopit, famous for its marble structure; and Wat Traimitr, with the five-ton golden Buddha. This tour does not include the Grand Palace.

Thai Dinner and Classical Dance. This evening tour includes a buffet-style Thai dinner with a show of classical dancing. You can manage it just as well on your own.

Exploring

Highlights for First-time Visitors

Damnoen Saduak floating market
(*see* Chapter 4, Excursions from Bangkok)

Ferry ride on the Chao Phraya River
(*see* Excursions from Bangkok)

Grand Palace and Wat Phra Keo (Temple of the Emerald Buddha) (*see* Tour 1)

Jim Thompson's House (*see* Tour 2)

National Museum (*see* Tour 2)

Wat Po (Temple of the Reclining Buddha) (*see* Tour 1)

Thai dance performance (*see* Tour 2)

Wat Traimitr (Temple of the Golden Buddha (*see* Tour 1)

Orientation

Because confusion is part of Bangkok's fascination, learning your way around is a challenge. It may help to think of Bangkok as an isosceles triangle with the base abutting the *S* curve of the Chao Phraya and the apex ending down Sukhumvit Road, somewhere around Soi 40.

Beginning at the apex of this conceptual triangle is Sukhumvit, once a residential neighborhood. In the last decade, it has developed into a district of hotels, shops, nightclubs, and restaurants while retaining some of its warm, residential atmosphere. Westward, toward the Chao Phraya, you come to spacious foreign embassy compounds, offices of large corporations, and modern international hotels. Slightly farther west, stores, offices, and more hotels are more closely packed. Now you reach the older sections of Bangkok. On the southern flank is Silom Road, a shopping and financial district. Parallel to Silom Road is Suriwongse Road with more hotels, and between the two is the entertainment district of Patpong. Continue farther and you reach two of the leading hotels on the riverbank: the Oriental and the Shangri-La.

Traveling down Rama I Road in the center of the triangle, you pass the Siam Square shopping area and the National Stadium. Continue in the direction of the Hualamphong Railway Station. Between Hualamphong and the river is Chinatown, a maze of streets with restaurants, goldsmiths, and small warehouses and repair shops.

In the northern part of the triangle, moving westward, you pass through various markets before reaching Thai government buildings, the Victory Monument, Chitlada Palace, the Dusit Zoo, the National Assembly, the National Library, and, finally, the river. Slightly to the south of this route are the Democracy Monument, the Grand Palace, and the Temple of the Emerald Buddha.

Knowing your exact destination, its direction, and approximate distance are important in negotiating taxi fares and planning your itinerary. Crossing and recrossing the city is time-consuming—many hours can be spent in frustrating traffic jams.

Numbers in the margin correspond to points of interest on the Bangkok map.

Tour 1: The River Tour

❶ Start the tour with breakfast on the terrace of the **Oriental Hotel,** overlooking the Chao Phraya River. The hotel itself is a Bangkok institution. To the side of the Oriental's entrance, a small lane leads to the river and a landing stage for the river buses that ply it. Take the river bus upstream to the Grand Palace and Wat Phra Keo.

❷ The **Grand Palace** is Bangkok's major landmark. This is where Bangkok's founder, King Rama I, built his palace and walled city in 1782. Subsequent Chakri monarchs enlarged the walled city, though today the buildings are used only for state occasions and royal ceremonies. The compound—but not all of the buildings—is open to visitors.

The official residence of the king—he actually lives elsewhere, at Chitlada Palace in Bangkok—is the Chakri Maha Prasart palace. Occasionally, its state function rooms are open to visitors, but most of the time only the exterior can be viewed. To the right of Chakri Maha Prasart is the Dusit Maha Prasart, a classic example of Thai royal palace architecture.

To the left of the palace is the Amarin Vinichai Hall, the original audience hall built by King Rama I and now used for the presentation of ambassadors' credentials. Note the glittering gold throne.

Visit this compound first, because none of these buildings excites such awe as the adjoining royal chapel, the most sacred temple in the kingdom, the **Temple of the Emerald Buddha** (Wat Phra Keo). No other wat in Thailand is so ornate and so embellished with murals, statues, and glittering gold. For many, it is overly decorated, and as your wat experience grows, you may decide that you prefer the simplicity of the lesser known wats, but you'll never quite get over the elaborate richness of Wat Phra Keo.

As you enter the compound, take note of a number of 6-m- (20-ft-) tall helmeted and tile-encrusted statues in traditional Thai battle attire standing guard and surveying the precincts. They set the scene—mystical, majestic, and awesome. Turn right as you enter, and notice along the inner walls the lively murals (re-

Bangkok

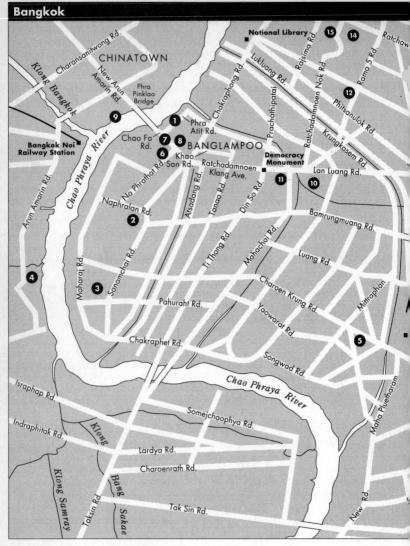

CHARANSANITWONG Rd.

Klong Bangkok

CHINATOWN

New Arun Amarin Rd.

Phra Pinklao Bridge

National Library

Lukluang Rd.

Chakraphong Rd.

Rajsima Rd.

Ratchaw

Prachathipatai

Ratchadamnoen Nok Rd.

Rama 5 Rd.

Phitsanulok Rd.

Krungkasem Rd.

Bangkok Noi Railway Station

Arun Amarin Rd.

Chao Phraya River

Chao Fa Rd.

Phra Atit Rd.

BANGLAMPOO

Khao San Rd.

Ratchadamnoen Klang Ave.

Democracy Monument

Lan Luang Rd.

Na Phrathat Rd.

Atsadang Rd.

Tanao Rd.

Din So Rd.

Bamrungmuang Rd.

Naphralan Rd.

Maharaj Rd.

Sanamchai Rd.

Ti Thong Rd.

Mohachai Rd.

Luang Rd.

Pahurat Rd.

Charoen Krung Rd.

Yaowarat Rd.

Mitraphan

Chakraphet Rd.

Songwad Rd.

Israphap Rd.

Chao Phraya River

Somejchaophya Rd.

Indraphitak Rd.

Klong

Bang

Maha Phuethoram

Lardya Rd.

Charoenrath Rd.

Klong Samray

Taksin Rd.

Sakae

Tak Sin Rd.

New Rd.

Ceremonial Barges, **9**

Chitlada Palace, **13**

Dusit Zoo, **14**

Grand Palace, **2**

Jim Thompson's House, **17**

Marble Temple, **12**

National Art Gallery, **8**

National Museum, **6**

National Theatre, **7**

Oriental Hotel, **1**

Suan Pakkard Palace, **16**

Temple of the Reclining Buddha (Wat Po), **3**

Vimarnmek Palace, **15**

Wat Arun, **4**

Wat Rachanada, **11**

Wat Sakret, **10**

Wat Traimitr, **5**

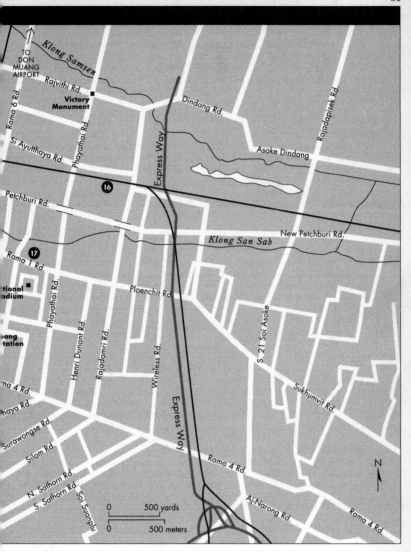

TO DON MUANG AIRPORT

Klong Samsen

Rajvithi Rd.

Victory Monument

Rama 6 Rd.

Phayathai Rd.

Si Ayutthaya Rd.

Dindang Rd.

Express Way

Asoke Dindang

Rajadapisek Rd.

Petchburi Rd.

16

New Petchburi Rd.

Klong San Sab

Rama 1 Rd.

17

tional adium

ong tation

Phayathai Rd.

Henri Dunant Rd.

Rajadamri Rd.

Ploenchit Rd.

Wireless Rd.

S. 21 Soi Asoke

Sukhumvit Rd.

Express Way

ma 4 Rd.

haya Rd.

Surawongse Rd.

Silom Rd.

N. Sathorn Rd.

S. Sathorn Rd.

Soi Suanplu

Rama 4 Rd.

Aj-Narong Rd.

Rama 4 Rd.

N

| 0 | 500 yards |
| 0 | 500 meters |

cently restored) depicting the whole *Ramayana (Ramakien* in Thai) epic.

The main chapel, with its gilded, glittering, three-tiered roof, dazzles the senses. Royal griffins stand guard outside, and shining gold stupas in the court establish serenity with their perfect symmetry. Inside sits the Emerald Buddha.

Carved from one piece of jade, the ¾-m- (31-in-) high figure is one of the most venerated images of the Lord Buddha. No one knows its origin, but history places it in Chiang Rai, in northeast Thailand, in 1464. From there it traveled first to Chiang Mai, then to Lamphun, and finally back to Chiang Mai, where the Laotians stole it and took it home with them. Eventually, the Thais sent an army into Laos to secure it. The statue reached its final resting place when King Rama I built the chapel. The statue is high above the altar and visitors can see it only from afar. What is most intriguing about the statue is the mystique surrounding it. Behind the altar and above the window frames are murals depicting the life and eventual enlightenment of the Lord Buddha.

Walk to the back of the royal chapel and you'll find a scale model of Angkor Wat. As Angkor Wat, in Kampuchea, is difficult to reach nowadays, this is a chance to sense the vastness of the old Khmer capital. *Admission charge. Open daily 8:30–11:30 and 1–3:30.*

Just to the east of the Grand Palace compound is the City Pillar Shrine that contains the foundation stone (Lak Muang) from which all distances in Thailand are measured. The stone is believed to be inhabited by a spirit that guards the well-being of Bangkok.

❸ When you leave the Grand Palace, walk south to the oldest and largest temple in Bangkok, the **Temple of the Reclining Buddha** (Wat Po, or Wat Phya Jetuphon). Much is made of the size of this statue—the largest in the country, measuring 46 m (151 ft) in length. Especially noteworthy are his 3-m- (10-ft-) long feet, inlaid with mother-of-pearl designs depicting the 108 auspicious signs of the Lord Buddha.

Walk beyond the chapel containing the Reclining Buddha and enter Bangkok's oldest open university. A hundred years before Bangkok was established as the capital city, a monastery was founded to teach classical Thai medicine. The school still gives instruction in the natural methods of healing. Around the walls are marble plaques inscribed with formulas for herbal cures, and stone sculptures squat in various postures demonstrating techniques for relieving muscle pain.

Don't be perturbed by the sculpted figures that good-naturedly poke fun at farangs. Referred to as Chinese rock sculptures, they are gangling 3.6-m- (12-ft-) high figures, the most evil of demons, which scare away all other evil spirits. With their top hats, they look farcically Western. In fact, they were modeled after the Europeans who plundered China during the Opium Wars.

These tall statues guard the entrance to the northeastern quarter of the monastery and a very pleasant three-tier temple. Inside are 394 seated Buddhas. Usually, a monk sits cross-legged at one side of the altar, making himself available to answer your questions (you will need to speak Thai or have a translator). On the walls, bas-relief plaques salvaged from Ayutthaya depict stories from the *Ramayana*. Around this temple area are four tall *chedis* (Thai-style pagodas where holy relics are kept), decorated with brightly colored porcelain, each representing one of the first four kings of the Chakri (present) dynasty. *Admission charge. Open daily 7–5.*

Time Out   The monks of Wat Po still practice ancient cures and have become famous for their massage technique. The massage lasts one hour, growing more and more pleasurable as you adjust to the technique. Masseurs are available 7–5. Cost: B150. When you're ready for refreshment, there is a pleasant snack bar in the northeastern compound, where the fare includes delicious chilled coconut milk.

From Wat Po, if you walk halfway back to the Grand Palace and then cut down to the river past a small market, you'll reach the jetty, Tha Thien, for the ferry to cross over the Chao Phraya to **❹ Wat Arun** on the western bank of the river.

Wat Arun means "Temple of the Dawn," and at sunrise, it is inspiring. It is even more marvelous toward dusk, however, when the setting sun casts its amber tones. Within the square courtyard, the temple's architecture is symmetrical, containing five Khmer-style prangs (stupas). The central prang, towering 86 m (282 ft), is surrounded by its four attendant prangs in the corners. All of the prangs are covered in mosaics of broken Chinese porcelain. The surrounding grounds are a peaceful haven in which to relax and watch the sun go down. The more energetic climb the steep steps of the central prang for the view over the Chao Phraya River. *Admission charge. Open 8–5:30.*

Wat Arun has a small park around it, and, by the river, is a pleasant spot in which to linger. However, if time is short, cross back to the eastern shore and wander inland through Chinatown. You may want to take a tuk-tuk as far as Pahurat Road.

The site of Bangkok's first tall buildings, **Chinatown** used to be the prosperous downtown neighborhood, but, as Bangkok has grown, new, taller office buildings have sprung up to the east, and Chinatown, losing some of its bustle and excitement, has become less the hub of activity. Red lanterns and Chinese signs still abound, and numerous modest Chinese restaurants line the streets. Pahurat Road is full of textile shops, with nearly as many Indian dealers here as Chinese. Down Pahurat Road, and a zigzag to the left, is Yaowarat Road, Chinatown's main thoroughfare, crowded with numerous gold and jewelry shops. Between Yaowarat and Charoen Krung roads is the so-called Thieves Market (Nakorn Kasem), an area of small streets with old wood houses, where you can buy all sorts of items ranging from hardware to porcelains. Bargains are hard to find nowadays; nevertheless, these small, cluttered streets are fascinating to walk through, and, who knows, a porcelain vase may take your fancy. Bargain hard!

South along Yaowarat Road is Charoen Krung (New Road). On **❺** the opposite corner is **Wat Traimitr** (Temple of the Golden Buddha). The main temple has little architectural merit, but off to the side, next to the money-changing wagon, is a small chapel. Inside is the world's largest solid-gold Buddha image, cast about nine centuries ago. Weighing 5½ tons and standing 3 m (10 ft) high, the statue gleams with such a richness and purity that even the most jaded are inspired by its strength and power. Sculpted in Sukhothai style, the statue is believed to have been brought first to Ayutthaya. When the Burmese were about to sack the city, the statue was covered in plaster. Two centuries later, the plaster still covering the image, it was regarded as just another Buddhist statue. Then, when it was being moved to a new temple in Bangkok, it slipped from the crane. Leaving the statue in the mud, the workmen called it a day. During the night, a temple monk dreamed that the statue was divinely inspired. First thing in the morning he went to see the Buddha image. Through a crack in the plaster, he saw the glint of yellow. Opening the plaster farther, he discovered that the statue was pure gold. *Admission charge. Open daily 9–5.*

Tour 2: Temples, Museums, and Villas

6 Unless you can get an early start to visit some temples and beat the heat, the **National Museum** should be your first stop. Try to make it on a Tuesday, Wednesday, or Thursday, when free, guided, 90-minute tours in English start at 9:30 AM. Volunteers who specialize in different aspects of Thai art explain the complexities of Thai culture and give visitors a general orientation to the vast collection of treasures in the museum. The tours meet at the entrance to the main building, which was originally built in 1783 as a palace for surrogate kings (a position abolished in 1874). The two new wings were added in 1966.

This extensive museum has one of the world's best collections of Southeast Asian art in general, and Buddhist and Thai art in particular. As a result, it offers the best opportunity to trace Thailand's long history, beginning with ceramic utensils and bronzeware from the Ban Chiang civilization, thought to have existed 5,000 to 6,000 years ago. To the left of the museum's ticket counter is an artifact gallery that depicts the history of Thailand. You may want to see this first for a historical overview. Afterward, explore the galleries that portray the early history of Thailand—the Dvaravati and Khmer periods of more than 1,000 years ago. These will prepare you for the complex of galleries displaying the different styles of Thai art from the Sukhothai period (1238–mid-14th century) and later. The majority of the great masterpieces created during the Sukhothai and Ayutthaya periods, as well as those works from the northern provinces, have found their way into the Bangkok National Museum. Consequently, up-country museums are rather bare of fine Thai art; so take the opportunity to see this collection if you can. A cafeteria is centrally located in the museum complex. *Admission charge. Open Tues.–Thurs. and weekends 9–noon and 1–4.*

7 Next door is the **National Theatre,** where classical Thai dance and drama performances are held (*see* The Arts and Nightlife, below).

8 Opposite is the **National Art Gallery,** with exhibits, both modern and traditional, by Thai artists. *Chao Fa Rd., tel. 02/281–2224. Admission charge. Open Tues.–Thurs. and weekends 9–noon and 1–4.*

9 Walk or take a tuk-tuk across the Phra Pinklao Bridge to the dockyard, where the royal **ceremonial barges** are berthed. The ornately carved barges, crafted in the early part of this century, take the form of famous mythical creatures featured in the

Ramayana. The most impressive is the red-and-gold royal flag barge, *Suphannahongse* (Golden Swan), used by the king on (very) special occasions. *Admission charge. Open Tues.-Thurs. and weekends 9–noon and 1–4.*

⑩ Back across the river is **Wat Sakret.** It's too far to walk; so take a tuk-tuk for B20. You'll first pass the tall and imposing Democracy Monument, and at the next main intersection, right across the street, will be Wat Sakret.

Wat Sakret (the Temple of the Golden Mount) is a notable landmark of the old city and was, for a long time, the highest building around. King Rama III started the building of this mound and temple, which were completed by Rama V. To reach the gold-covered chedi, you must make an exhausting climb up 318 steps winding around the mound. Don't even attempt it on a hot day, but on a cool, clear day, the view over Bangkok from the top is worth the effort. Every November, the temple compound is the site of Bangkok's largest temple fair, with food stalls, stage shows, and merrymaking. *Admission charge. Open daily 8–5.*

⑪ Across from Wat Sakret is **Wat Rachanada,** built to resemble the mythical castle of the gods. According to legend, a wealthy and pious man built a fabulous castle, Loha Prasat, following the design laid down in Hindu mythology for the disciples of the Lord Buddha. Wat Rachanada, built in metal, is meant to duplicate that castle and is the only one of its kind remaining. In its precincts are stalls selling amulets that protect the wearer from misfortune—usually of the physical kind, though love amulets and charms are also sold. They tend to be rather expensive, but that's the price of good fortune. *Admission charge. Open daily 8–6.*

⑫ A short tuk-tuk ride away—no more than B20—is one of Bangkok's most photographed temples, the **Marble Temple** (Wat Benjamabophit), built in 1899. Go north from Wat Rachanada, up Ratchadamnoen Nok Road and past the Tourist Authority of Thailand office, toward the equestrian statue of King Chulalongkorn. Just before the statue is Si Ayutthaya Road. Take a right, and Wat Benjamabophit will be on your right.

With its statues of Buddha lining the courtyard and magnificent interior with crossbeams of lacquer and gold, Wat Benjamabophit is more than a splendid temple. The monastery is a seat of learning that appeals to Buddhist monks with intellectual yearnings. It was here that Thailand's present king came to spend his days as a monk before his coronation. *Admission charge. Open daily 7–5.*

Leaving Wat Benjamabophit, you can take another short tuk-tuk ride to Vimarnmek Palace. Ask the driver to go there by **⑬** way of Rama V Road past **Chitlada Palace,** one of the king's residences. The palace will be on the right. On the left will be the **⑭** **Dusit Zoo,** a place to visit perhaps when you are exhausted by Bangkok's traffic and want to rest in a pleasant expanse of greenery. *Admission charge. Open daily 8–6.*

⑮ **Vimarnmek Palace** is the largest teak structure in the world. This four-story palace was built by King Rama V, grandfather of the present king, as a suburban palace. Now, with the capital's growth, it's in the center of administrative Bangkok, right next door to the entrance of the National Assembly building.

The Vimarnmek Palace fits its name, "Castle in the Clouds." Its extraordinarily light and delicate appearance is enhanced by the adjacent reflecting pond. King Rama's fascination with Western architecture shows in the palace's Victorian style, but the building retains an unmistakable Thai delicacy. Most of the furniture was either purchased in the West or given as gifts by European monarchs. Some of the exhibits by late 19th-century craftsmen are exquisite—porcelain, handcrafted furniture, and crystal—and some have more novelty value, such as the first typewriter to have been brought to Thailand. *Admission charge. Open daily 9:30–4.*

16 By way of contrast with Vimarnmek Palace, visit the **Suan Pakkard Palace** next. You'll need a taxi or a tuk-tuk; it's a good B30 ride due east down Ayutthaya Road. Five traditional Thai houses, built high on teak columns, adorn the perfectly kept grounds, which include undulating lawns, shimmering lotus pools, and lush shrubbery. The center of attraction, the Lacquer Pavilion, is at the back of the garden. Inside is gold-covered paneling with scenes from the life of Buddha. On display in the houses are porcelain, Khmer stone heads, old paintings, and statues of Buddha. The serene atmosphere of the houses and grounds makes Suan Pakkard one of the most relaxing places in which to absorb Thai culture. *Admission charge. Open Mon.–Sat. 9–4.*

17 Another compound of traditional Thai architecture and Southeast Asian furnishings—**Jim Thompson's House**—is fairly close, no more than a B30 tuk-tuk ride away. Go south on Phayathai Road and then west (right) on Rama I. Bargain lovers may want to make an interim stop at the Praturnam Market, just before the Rama I junction and after the Indra Regent Hotel. Hundreds of stalls and shops jam the sidewalk vying for shoppers' attention. The stacks of merchandise, consisting primarily of inexpensive clothing, are overwhelming, and the prices are irresistible—jeans for $5 and shirts for $4.

The entrance to Jim Thompson's House is easy to miss. Walk down Soi Kasemsong, an unprepossessing lane leading off to the right of Rama I as you come from Phayathai. At the end of the lane, the entrance is on your left.

American Jim Thompson was once an architect in New York; he joined the OSS in World War II and went to Asia. After the war, he stayed in Thailand and took it upon himself to revitalize the silk industry, which had virtually become extinct. His project and product met with tremendous success. That, in itself, would have made Thompson into a legend, but, in 1967, he went to the Malaysian Cameron Highlands for a quiet holiday and was never heard from again.

Aside from reestablishing the Thai silk industry, Thompson also left us his house. Using parts of old up-country houses, some as old as 150 years, he constructed a compound of six Thai houses, three of which are exactly the same as their originals, including all the details of the interior layout. With true appreciation of Southeast Asian art, Thompson then set out to collect what are now priceless works of art to furnish his home. *Tel. 02/215–0122. Admission charge. Open Mon.–Sat. 9–4:30.*

Both of the tours above are long, full-day ventures. Each would be managed more comfortably in two days, allowing time to discover your own Bangkok. Moreover, these tours have left out at least 290 other Buddhist temples!

Off the Beaten Track

A relaxing way to see Bangkok is to hire a motorboat for an hour or two and explore the small canals (klongs). The cost is about B250, and a boat can seat four easily.

Alternatively, you can travel on the Chao Phraya River on the ferryboats. One good trip past waterside temples, Thai-style houses, the Royal Barge Museum, and Khoo Wiang Floating Market starts at the Chang Pier near the Grand Palace and travels along Klong Bang Khoo Wiang and Klong Bang Yai. Boats leave every 20 minutes between 6:15 AM and 8 PM and cost B10.

Stroll around the **Banglampoo** section of Bangkok, the area where the backpackers gravitate. The main thoroughfare, Ko Sahn Road, is full of cafés, secondhand bookstalls, and inexpensive shops. In the evening, the streets are full of stalls and food stands serving the needs of young Westerners on their grand around-the-world tour.

Visit the **Pratunam night market** at the junction of Phetchaburi and Rajaprarop roads. Locals come here for noodles and other tasty dishes after an evening out at the cinema. The market is a good place to meet Thais and eat inexpensive Thai and Chinese food.

Shopping

Bangkok, with its range of goods produced in all regions of the country and offered at competitive prices, is a shopper's paradise.

Shopping Districts

The main shopping areas are along Silom Road and at the Rama IV end of Suriwongse for jewelry, crafts, and silk; along Sukhumvit Road for leather goods; along Yaowarat in Chinatown for gold; and along Silom Road, Oriental Lane, and Charoen Krung Road for antiques. The Oriental Plaza (across from the Oriental Hotel) and the River City Shopping Centre next to the Sheraton Orchid Hotel have shops with collector-quality goods ranging from antiques to fashion. The shops around Siam Square and at the new World Trade Centre attract middle-income Thais and foreign shoppers. The newest and glitziest shopping complex is Thaniya Plaza, located between Silom and Suriwong roads, near Patpong.

Duty-free Shopping Despite protests from shopkeepers, **TAT** (888 Ploenchit Rd., Lumpini, Patumwan, Bangkok 10330, tel. 02/253–0347) opened a duty-free shop that carries everything from fresh fruits to handicrafts, fashion goods to imported perfumes. Store personnel speak English and other languages. Prices are not particularly inexpensive, however, and you miss out on the cultural experience of shopping in a foreign country. Purchasers need their passports and airline tickets. *Open daily 9:30 AM–10:30 PM.*

Street Markets

Bangkok's largest street market is the **Weekend Market,** where virtually everything is offered for sale. When it was located near Wat Phra Keo, it had the excitement of a lively bazaar, but at its new quarters at Chaturhak Park (on Paholyothin Road opposite the Northern Bus Terminal), it lacks an exotic character. While there is still a great deal of activity from Saturday morning until closing on Sunday evening, the market is more like an open-air department store, selling a range of goods, most of them mass-produced items for local consumption. If you are looking for inexpensive chinaware or a tough pair of boots, this market will suit your needs. *Open weekends 9–9.*

The other all-purpose market is **Pratunam Market** along Ratchaprarop Road. This is a beehive of activity on and off the sidewalk. It is best for deeply discounted clothing. *Open daily 9–8.*

Another lively market for goods that are cheap, but inflated for the tourist, is in **Patpong.** Along Silom Road, stalls are set up in the afternoon and evening to sell tourists everything from "Rolex" watches to leather belts and knockoff designer shirts. **Thieves Market** in Chinatown, at the northwestern end of Yaowarat Road, once a place for bargains in antiques, has become more utilitarian in its wares, but is still fun to browse through. *Open daily 8–6.*

Department Stores

Good-quality merchandise may be found at **Robinson Department Store** (459 Rajavithi, tel. 02/246–1624), which has several locations, including one at the top of Silom Road. For Japanese-inspired goods, **Sogo** (Amarin Plaza, Ploenchit Rd., tel. 02/256–9131) presents its wares in modern glitter. However, the locals shop at the **Central Department Store** (306 Silom Rd., tel. 02/233–6930; 1691 Phaholyothin Rd., tel. 02/513–1740; and 1027 Phoenchit Rd., tel. 02/251–9201). Prices are good and the selection is extensive.

Specialty Stores

Art and Antiques Suriwongse Road, Charoen Krung Road, and the Oriental Plaza (across from the Oriental Hotel) have many art and antiques shops. You will also find quality artifacts in the shops at the **Riverside Shopping Plaza,** next to the Royal Orchid Sheraton Hotel. **Peng Seng** (942 Rama IV, tel. 02/234–1285), at the intersection of Suriwongse Road, is one of the most respected dealers in Bangkok. The price may be high, but the article is likely to be genuine. Thai antiques and old images of Buddha need a special export license.

Clothing and Fabrics Thai silk gained its world reputation only after World War II, when technical innovations were introduced to its silk-weaving industry. Two other Thai fabrics are worth noting: Mudmee (tie-dyed) silk is produced in the northeast of Thailand; Thai cotton is soft, durable, and easier on the wallet than silk.

The Jim Thompson Thai Silk Company (9 Suriwongse Rd., tel. 02/234–4900), begun by Jim Thompson, has become *the* place for silk by the yard and for ready-made clothes. There is no bargaining and the prices are high, but the staff is knowledgeable and helpful. A branch store has opened in the Oriental Hotel's shopping arcade. **Choisy** (9/25 Suriwongse, 02/233–7794) is run by a French woman who offers Parisian-style ready-to-wear dresses in Thai silk. **Design Thai** (304 Silom Rd., tel. 02/235–1553) has a large selection of silk items in all price ranges—a good place for that gift you ought to take home. (It's not standard practice, but you can usually manage a 20% discount here.)

For factory-made clothing, the **Indra Garment Export Centre** is behind the Indra Regent Hotel on Ratchaprarop Road, where you can visit hundreds of shops selling discounted items, from shirts to dresses.

The custom-made suit in 48 hours is a Bangkok specialty, but the suit often hangs on the shoulders just as one would expect from a rush job. If you want a custom-made suit of an excellent cut, give the tailor more time. The best in Bangkok is **Marco Tailor** (430/33 Siam Sq., Soi 7, tel. 02/252–0689), where, for approximately B10,000, your suit will equal those made on Savile Row.

Jewelry   While the government **Narayana-Phand** store (295/2 Rajaprarop, Payatai, tel. 02/245–3293) has a selection of handcrafted jewelry, **Polin** (860 Rama IV Rd., tel. 02/234–8176), close to the Montien Hotel, has jewelry of interesting design, and the **A.A. Company** (in the Siam Centre, tel. 02/251–7283), across from the Hotel Siam Intercontinental, will custom-make your jewelry.

Leather   Leather is a good buy in Bangkok, with possibly the lowest prices in the world, especially for custom work. Crocodile leather is popular, but be sure to obtain a certificate that the skins came from a domestically raised reptile; otherwise U.S. Customs may confiscate the goods. For shoes, try **River Booters** at the River City Shopping Centre (tel. 02/235–2966), next to the Sheraton Orchid Hotel.

Silverware,   You may wish to wait until you travel to Chiang Mai for these
Nielloware,   goods. However, **Anan Bronze** (157/11 Petchburi Rd., tel. 02/
and Bronzeware   215–7739) and **S. Samran** (302/8 Petchburi Rd., tel. 02/215–8849) have good selections at fair prices. Both will arrange for shipping purchases home.

Sports and Fitness

Golf   Although weekend play requires advance booking, tee times are usually available during the week. Three good golf courses are the **Krungthep Sports Golf Course** (522 Gp 10 Huamark, tel. 02/374–0491), with fairways flanked by bougainvillea and pine trees, and elevated greens surrounded by sandtraps; the **Navatanee Golf Course** (22 Mul Sukhaphiban 2 Rd., Bangkapi, tel. 02/374–6127), designed by Robert Trent Jones; and the **Rose Garden Golf Course** (4/8 Soi 3 Sukhumvit, tel. 02/253–0295), a pretty course with other leisure activities within the same complex. Greens fees are approximately B250 weekdays and B500 weekends.

Jogging Because of the heat, the humidity (which rarely falls below 60%), the crowds, and the air pollution, the best time to run is early in the morning. For a quick jog, the small running track featured at many hotels may be the best bet. The **Siam Inter-Continental Hotel** has a 700-m (½-mi) jogging track in its parkland gardens. But **Lumphini Park,** whose pathways are paved, is 52 acres and about 1.25 km (2 mi) around. Many hotels are nearby. **Chatuchak Park,** twice as large, is north of the city, and also a popular place for running. A third park is **Sanam Luang,** in front of the Grand Palace. There is grass in the middle, but as in all city parks, follow Thai runners, and stay off the grass. Some people like to jog around Chitlada, the Thai royal residence. It is best not to run in the parks at night, but women can run alone safely during the day.

Spectator Sports

Horse Racing Horse races are held every Sunday at the **Royal Bangkok Sports Club** (02/251–0181) or the **Royal Turf Club** (02/280–0020), alternately. Each meeting has up to 12 races, and public betting is permitted.

Thai Boxing The two main Bangkok stadiums are **Lumphini** (tel. 02/251–4303) on Rama IV Road and **Ratchadammon** (tel. 02/281–4205) on Ratchadammon Nok Road near TAT. The latter has bouts every Monday, Wednesday, and Thursday; Lumphini has bouts every Tuesday, Friday, Saturday, and Sunday. Evening bouts begin at 6 PM, Sunday bouts at 1 PM. Tickets may be purchased at the gates for B100–B500. Understanding the rules of this sport is close to impossible. All manner of punches seem to fly from feet as well as fists, and sometimes more than two boxers are in a ring at once. Though you will probably find a TV channel covering Thai boxing during your visit, try to attend a live match. It's fast and furious, and the playing of traditional music only heightens the drama of this intense sport.

Dining

by Robert Halliday

Robert Halliday has lived in Thailand for 20 years and writes about Thai food for many publications, most recently as food editor of the Bangkok Post.

Thais are passionate about food. Eating, like politics or boxing, is a perpetual subject for discussion, and everyone has very definite ideas on which restaurant is best at what. What's more, there is no such thing as a standard Thai recipe, so that even the most common dish can surprise you in a creative new interpretation at some obscure little shop. In Thailand, seeking out the out-of-the-way food shop that prepares some specialty better than anyone else, then dragging friends off in groups to share the discovery, is a national pastime.

Some of Bangkok's best restaurants are in the big hotels, and many visitors will be content to look no further. But the gastronomically curious will be eager to get out and explore. Wonders await those prepared to try out small, informal eating places, but there are also dangers.

As a general rule, steer clear of open outdoor stands in markets and at roadsides. Most of these are safe, but you're far better off sticking to the clean, well-maintained food shops on major roads and in shopping centers. These rarely cause problems and will give you a chance to taste the most popular Thai dishes in authentic versions, and at very low prices.

Water is much less of a problem these days than in the past, but it's best to drink it bottled or boiled. Clear ice cubes with holes through them are safe, and most restaurants use them.

In compiling the following list, we have placed the emphasis on those restaurants that prepare Thai food authentically and deliciously, but will not sabotage your vacation with anything your fresh-off-the-plane stomach can't handle. Also included is a smattering of the city's best Western-style dining rooms and others that feature non-Thai Asian cuisines. Another popular category of Thai eating place, the seafood restaurant, is represented by only an example or two, although many excellent ones exist.

A word should also be said about price categories. No restaurant in Bangkok is very expensive in the sense one understands the term in New York, London, or Paris. Even the priciest dining rooms in the city will rarely go above $50 per person, unless one is *determined* to spend more. There are individual luxury dishes like the famous Chinese pot dish *phra kradode kamphaeng* ("monk jumps over the wall"), a mixture of everything expensive—abalone, fancy mushrooms, large shrimp, lobster—that can run to $400 or more for a party of four or five. In the inexpensive places, a large and tasty meal can be had for as little as a dollar or two. Most restaurants stop serving dinner at 10:30 PM.

Highly recommended restaurants are indicated by a star ★. For Bangkok restaurants, the following price categories apply.

Category	Cost*
Very Expensive	over B1,000 ($40)
Expensive	B500–B1,000 ($20–$40)
Moderate	B100–B500 ($4–$20)
Inexpensive	under B100 ($4)

per person without tax, service, or drinks

Thai

★ **Lemongrass.** Elegance and a certain adventurousness have made this restaurant a favorite with both Thais and resident Westerners. Embellished with Southeast Asian antiques, the dining rooms and the outdoor-garden dining area all have plenty of atmosphere. Among regional specialties, two southern Thai favorites are the notoriously hot fish curry, *kaeng tai plaa*, a good point of departure for those ready to explore, and the *kai yaang paak phanan*, a wonderfully seasoned barbecued chicken-type dish. Be sure to try a glass of *nam takrai*, the cold, sweet drink brewed from lemongrass. *5/1 Sukhumvit Soi 24, tel. 02/258–8637. Reservations suggested. Dress: casual. AE, DC, MC, V. Moderate.*

My Choice. Middle-class Thais with a taste for their grandmothers' traditional recipes flock to this restaurant throughout the day. Particularly popular is *ped aob*, a thick soup made from beef stock, but foreigners may prefer the *tom khaa tala*, a hot-and-sour dish with shrimp served with rice. The attraction is the food and camaraderie of the diners, not the surroundings. The interior decor is plain and simple, and the outside tables

Bangkok Dining and Lodging

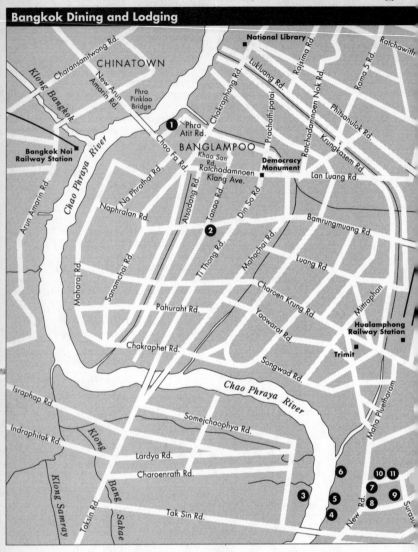

Dining
Coca Noodles, **16**
Genji, **23**
Himali Cha Cha, **8**
Le Dalat, **32**
Lemongrass, **36**
Le Normandie, **5**
Mandalay, **28**
My Choice, **35**
Pan Pan, **25, 34**
The Regent Grill, **21**
River City Bar-B-Q, **6**

Royal Kitchen, **19**
Sala Rim Naam, **3**
Salathip, **4**
Sanuknuk, **38**
Saw Ying Thai, **2**
Soi Polo Fried
Chicken, **30**
Spice Market, **21**
Thai Room, **18**
Thong Lee, **33**
Ton Po, **1**
Tumnak Thai, **39**

Lodging
Airport Hotel, **14**
Ambassador Hotel, **27**
Century Hotel, **23**
Dusit Thani, **20**
The Executive
House, **11**
First House, **22**
Hilton
International, **24**
Imperial Hotel, **26**
Landmark Hotel, **29**
Manohra Hotel, **10**

Mermaid's, **31**
Montien, **17**
Narai Hotel, **13**
New Trocadero, **7**
Oriental Hotel, **5**
La Residence, **12**
Shangri-La Hotel, **4**
Siam Inter-
Continental, **15**
Silom Plaza Hotel, **9**
Tara Hotel, **37**

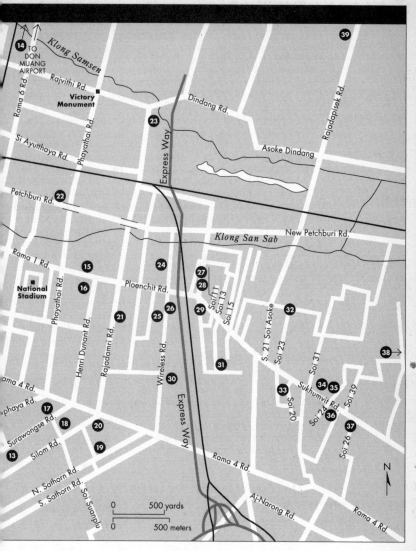

TO
DON
MUANG
AIRPORT

Klong Samsen

Rajvithi Rd.

Rama 6 Rd.

Victory
Monument

Phoyathai Rd.

Si Ayutthaya Rd.

Express Way

Dindang Rd.

Asoke Dindang

Rajadapisek Rd.

Petchburi Rd.

Rama 1 Rd.

Klong San Sab

New Petchburi Rd.

National
Stadium

Phoyathai Rd.

Ploenchit Rd.

Soi 11
Soi 13
Soi 15

S. 21 Soi Asoke

Soi 23

Soi 31

Henri Dunant Rd.

Rajadamri Rd.

Wireless Rd.

Sukhumvit Rd.

Soi 39

Rama 4 Rd.

Surawongse Rd.

Silom Rd.

Soi 20

Soi 24

Soi 26

N. Sathorn Rd.

S. Sathorn Rd.

Soi Suanplu

Express Way

Rama 4 Rd.

Aj-Narong Rd.

Rama 4 Rd.

0   500 yards

0   500 meters

N

face the car park. *Soi 33 Sukhumvit, tel. 02/258–5726. No reservations. Dress: casual. AE, DC, MC, V. Moderate.*

Sala Rim Naam. Definitely a tourist restaurant, but with style to spare. This elegant *sala* (room), on the bank of the Chao Phraya River across from the Oriental Hotel, realizes many of the images that come to mind with the word *Siam*. Thais place great importance on the visual presentation of food, and here some dishes are so beautifully prepared that eating them feels like vandalism. Try some of the hot-and-sour salads, particularly the shrimp version called *yam koong*. The excellently staged Thai dancing will be either a bonus or a distraction, depending on preferences. *Use free boat service from the Oriental Hotel, tel. 02/437–6211. Reservations required on weekends and Oct.–late Feb. Dress: casual. AE, DC, MC, V. Moderate.*

Salathip. Built as a Thai pavilion, with an outside veranda facing the Chao Phraya River, the restaurant provides an ambience that guarantees a romantic evening. Be sure to reserve a table outside. Though the Thai cooking may not have as much hot chili as some like, the food hasn't been adulterated to suit Western tastes. On Sundays, the restaurant offers possibly the best buffet in Bangkok, allowing customers to sample some of the finest Thai cuisine in the country. *Shangri-La Hotel, 89 Soi Wat Suan Phu, New Rd., tel. 02/236–7777. Reservations are essential for a veranda table. Dress: casual but neat. Dinner only. AE, DC, MC, V. Moderate.*

★ **Sanuknuk.** Named for one of the oldest surviving works of Thai literature, Sanuknuk was originally conceived as a drinking place for the city's intellectual community, particularly writers and artists. Its unique menu includes dishes that had been virtually forgotten until they were resurrected by the owner and his wife through interviews with old women in up-country areas. The eccentric decor—which features original work by the artist owner and many others among the city's most prominent creative figures—is of near-museum quality. Sanuknuk's writer-artist crowd drinks a good deal and keeps things lively. Go with a Thai friend if you can, as the menu—a series of cards in a tape cassette box—is written only in Thai. Especially good are the many types of *nam phrik* and the soups like *tom khaa kai*, chicken with coconut cream, chili, and lime juice. *411/6 Sukhumvit Soi 55 (Soi Thong Law) at the mouth of Sub-soi 23, tel. 02/390–0166 or 392–2865. Reservations suggested on weekends. Dress: very casual. DC, MC, V. Dinner only, but open until midnight. Closed 3rd and 4th Sun. of each month. Moderate.*

★ **Spice Market.** Here is Thai home cooking as it was when domestic help was cheap. The decor re-creates a once-familiar sight— the interior of a well-stocked spice shop, with sacks of garlic, dried chilies, and heavy earthenware fish-sauce jars lined up as they were when the only way to get to Bangkok was by steamer. The authentic recipes are prepared full-strength; a chili logo on the menu indicates peppery dishes. The Thai curries are superb, and there is a comprehensive selection of old-fashioned Thai sweets. From mid-January to the end of March, try the *nam doc mai* (Thai mango) with sticky rice and coconut milk; foreign businessmen arrange trips to Bangkok at this time of year just for this dessert. *Regent of Bangkok Hotel, 155 Rajadamri Rd., tel. 02/251–6127. Reservations suggested on weekends. Dress: casual. AE, DC, MC, V. Moderate.*

Ton Po. This is open-air riverside dining without tourist trappings. Ton Po (Thai for the Bo tree, of which there is a large, garlanded specimen at the entrance) takes the form of a wide, covered wooden veranda facing the Chao Phraya. To get the breeze that blows even in the hottest weather, try to wangle a riverside table. Many of its dishes are well-known, none more so than the *tom khlong plaa salid bai makhaam awn*, a delectable, but very hot and sour soup made from a local dried fish, chili, lime juice, lemongrass, tender young tamarind leaves, mushrooms, and a full frontal assault of other herbal seasonings. Less potent but equally good are the *kai haw bai toei* (chicken meat wrapped in fragrant pandanus leaves and grilled) and *haw moke plaa* (a type of curried fish custard, thickened with coconut cream and steamed in banana leaves). *Phra Atit Rd., no phone. No reservations. Dress: casual. AE, DC, MC, V. Moderate.*

River City Bar B-Q. Seated on the roof of the River City Shopping Center, guests do their own cooking. Waiters bring the burner and hot plate, and a mound of different meats and vegetables. Guests use their chopsticks to grill the foods to their liking. Order some appetizers to nibble on while dinner is cooking—the northern Thai sausage is excellent. Request a table at the edge of the roof for a romantic view of the Chao Phrao River. *5th floor, River City Shopping Center, tel. 02/237-0077, ext. 240. Reservations accepted. Dress: casual. MC, V. Inexpensive–Moderate.*

Tumnak Thai. The biggest restaurant in the world, according to the *Guinness Book of World Records*, Tumnak Thai seats 3,000 in several pavilions (each representing a different regional architectural style) and is so extensive that the staff zips around on roller skates. The menu attempts to encompass the cuisine of the entire country and, not surprisingly, some dishes come off much better than others. Well worth trying are dishes based on rare freshwater fishes, which are now being farmed in Thailand. The bizarre *plaa buek*, a type of firm-fleshed, white, slightly sweet-flavored catfish that also makes the *Guinness Book* as the world's biggest freshwater fish, is featured in several dishes, including a tasty tom yam. Also worth trying is the sweet-fleshed *plaa yeesok* fish. Several of the pavilions overlook a small artificial lake with a stage, where classical Thai dance is sometimes performed. *131 Rajadapisek Rd., tel. 02/ 276-1810. No reservations. Dress: casual. AE, DC, MC, V. Inexpensive–Moderate.*

★ **Soi Polo Fried Chicken.** Although its beat-up plastic tables, traffic noise, and lack of air-conditioning make this small place look like a sure thing for stomach trouble, it is one of the city's most popular lunch spots for nearby office workers. The reason: its world-class fried chicken flavored with black pepper and plenty of golden-brown, crisp-fried garlic. The chicken should be sampled with sticky rice and perhaps a plate of the restaurant's excellent *som tam* (hot-and-sour raw papaya salad, a hydrogen bomb of a hot coleslaw from the northeast). Try to get there a bit before noon, or landing a table will be a problem. *Walk into Soi Polo from Wireless Rd. (the restaurant is the last in the group of shops on your left as you enter the soi), no phone. No reservations. Dress: very casual. No credit cards. No dinner. Inexpensive.*

Saw Ying Thai. Unless you speak Thai or are accompanied by a Thai friend, it may not be worth your while to track down this place. Saw Ying Thai has been open for almost 60 years and has an extremely devoted clientele, many of whom have been regulars for decades. It is rare to find a tourist at Saw Ying Thai, and the circle of even long-term expatriate customers is small. The menu, written on placards on the wall, is in Thai only, and none of the staff speaks English. If you do go, be sure to order the *kai toon*, a chicken soup with bamboo sprouts; *plaa du thawd krawb phad phed*, crisp-fried catfish stir-fried with curry spices and herbs; and *khai jio neua puu*, an omelet full of crabmeat. For many years, the decor consisted of long-out-of-date posters on the walls. Recently, it has been spiffed up, but the charm remains the same. This restaurant would rate a star were it more accessible. *Corner of Bamrungmuang and Tanao Rds., no phone. No reservations. Dress: casual. No credit cards. Inexpensive.*

Thong Lee. This small but attractive shop-house restaurant has an air-conditioned upstairs dining area. Although prices are very low, Thong Lee has a devoted upper-middle-class clientele. The menu is not adventurous, but every dish has a distinct personality—evidence of the cook's artistry and imagination. Almost everyone orders the *muu phad kapi* (pork fried with shrimp paste); the *yam hed sod* (hot-and-sour mushroom salad) is memorable but very spicy. *Sukhumvit Soi 20, no phone. No reservations. Dress: casual. No credit cards. Inexpensive.*

Non-Thai Asian

Genji. Bangkok has many good Japanese restaurants, although a number of them give a chilly reception to those not of the city's insular Japanese community. Genji is a happy exception. Although culinary purists may wince to learn that it is located in a large international hotel, they would be wrong to stay away. There is an excellent sushi bar and several small, private rooms. Try some of the sushi, especially the succulent grilled eel. Set menus for lunch and dinner are well conceived. Japanese breakfasts are also served. *Hilton International, 2 Wireless Rd., tel. 02/253–0123. Reservations recommended. Dress: casual. AE, DC, MC, V. Expensive.*

★ **Royal Kitchen.** Perhaps the most elegant of Bangkok's many Chinese restaurants, the Royal Kitchen consists of a number of small, atmospherically decorated dining rooms where everything, right down to the silver chopsticks on the tables, has been carefully considered. The menu is a reference resource for southern Chinese delicacies, including such offerings as *Mieng nok*, with finely minced, seasoned pigeon served on individual fragrant leaves. At lunchtime, dim sum is served, and it, too, is probably Bangkok's best, as beautiful to look at as it is subtle in taste. *N. Sathorn Rd., opposite YWCA and Thai Oil, tel. 02/ 234–3063. Reservations required. Jacket and tie suggested. AE, DC, MC, V. Expensive.*

Himali Cha Cha. Cha Cha, who prepares the food at this popular Indian restaurant, was once Nehru's cook. He serves up northern Indian cuisine in a pleasantly informal setting with the usual decor. Far from usual, however, is the quality of the food, which has kept the place a favorite for a decade. The tandoori chicken is locally famous, and there are daily specials that Cha Cha himself will recommend and explain. Always good are the breads and the fruit-flavored *lassis* (yogurt drinks—the mango ones are especially successful). *1229/11 New Rd., tel. 02/235–1569. Reservations recommended for dinner. Dress: casual. AE, DC, MC, V. Moderate.*

★ **Le Dalat.** Once a private home and now a very classy Vietnamese restaurant, Le Dalat consists of several intimate and cozily decorated dining rooms. Much Vietnamese cuisine is based on flavor juxtapositions striking to the Western palate, and here it's all served up with style. Try *naem neuang*, which requires you to take a garlicky grilled meatball and place it on a round of *mieng* (edible thin rice paper used as a wrapper), then pile on bits of garlic, ginger, hot chili, star apple, and mango, spoon on a viscous sweet-salty sauce, and wrap the whole thing up in a lettuce leaf before eating. The restaurant has become a favorite with Bangkok residents. *51 Sukhumvit Soi 23, opposite Indian Embassy, tel. 02/258–4192. Reservations suggested. Dress: casual. AE, DC, MC, V. Moderate.*

★ **Mandalay.** One of only two Burmese restaurants in Thailand, Mandalay offers food that looks similar to Thai, but tastes very different indeed. Many of the highly seasoned, saladlike dishes are real surprises. One marvel called *lo phet* (made from marinated young tea leaves, peanuts, sesame, garlic, toasted coconut, and several aromatic herbs) is a stunner, but remember the caffeine content of the tea leaves—too much will keep you awake. Also available are excellent, very thick beef and shrimp curries and an unusual pork curry called *hangle*. On the walls are Burmese antiques from the owner's famous shop, Elephant House, and taped Burmese popular music plays in the background. An unusual touch is a plate of Burmese cheroots and lumps of coconut sugar placed on the table after the meal. *77/5 Soi Ruamrudee [Soi 11] Sukhumvit (behind the Ambassador Hotel), tel. 02/250–1220. Reservations recommended on weekends. Dress: casual. AE, DC, MC, V. Moderate.*

Coca Noodles. This giant, raucous restaurant is as high-spirited as any in town. On evenings and weekends, it is full of Chinese families eating a daunting variety of noodle dishes with noisy gusto. Both wheat- and rice-based pastas are available in abundance, in combination with a cornucopia of meats, fish, shellfish, and crunchy Chinese vegetables. Try some of the green, wheat-based noodles called *mee yoke*, topped with a chicken thigh, red pork, or crabmeat. Also, on a gas ring built into the table, you can prepare yourself an intriguing Chinese variant of sukiyaki. *In Siam Square Shopping Center facing 461 Henri Dunant Rd., tel. 02/251–6337 or 02/251–3538. Another branch is on Suriwongse Rd., tel. 02/236–0107. Reservations suggested on weekends. Dress: casual. No credit cards. Inexpensive.*

Western Cuisine

★ **Le Normandie.** Perched atop the Oriental Hotel, this legendary Bangkok restaurant commands a panoramic view across the Chao Phraya River. Periodically, it persuades the most highly esteemed chefs in France to temporarily abandon their three-star restaurants and take over in Le Normandie's kitchen. Recently, Michelin three-star chef Georges Blanc was appointed the restaurant's permanent consultant. These artists usually import ingredients from home, and at such times the restaurant's patrons enjoy what is literally the finest French food in the world. Even when no superstar chef is on the scene, the cuisine is unforgettable, with the menu often including rare dishes taught to Le Normandie's own master chef by the visiting chefs. *48 Oriental Ave., tel. 02/234–8690. Reservations re-*

quired one or two days in advance. Jacket and tie. AE, DC, MC, V. Dinner only on Sun. Very Expensive.

The Regent Grill. This is a strikingly designed, high-fashion French restaurant that resembles the interior of a Siamese palace. Appearing on the menu from time to time are such memorable dishes as fresh goose liver in raspberry vinegar (this can be specially prepared if requested a day or so in advance). Excellent endive salads and lobster dishes, one with a subtle goose liver sauce, are regularly featured on the menu. In addition to changing its name from Le Cristal, the Regent Grill has been enlarged to encompass an outdoor terrace overlooking the imaginatively landscaped grounds of the Regent of Bangkok Hotel, where it is located. The renovated restaurant is now putting more emphasis on grilled dishes. *155 Rajadamri Rd., tel. 02/251-6127. Reservations required. Jacket and tie required. AE, DC, MC, V. Dinner only on weekends. Very Expensive.*

Pan Pan. Both branches of this Italian-food-and-ice-cream chain are among the most popular restaurants in Bangkok. They are pleasingly decorated with Italian kitchen items and spices. Tables are comfortable, and the relaxed feeling in both places invites long, intimate talks. The long list of pasta includes generous and delicious dishes: linguini with a sauce of salmon, cream, and vodka that is a taste of high-calorie heaven; or "Chicken Godfather," with its cream-and-mushroom sauce, which is similarly disappointment-proof. But save room for the ice cream. It is of the thick, dense Italian type, and there is a fine durian-flavored one for those who dare. The branch on Sukhumvit Road offers a buffet-style antipasto and a large selection of extremely rich desserts. *6-6/1 Sukhumvit Rd., near Soi 33, tel. 02/258-9304 or 258-5071; or 45 Soi Lang Suan, off Ploenchit Rd., tel. 02/252-7104. Reservations suggested. Dress: casual. AE, DC, MC, V. Moderate-Inexpensive.*

Thai Room. A time capsule that has remained virtually unchanged since it opened during the Vietnam War, in 1966, the Thai Room was usually packed in the evening with GIs on R&R. Not a molecule of the decor has changed since then, and it is not unusual to see a veteran of that war quietly reminiscing. Around him, however, will be local residents and tourists in from the tawdry riot of Patpong. The Mexican food is a peculiar hybrid of Mexican and Thai cuisines, and the result is not unpleasing. Some of the Italian items, like the eggplant parmigiana, are very good by any standard, however, and the Thai food can be excellent. Local clients feel great affection for this one-of-a-kind restaurant, which stays open until midnight. *30/37 Patpong 2 Rd. (between Silom and Suriwongse Rds.), tel. 02/233-7920. No reservations. Dress: casual. AE, DC, MC, V. Inexpensive.*

Lodging

The surge in tourism has taxed Bangkok's hotels to the limit, but the situation is improving as new hotels open. The major hotel opening was the Grand Hyatt Erawan on the site of the old Erawan Hotel along Rajadamri Road. Designed with a four-story atrium decorated to emulate a palatial Thai residence, the hotel has more than 400 guest rooms on concierge floors, tended by a private butler. Even with the new Hyatt and other hotels, such as the Siam Lodge Group's projected

1992 opening of the 553-room Watergate Hotel in Praturnam and the 600-room Atrium Hotel on New Petchaburi Road, you may find reservations hard to come by during the peak season, from November through March. That is not to say you will be unable to find shelter, but perhaps not at the hotel you might have preferred, or even chosen.

Room prices in Bangkok (and throughout Thailand) have escalated in recent years, and you will often find that, in all but the very expensive category, hoteliers have not reinvested their profits in refurbishment. Carpets tend to have stains, plasterwork is patched, and, if your room faces the street, the only way to deaden the traffic noise is to hope the air conditioner works and that its clanking will drown out the street noise. With the opening of new properties and insufficient hotel schools to supply the staff for them, service may falter for a few years even in the top hotels.

That said, Bangkok hotels are not expensive by European standards, and the deluxe hotels are superb. Indeed, in the past, the Oriental Hotel has been rated by some as the world's best hotel, and the Shangri-La and the Dusit Thani are also in the running for that position. Such hotels are about $250 for a double. An equivalent hotel in Paris would be close to $450.

There are many hotels in the $80–$100 range, and these, too, have every modern creature comfort imaginable, with fine service, excellent restaurants, health centers, and facilities for businesspeople. For $50, you can find respectable lodgings in a hotel with an efficient staff. Rooms in small hotels with limited facilities are available for around $10, and, if you are willing to share a bathroom, guest houses are numerous.

The four main hotel districts are next to the Chao Phraya and along Silom and Suriwongse roads; around Siam Square; in the foreign-embassy neighborhood; and along Sukhumvit Road. Other areas, such as Khao San Road for inexpensive guest houses favored by backpackers, and across the river, where modern high-rise hotels are sprouting up, are not included in the following list. The latter are inconveniently located, and finding a room in Khao San, especially in the peak season, requires going from one guest house to another in search of a vacancy—which is best done around breakfast, as departing residents check out.

Very Expensive

★ **Dusit Thani.** At the top end of Silom Road, this low-key 23-story hotel with distinctive, pyramid-style architecture is the flagship property of an expanding Thai hotel group. An extensive shopping arcade, a Chinese restaurant, and an elegant Thai restaurant are at street level. One floor up is the lobby, reception area, and a delightful sunken lounge, especially pleasant for enjoying afternoon tea while listening to piano music and looking out over a small courtyard garden. The pool area is built within a central courtyard filled with trees and serves as a peaceful oasis amid Bangkok's frenzy. Rooms are stylishly furnished in pastels, and the higher floors have a panoramic view over Bangkok. The Dusit Thani is particularly noted for the spaciousness and concierge service of its Landmark suites, and for the tremendous detail paid to every possible amenity. *Rama IV Rd., Bangkok 10500, tel. 02/233–1130, 800/223–5652,* *or in NY, 212/593–2988. 525 rooms, including 15 suites. Facilities: 7 restaurants, 24-hr coffee shop, disco, cocktail lounge, small outdoor pool, health center, business center, meeting and banquet rooms, shopping arcade. AE, DC, MC, V.*

Hilton International. This five-story hotel in the embassy district opened in 1983. Its most notable feature is the 8½ acres of landscaped gardens, which, aside from the large swimming pool and the poolside terrace restaurants, contain a wonderful retreat of greenery—mango, rose apple, broad-leaf breadfruit, durian, sapodilla, and mangosteen trees. The public areas front the garden, and light floods in through the high windows, giving the hotel a feeling of spaciousness. Some rooms, decorated in soft pastels, have bougainvillea-draped balconies that overlook the garden. All rooms have individual safes. The French restaurant, Ma Maison, has won local awards for its cuisine, and revelers seem to enjoy Juliana's of London, the hotel's nightclub. Construction is planned for a shopping mall on the Hilton grounds, which may cause inconvenience for guests until the mall's projected completion in 1993. *2 Wireless Rd., Bangkok 10330, tel. 02/251–1711. 389 rooms and suites. Facilities: concierge floor, 4 restaurants, music bar, pool terrace bar, outdoor pool, fitness center, 2 tennis courts, squash courts, drugstore, French pastry shop, shopping arcade. AE, DC, MC, V.*

Landmark Hotel. Calling itself Bangkok's first high-tech hotel, it has created an ambience suggestive of a grand European hotel by the generous use of teak in its reception areas. Guest rooms are unobtrusively elegant, geared to the international business traveler, and include a good working desk and a TV/video screen that can be tuned into information banks linked to the hotel's business center. With a staff of 950 to manage this 450-room hotel, service is swift and attentive. Its Hibiscus restaurant has a view of the city to accompany European fare and an elegant setting. The Huntsman Pub has a jazz trio to accompany drinks and light meals. *138 Sukhumvit Rd., Bangkok 10110, tel. 02/254–0404. 395 rooms and 55 suites. Facilities: 4 restaurants, 24-hr coffee shop, outdoor pool with snack bar, fitness center, 2 squash courts, sauna, shopping complex, business center, meeting rooms. AE, DC, MC, V.*

★ **Oriental Hotel.** Often cited as the best hotel in the world, the Oriental has set the standard toward which all other Bangkok hotels strive. Part of its fame stems from its past roster of famous guests, including Joseph Conrad, Somerset Maugham, and Noël Coward. Today's roster is no less impressive, though it now features heads of state and film personalities. The Oriental's location overlooking the Chao Phraya River is unrivaled. The Garden Wing, with duplex rooms looking out on the gardens and the river, has been refurbished, and these rooms—along with the main building's luxury suites—are the hotel's best, though their price has now climbed to $275 a night. The hotel has several well-known restaurants, including the China House, which opened in 1990 with Cantonese cuisine prepared by four master chefs from Hong Kong. The ambience is that of an elegant private residence. The Sala Rim Naam is well known for its Thai food, while Le Normandie ranks as the best French restaurant in Bangkok (*see* Dining, above). In addition, the hotel has a riverside barbecue every night. The Oriental radiates elegance and provides superb service, though in recent years some of the crispness and panache have disappeared, perhaps because the staff is continually wooed away by other hotels. In the attempt to offset travelers switching their allegiance to either the Shangri-La or the Dusit Thani, the Oriental instituted a Thai cooking school and, more recently, afternoon seminars explaining Thai culture for the benefit of tourists and businessmen. *48 Oriental Ave., Bangkok 10500, tel. 02/236–0400. 398 rooms. Facilities: 3 restaurants, outdoor pool, 2 tennis courts, jogging track, golf practice nets, 2 squash courts, health club, disco/nightclub, business center. AE, DC, MC, V.*

★ **Shangri-La Hotel.** For decades the Oriental could safely claim to be Bangkok's finest hotel, but the 25-story Shangri-La successfully challenges this position. Service is excellent (many top staff from the Oriental were enticed to the Shangri-La). The facilities are impeccable, and the open marble lobby, with crystal chandeliers, gives a feeling of spaciousness that is a relief from the congestion of Bangkok. The lobby lounge, enclosed by floor-to-ceiling windows, looks over the Chao Phraya River. The gardens, with a swimming pool alongside the river, are a peaceful oasis, interrupted only by the river boat traffic. The spacious guest rooms are decorated in pastels. On the Horizon floor (21st floor), the executive floor, the rooms have outstanding views of the river, and their teak paneling adds warmth and intimacy. By the end of 1991, the 16-story Krungthep Wing will be open. Designed primarily for business travelers, the new wing will add 161 rooms and 13 suites, all with a view of the river and with on-floor butler service. With its own three-story atrium lobby, pâtisserie, dining room, club bar, and executive center, the Krungthep Wing serves as a hotel within a hotel. *89 Soi Wat Suan Phu, New Rd., Bangkok 10500, tel. 02/236–7777. 650 rooms and 47 suites. Facilities: 4 restaurants, 24-hr coffee shop, 2 bars, outdoor pool, 2 lighted tennis courts, 2 squash courts, extensive fitness center, sauna, massage, business center. AE, DC, MC, V.*

Siam Inter-Continental. In the center of Bangkok on 26 landscaped acres, the Siam Inter-Continental has a soaring pagoda roof. The lobby, with its lofty space and indoor plantings and cascades, echoes the pagoda roof and the gardens. Its modern Thai-style architecture and feeling of space make this hotel stand out from all others in Bangkok. Each of the air-conditioned rooms is stylishly decorated with teak furniture and trim, upholstered wing chair and love seat, and a cool, blue color scheme. Especially attractive are the teak-paneled bathrooms with radio, telephone extension, and built-in hair dryer. *967 Rama 1 Rd., Bangkok 10330, tel. 02/253–0355. 411 rooms and suites. Facilities: 4 restaurants, 2 bars, conference rooms, 24-hr room service, swimming pool, .8-km (½-mi) jogging track, putting green and driving range, outdoor gym with workout equipment. AE, DC, MC, V.*

Expensive

Airport Hotel. If you need to stay within walking distance of the airport, this is your only option. The hotel is modern and utilitarian, with a helpful staff. In contrast to the exotic surroundings of Thailand, however, it is a bit boring. Rooms are functional and efficient. Daytime rates for travelers waiting for connections are available, and video screens in the public rooms display the schedules of flight arrivals and departures. A 140-room extension is in the works and is scheduled to be completed by the end of 1991. *333 Chert Wudhakas Rd., Don Muang, Bangkok 10210, tel. 02/566–1020. 440 rooms. Facili-*

ties: 2 restaurants, 24-hr coffee shop, disco, outdoor pool, free shuttle bus to town, conference rooms. AE, DC, MC, V.

Ambassador Hotel. This hotel, with three wings of guest rooms, a complex of restaurants, and a shopping center, is virtually a minicity, which perhaps explains the impersonal service and limited helpfulness of the staff. Milling convention delegates contribute to the impersonal atmosphere. Guest rooms are compact, decorated with standard pastel hotel furnishings. There is plenty to keep you busy at night: the Dickens Pub garden bar, the Flamingo Disco, and The Club for rock music. The 5,000-room Ambassador City on Jontien Beach, Pattaya, is a sister hotel. *171 Sukhumvit Rd., Soi 11–13, Bangkok 10110, tel. 02/254–0444. 1,050 rooms, including 24 suites. Facilities: 12 restaurants, 24-hr coffee shop, 24-hr room service, outdoor pool, poolside snack bar, health center with massage, 2 tennis courts, business center with secretaries, 60 function rooms. AE, DC, MC, V.*

★ **Imperial Hotel.** After a major renovation in 1989, the Imperial became the smartest hotel in this price category. The restored lobby's grand, high ceiling is magnificent, and the staff is friendly and eager to please. Located on six acres in the embassy district, the hotel is separated from the main road by expansive lawns. The inner gardens surround the pool and arcades. Guest rooms facing the garden are most preferred. The rooms are decorated with pale cream walls accented by bright, often red, bedspreads and draperies. *Wireless Rd., Bangkok 10330, tel. 02/254–0023. 400 rooms. Facilities: 4 restaurants (Chinese, Japanese, Thai, Western), tennis court, 2 squash courts, outdoor pool, fitness center, sauna, putting green, shops. AE, DC, MC, V.*

Montien. Across the street from Patpong, this hotel has been remarkably well maintained over its two decades of serving visitors, especially those who want convenient access to the corporations along Silom Road. The concierge is particularly helpful. The guest rooms are reasonably spacious, though not decoratively inspired. They do, however, offer guests private safes. New this year are in-house fortune-tellers who will read your palm or stars in the evening for B250. *54 Surawongse Rd., Bangkok 10500, tel. 02/234–8060. 500 rooms. Facilities: 2 restaurants, 24-hr coffee shop, disco with live music, outdoor pool with pool bar, business center, banquet rooms. AE, DC, MC, V.*

Narai Hotel. Conveniently located on Silom Road near the business, shopping, and entertainment areas, this friendly, modern hotel offers comfortable, utilitarian rooms, many of which are decorated with warm, rose-colored furnishings. At the low end of this price category, the hotel is a good value given its cheerful rooms and high level of service. The most distinguishing feature of the hotel is Bangkok's only revolving restaurant, La Rotunde Grill, on the 15th floor. *222 Silom Rd., Bangkok 10500, tel. 02/257–0100. 500 rooms, including 10 suites. Facilities: 3 restaurants, 24-hr coffee shop, nightclub, outdoor pool, small fitness center, business center. AE, DC, MC, V.*

Moderate

Century Hotel. The hotel's location in the northern part of downtown is convenient for those who are only staying overnight in Bangkok and don't want to risk a long drive to the airport in the morning. The rooms, though neat and clean, are small and dark. The coffee shop/bar is open 24 hours, an added plus for travelers with early morning flights. *9 Rajaprarob Rd., Bangkok 10400, tel. 02/246–7800. 240 rooms. Facilities: 24-hr coffee shop/bar/restaurant, outdoor pool. AE, DC, MC, V.*

La Residence. You would expect to find this small town-house-type hotel on the Left Bank of Paris, not in Bangkok. Though a little overpriced, La Residence suits the frequent visitor to Bangkok looking for a low-key hotel. The staff members, however, can be abrupt at times. The guest rooms are small, but the furnishings, from light-wood cabinetry to pastel drapes, give them a fresh, airy feel. The newness of the hotel, which only opened in 1989, adds to the freshness. The restaurant serves Thai and European food, and, since there is no lounge or lobby area in the hotel, it often acts as a sitting area for guests. *173/8–9 Suriwongse Rd., Bangkok 10150, tel. 02/233–3301. 23 rooms. Facilities: restaurant, laundry service. AE, DC.*

Manohra Hotel. An expansive marble lobby characterizes the pristine efficiency of this hotel located between the river and Patpong. Rooms have pastel walls, rich patterned bed covers, and dark-green carpets. If you can take Bangkok's polluted air, there is a roof garden for sunbathing. For evening action, there is the Buccaneer Night Club. A word of caution: If the Manohra is fully booked, the staff may suggest its new sister hotel, the Ramada (no relation to the American-managed Ramada), opposite the general post office at 1169 New Road (tel. 02/234–897). Unless you are desperate, decline. The Ramada is overpriced and has small, poorly designed rooms. The Manohra, on the other hand, is attractive and well run, with a helpful, friendly staff. *412 Surawongse Rd., Bangkok 10500, tel. 02/234–5070. 230 rooms. Facilities: 2 restaurants, coffeehouse, nightclub, indoor pool, meeting rooms. AE, DC, MC, V.*

Silom Plaza Hotel. Opened in 1986 in the shopping area close to compact rooms with modern decor in soft colors. The more expensive rooms have river views. The hotel caters to business travelers who want to be close to Silom Road. Service is quick. The facilities are limited, but nearby is all the entertainment you could wish for. *320 Silom Rd., Bangkok 10500, tel. 02/236–0333. 209 rooms. Facilities: Chinese restaurant, coffeeshop, 24-hr room service, indoor pool, poolside bar, gym, sauna, 4 function rooms. AE, DC, MC, V.*

★ **Tara Hotel.** Brand-new in 1989, the Tara is in the developing restaurant-and-nightlife section of Sukhumvit Road. Guests register in a check-in lounge, with tea or coffee served while the formalities are completed. The lobby is spacious, lined with teakwood carving. Guest rooms, which are on the small side, are decorated with pale pastels, and many overlook the eighth-floor outdoor swimming pool. *Sukumvit Soi 26, Bangkok 10110, tel. 02/259–0053. 200 rooms and 20 suites. Facilities: restaurant, 24-hr coffee shop, outdoor pool, poolside bar, banquet room. AE, DC, MC, V.*

Inexpensive

The Executive House. Though it offers only limited services, this hotel has a friendly staff at the reception desk that will help with travel questions and a coffee shop that will deliver food to your room until midnight. The rooms are spacious for the price, the air-conditioning works, and, even if the decor is drab and a bit run-down, the rooms on the upper floors have plenty of light. The penthouse rooms—on the 16th–18th floors—are spacious and include a small kitchen; they're also flooded with light. Rooms with a river view are B200 more than those with a city view. The hotel is next to the Manohra Hotel, down a short driveway. *410/3–4 Surawongse Rd., Bangkok 10500, tel. 02/235–1206. 120 rooms. Facilities: coffee shop, small business center. AE, DC, MC, V.*

First House. Tucked behind the Praturnam market on a soi off Petchburi, the First House offers excellent value for a full-service hotel in this price range. The small lobby/sitting area serves as a meeting place where guests can read the complimentary newspapers. Off to the left, the Saranyuth coffee house/restaurant, open 24 hours, serves Thai and Western dishes. The compact rooms are carpeted and amply furnished, but the lack of daylight from windows can be depressing during the day. Bathrooms are clean, though rough plaster patchings and the drab fixtures don't encourage leisurely grooming. However, the reasonable rates, the security, and the helpfulness of the staff all contribute to making this hotel worth noting. *14/20–29 Petchburi Soi 19, Praturnam, Bangkok 10400, tel. 02/254–0303. 84 rooms. Facilities: 24-hr coffee shop and tour desk. AE, DC, MC, V.*

New Trocadero. This hotel, between Patpong and the Chao Phraya River, has been a Westerner's standby for six decades. Recently refurbished, it offers big double beds in smallish rooms and clean bathrooms. Service is friendly, with a helpful travel/tour desk in the lobby. *343 Surawongse Rd., Bangkok 10500, tel. 02/234–8920. 130 rooms. Facilities: 24-hr coffee shop, small outdoor pool. AE, DC, MC, V.*

Budget

Mermaid's. Down a small, partly residential street off Sukhumvit Road near the Ambassador Hotel, this Scandinavian-owned hotel seems more like a guest house. The value is good, even if the staff's attitude is a little perfunctory at times. Rooms are clean and neat, and each of the more expensive ones has a private balcony. *39 Sukhumvit Soi 8, Bangkok 10110, tel. 02/253–3410. 70 rooms with fan or air-conditioning, some with private bath. Facilities: restaurant, lounge with video, small outdoor pool, travel desk. AE, DC.*

In the neighborhood of Khao San Road, there are hundreds of small guest houses where the price of a room and shared bathroom is about B60. The best guest houses are close to this area, but sufficiently far away from backpacking groups. The **C&C Guest House** (12 Wisut Kasat Rd., Bang Khunprom, Bangkok 10200, tel. 02/282–4941) is located near Wat In and has clean rooms, a coffee lounge, a small garden, and a friendly staff. The same can be said for the **Shanti Lodge** (37 Sri Ayutthaya, Bangkok 10200, tel. 02/281–2497), located behind the National Library.

The Arts and Nightlife

The English-language newspapers, the *Bangkok Post* and *The Nation*, have good information on current festivals, exhibitions, and nightlife. TAT's weekly *Where* also lists events.

The Arts

Classical Thai Dance Thai classical dance is the epitome of grace. Themes for the dance drama are taken from the *Ramayana* (*Ramakien* in Thailand). A series of controlled gestures uses eye contact, ankle and neck movements, and hand and finger gestures to convey the stories' drama. The accompanying band consists of a woodwind instrument called the piphat, which sounds like an oboe, and percussion instruments.

Thai dance drama comes in two forms, the *khon* and the *lakhon*. In khon, the dancers (originally all men) wear ferocious masks, and in the lakhon, both male and female roles are played by women. In the old days of the courts of Siam, the dance drama would last for days. Now, seen mostly at dinner shows in hotels, only a few selected scenes are presented about how Rama (a reincarnation of Vishnu) battles with the demon king Ravana and how he frequently has to rescue the beautiful princess Sita.

Occasionally, you may find a performance of *nang taloung*, a form of shadow puppet theater using silhouettes made from buffalo hide. These plays are similar to those found in Java and Bali, Indonesia.

Various restaurants, such as the **Baan Thai** (Soi 22, Sukhumvit Rd., tel. 258–5403) and the **Sala Rim Naam** (Oriental Hotel, 489 Charoen Nakom Rd., tel. 02/437–6211), offer a classical dance show with dinner. At the **National Theatre** (Na Phra That Rd., tel. 02/221–5861 or 224–1342), performances are given most days at 10 AM and 3 PM. Special performances of Thai classical dancing and music are also held on the last Friday of each month at 5:30 PM.

Nightlife

Most of Bangkok's nightlife is geared to the male tourist. Unfortunately, tourism has propagated its most lurid forms. Live sex shows, though officially banned, are still found in Patpong and other areas. Expect to be ripped off if you indulge.

Cabaret Most of the nightlife will be found on three infamous side streets that link Surawongse and Silom roads. Patpong I and II are packed with go-go bars with hostesses by the dozen. The obscene club acts are generally found one flight up and, despite promises to the contrary by tour guides, usually require a hefty cover charge. Patpong III caters to homosexuals. Patpong is quite safe, well patrolled by police, and even has a night market where Thai families shop. A quieter version of Patpong is Soi Cowboy, off Sukhumvit Road at Soi 22, where bars have more of a publike atmosphere. Nana Plaza, at Soi 4 off Sukhumvit Road, is another party area, with 20 bars that cater mostly to the spirited male, but also a few geared more to the family-oriented visitor. The largest troupe of performing transvestites is reputed to be on stage at the **Calypso Garden** (688 Sukhumvit Rd., between Soi 24 and 26, tel. 02/258–8987) with nightly shows at 8:15 and 10. For less ribald entertainment with live bands and internationally known nightclub artists, try the **Tiara** penthouse restaurant at the Dusit Thani Hotel.

Bars Just beyond Soi Cowboy in the curving side streets (Soi 23 to Soi 31) off Sukhumvit are several small, pleasant bars, often with a small live band playing jazz or country music. **Rang Phah** (16 Sukhumvit 23 Soi, tel. 02/258–4321) is a restaurant with excellent Thai food, but you can sit in the garden outside the marvelous Thai house and drink, eat a little, and gaze at the stars. **September** (120/1 Sukhumvit 23, tel. 02/258–5785), another restaurant, is designed in a Victorian Thai style with a heavy teak bar. **Fred and Barts** (123/1 Sukhumvit, tel. 02/258–4541), a modern bar with stainless-steel furnishings, has enthusiastic hostesses if you need companionship. Around the corner the friendly and cozy **Drunken Duck Pub** (59/4 Soi 31, Sukhumvit Road, tel. 02/258–4500) has a three-piece band playing popular jazz. A country-and-western band plays at the nearby **Trail Dust** (43/2 Sukhumvit 31, tel. 02/258–4590), a large tavern with tables both in its patio garden and inside.

Friendly pubs and cafés, popular with Yuppie Thais and expats, can be found along Sarasin Road (north of Lumphini Park). The three best are **Brown Sugar** (231/20 Soi Sarasin, tel. 02/250–0103), which has a clutter of small rooms humming with animated conversation; the **Old West Saloon** (231/17 Soi Sarasin, tel. 02/252–9510), which re-creates the atmosphere of America's Old West aided by a four-piece band; and the **Burgundy Pub** (231–18 Soi Sarasin, tel. 02/250–0090), good for conversation and relaxation. **The Hemingway Bar & Grill** (159/5 Sukhumwit, Soi 55, tel. 02/392–3599) is popular with Thais and expats for an evening of fellowship in log cabin-style ambience.

At **Summertime** (133/19 Kesorn Rd., Rajprasong, near the Erawan Hyatt, tel. 02/253–7604), which has a solid-mahogany bar and features Italian food, the collectibles decorating the walls are for sale. Across the street is the seafood restaurant **Moon Shadow** (tel. 02/253–7553), which features live jazz in an upstairs lounge, in addition to excellent fresh fish served in a publike setting. **Witch's Tavern** (Soi Thonglor, Sukhumvit Rd., tel. 02/391–9791) offers classical jazz in a cozy Victorian atmosphere where you can just order a beer or hearty English fare.

Discos Most of the large hotels have their own disco/nightclubs. Two of the best known are **Juliana's of London** at the Hilton and **Diana's** at the Oriental, which is said to be Bangkok's most extravagant club. Lately the sparklingly refurbished **Bubbles,** at the Dusit Thani (tel. 02/233–1130), attracts the Thai BMW set. If you wish to venture elsewhere, head for **Silom Plaza** (320/14 Silom Road, tel. 02/234–2657 and nearly opposite the Patpong District), the hot new disco and pub center. Discos, such as the **Virgin,** and bars thumping out music from loud stereos line either side of the plaza both at ground level and one story up. In the center of the plaza are tables where you can also drink and eat while watching the comings and goings of young Thais swinging to the latest beat.

Dinner Cruises Strictly for tourists are the dinner cruises on the Chao Phraya River. Boats such as the *Wan Foh* (tel. 02/433–5453)—built to look like a traditional Thai house—start at the Mae-Nam Building near the Shangri-La Hotel. During the two-hour trip, a Western/Thai dinner is served. Your hotel staff will make reservations. The difference between one ship and another is marginal. Cost: B450 per person.

Cultural Shows   **Silom Village** (286 Silom Rd., tel. 02/234–4448) may perhaps be rather touristy, but its appeal also reaches out to Thais. The block-size complex, open 10 AM–10 PM, has shops, restaurants, and performances of classical Thai dance. A couple of the restaurants feature chefs cooking tasty morsels in the open, and you may select from them what takes your fancy or order from a menu. The best cultural show is at the dinner restaurant **Ruan Thep** (reservations, tel. 02/234–4581). Dinner starts at 7 and showtime is at 8:20. Cost: dinner and show, B350; show only, B200.

4 Excursions from Bangkok

Damnoen Saduak and Nakhon Pathom

by Nigel Fisher

Don't bother visiting the floating market in Bangkok. It was a real market 20 years ago, when vendors sold their wares and vegetables from boats. Since then, it has withered to one or two boats that, it has been suggested, are paid by the tour operators to paddle around. Instead, head for Damnoen Saduak, 109 km (65 mi) southwest of Bangkok in the province of Rajburi. The colorful floating market there, with its multitude of vendors paddling their small boats, is a photographer's fantasy. About 30 minutes from Damnoen Saduak is Nakhon Pathom, the oldest city in Thailand. The bridge over the River Kwai at Kanchanaburi is another worthwhile stop, though Kanchanaburi Province is so full of natural beauty that you may want to visit the area and the famous bridge during separate excursions.

Guided Tours

All of the major hotels have arrangements with a tour operator who organizes morning trips to Damnoen Saduak. These operators collect you from your hotel about 8 AM. The cost varies, but plan to spend about B700. If your hotel does not have an arrangement with a tour operator, use the travel/tour desk at the nearest major hotel. Alternatively, contact a Bangkok tour operator, such as **P.B.R. Travel Service** (888/29 Ploenchit Rd., Bangkok 10110, tel. 02/252–0096).

Damnoen Saduak Floating Market Tour. With the wilting of Bangkok's floating market, Damnoen Saduak offers one of the most exotic and colorful sights of vendors selling produce from sampans. The tour leaves around 8 AM to cover the 100 km (62 mi) to Damnoen Saduak by 9:30, when the market is bustling. This tour may be combined with a visit to the Rose Garden, or Kanchanaburi, and the Bridge over the River Kwai (*see* below).

Rose Garden Tour. On Bangkok Road, 20 km (12 mi) east of Nakhon Pathom, is a complex that commercially replicates a Thai village. Amid flowers and gardens containing 20,000 rose bushes, there are traditional Thai houses and a stage where a "cultural show" of dance, Thai boxing, sword fighting, and a wedding ceremony are performed at 2:15 and 3:15. The park also contains hotels, restaurants, swimming pools, and other playground activities. Though this afternoon tour is popular, the Rose Garden is a sterile tourist resort. Should you wish to go there independently, reserve through the *Rose Garden booking office, 26414 Siam Sq., tel. 02/253–0295.*

Getting There

By Taxi Most Bangkok hotels can arrange for you to be picked up, either by a regular tour bus or by private car/taxi. It is cheaper to negotiate with a car firm outside your hotel. Speak to the concierge "on the quiet"—nine times out of 10, he or she will have a good resource. A private car or taxi is far superior to a tour bus because you can reach the Damnoen Saduak market by 9 AM, before the tours arrive. The cost for two people sharing a private car will be no more than the tour bus. Round-trip fare from Bangkok to Damnoen Saduak can be as low as B600. If you keep the car to visit both Nakhon Pathom and Kanchanaburi in a one-day excursion, the rate will be about B1,000.

By Bus Public buses, some air-conditioned, leave from the Southern Bus Terminal on Charan Sanitwong Road for Damnoen Saduak every 20 minutes from 6 AM. The fare on an air-conditioned bus is B50; B30 for a nonair-conditioned one. From the Damnoen Saduak Bus Station, walk for 1½ km (1 mi) on the path running along the right-hand side of the canal, or take a taxi boat at the pier to the nearby floating market for B10. Buses are also available to Nakhon Pathom.

By Train Trains from the Bangkok Hua Lunphong and Bangkok Noi stations stop in Nakhon Pathom.

Exploring

Damnoen Saduak Once at Damnoen Saduak, hire a *ruilla pai* (sampan) for about B300—an outrageous sum, but so many tourists will pay the price that you cannot negotiate a much lower rate. Then, for an hour or more, lazily travel the canal. If you think Bangkok traffic is bad, witness true gridlock from a sampan in the middle of a mess of boats, each trying to shove its way along the *klong* (canal). The traffic jams of sampans, with vendors selling fresh vegetables, meats, and clothes, are a memorable sight. Farmers' wives dressed in baggy pants, long-tailed shirts, and straw hats sell their produce from their sampans, paddling back and forth, or rather pushing and barging their way through the congestion. Other women, cooking tasty treats on their little stoves, sit ready to ferry sustenance to the hungry, either in other boats or on the shore. It's an authentic and colorful slice of Thai life.

If you want to rest, a wharf alongside the klong has tables and chairs. Buy your drinks from the stall and your food from any one of the ruilla pai. By 11 AM, you will have seen the best of Damnoen Saduak.

Nakhon Pathom Nakhon Pathom is reputed to be Thailand's oldest city, dating from 150 BC. Its main attraction is **Phra Pathom Chedi,** the tallest Buddhist monument in the world—at 417 feet, it stands a few feet higher than the Shwe Dagon Chedi of Burma. The first *chedi* (Thai pagoda where holy relics are kept) on this site was erected in the 6th century, but today one sees a larger chedi, built in 1860, that encases the ruins of the original. Phra Pathom Chedi also marks the first center of Buddhist learning on the Thai peninsula, established here about 1,000 years ago.

The man responsible for reconstructing the chedi was King Monghut, a Buddhist monk who saw the Phra Pathom Chedi as crucial to the establishment of Buddhism in Thailand. Believing that the chedi, then in a state of disrepair, contained Buddha's holy ashes, he ordered the existing chedi to be incorporated into the new one. In the outer courtyard are four *viharn* (halls) facing in different directions and containing images of Buddha in various postures. The eastern viharn depicts Buddha beneath a boa tree; the western viharn shows Lord Buddha in a reclining position (symbolizing his imminent death), surrounded by his disciples; in the southern viharn, Buddha is being protected by a Naga; and in the northern viharn, Buddha is standing. At the base of this image are the ashes of King Vajiravudh. The terraces around the temple complex are full of fascinating statuary, including a Dvaravati-style Buddha seated in a chair, and the museum contains some interesting Dvaravati (6th–11th century) sculpture. Occasionally classical Thai dances are performed in front of the temple, and during the Lai Krathong festival, bazaars and a fair are set up in the adjacent park. *Museum open Wed.–Sun. 9–noon and 1–4.*

Sanan Chan Palace, just west of Phra Pathom Chedi, was built during the reign of King Rama IV. The palace is closed to the public, but the surrounding park is a lovely place to relax in between Damnoen Saduak and Bangkok.

Another potential stopping point on the return trip to Bangkok or en route to Kanchanaburi is the **Rose Garden.** Located on Bangkok Road 20 km (13 mi) east of Nakhon Pathom, the Rose Garden is a 60-acre resort complex. In addition to its hotel, swimming pool, and golf course, the resort has a Thai Cultural Village, which presents an afternoon show. Popular with bus tours from Bangkok, the Rose Garden is quite commercialized. *Tel. 02/253–0295 for reservations. Admission charge. Show at 3 PM.*

Equally commercial are the elephant roundups and crocodile shows at the neighboring **Samphran Elephant Ground & Zoo.** The elephants are hard to resist, however, as they perform dutifully every day at 1:45 and 3:30; an additional performance is given at 11 AM on weekends. Less appetizing are the crocodile wrestling demonstrations, during which trainers put their heads into the open mouths of well-behaved crocodiles each day at 12:45, 2:40, and 4:20. *Tel. 02/284–1873 for reservations. Admission charge. Grounds and zoo open daily 9–6.*

Kanchanaburi

The movie *The Bridge Over the River Kwai*, adapted from Pierre Boulle's novel, gave the area of Kanchanaburi a certain fame—or, more accurately, the Japanese gave the area the dubious distinction of being the site of the Death Railway. Even without this publicity, however, Kanchanaburi province would attract tourists. Lush tropical vegetation and rivers with waterfalls and gorges make it one of the most beautiful national parks in Thailand. The town of Kanchanaburi has little architectural merit, but its location, situated where the Kwai Noi and Kwai Yai rivers meet to form the Mae Khlong River, is splendid.

Tourist Information

The TAT office (Saeng Chuto Rd., Kanchanaburi, tel. 034/511–200) has good maps and brochures, as well as a knowledgeable and helpful staff. If you wish to take a minibus tour, daily guide services are available from B.T. Travel (Saeng Chuto Rd., Kanchanaburi, tel. 034/511–967), next door to the TAT.

Guided Tours

Kanchanaburi and the Bridge over the River Kwai. Usually a full day is necessary to travel the 140 km (87 mi) to Kanchanaburi to visit the Allied war cemeteries, the infamous bridge over the

river, and to tour the lush tropical countryside. Speak to your
hotel tour desk or any operator in Bangkok to arrange a visit.

Getting There

You can visit Kanchanaburi on the same excursion as Damnoen
Saduak or come straight from Bangkok.

By Train From Bangkok's Noi Thonburi Station (tel. 02/411–3102), the
train for Kanchanaburi leaves at 8 AM and 1:55 PM. The State
Railway of Thailand also offers a special excursion train every
Saturday, Sunday, and on holidays; it leaves Hualumpong Railway Terminal at 6:15 AM and returns at 7:30 PM. On the program are stops at Nakhon Pathom, the River Kwai Bridge, and
Nam-Tok, from which point minibuses continue on to Khao
Phang Waterfall. Tickets for this full-day, round-trip outing
may be purchased at Bangkok Railway Station (tel. 02/223–
7010), and advance booking is recommended. Cost: B75 for
adults, B40 for children.

By Bus Air-conditioned and nonair-conditioned buses leave the Southern Transportation Bus Station, Charansanitwong Road, near
Tha Phra intersection (tel. 02/411–0511 or 411–4978), every
half hour. The journey takes about 2½ hours.

Getting Around

Attractions around Kanchanaburi town are accessible either on
foot or by *samlor* (small three-wheel cabs). A hired car with a
driver is the most convenient means of transportation. Buses
leave from the town's terminal on Saeng Chuto Road (tel. 034/
511–387) every 30 minutes to most of the popular destinations.

By Raft For rafting on either the Kwai Yai or Mae Khlong rivers, make
advance reservations through the TAT office or a travel agent.
These trips, which take at least a full day, let you experience
the tropical jungle in a leisurely way. The rafts, which resemble houseboats, are often divided into sections for eating, sunbathing, and diving. If you decide to go for a swim, be careful—
the currents can have a whirlpool effect that will suck a swim-
mer down. For one-day rafting trips, the cost is approximately
B300. Longer trips are also offered. If you book through a responsible travel agent, you may have to pay a bit more, but
you'll also be more likely to get a raft in good condition and a
skipper familiar with the currents.

Exploring

One may forgive, but one cannot forget, the inhumanity that
caused the death, between 1942 and 1945, of more than 16,000
Allied prisoners of war and 49,000 impressed Asian laborers.
Forced by the Japanese, under abysmal conditions, to build a
railway through the jungle from Thailand into Burma, one person died for every railway tie on the track.

A reconstruction of the now famous bridge (it was successfully
bombed by the Allies toward the end of the war) stands just
north of the small, sleepy town of Kanchanaburi. Nearby are
two Allied war cemeteries with the remains of 8,732 POWs. To
reach the bridge, go through town on Saeng Chuto Road, the
main street.

Kanchanaburi War Cemetery is on the left. In row upon row of neatly laid-out graves rest 6,982 American, Australian, British, and Dutch prisoners of war. A commemorative service is held every April 25. After the cemetery, take the next road to the left and make a right at the *T* junction. Notice the **Japanese War Memorial Shrine** at the junction. Be sure to read the plaque—it has an English translation.

Just up the street from the memorial, the road opens out to a plaza—**the bridge** is on the left. Built with forced labor toward the end of the war, the bridge has steel girders, the center spans of which were knocked out by Allied bombs and replaced after the war with girders made in Japan. The other steel spans are the original ones. You can walk across the bridge to the opposite bank. The wooden bridge associated with the movie was located a mile or two downstream.

Restaurants, souvenir shops, and jewelry stores are located in the plaza before the bridge. Blue sapphires from the Bor Ploy mines, 45 km (28 mi) north of Kanchanaburi, are generally a good buy, but prices are marked up at these shops. You're better off buying the sapphires at the small shops in the center of town.

Upriver, on the road leading back to town, is the **JEATH War Museum** ("JEATH" is an acronym for Japan, England, America, Australia, Thailand, and Holland). Founded by a monk from the adjoining temple, the museum consists of a reconstructed bamboo hut—the type used to house the POWs—and a collection of utensils, railway spikes, clothing, aerial photographs, newspaper clippings, and illustrations designed to show the atrocities inflicted on the POWs by the Japanese. *Admission charge. Open daily 8–5.*

Another Allied burial ground, the **Chong-Kai War Cemetery,** lies across the river. To get there, take the ferry from the pier below the park off Patana Road.

A 1-km (½-mi) walk inland from Chong-Kai is **Wat Thum Khao Pun,** one of the best cave temples in the area. A small temple stands outside and a guide entices you into the cave, where serene images of Buddha sit between the stalagmites and stalactites.

Kanchanaburi province is more than the Death Railway. It is also spectacular countryside. The **Erawan Waterfall,** perhaps the most photographed waterfall in Thailand, is worth the trip. Located in the beautifully forested Khao Salop National Park, the falls are at their best in early autumn. To reach the falls, located 65 km (40 mi) from Kanchanaburi on the Kanchanaburi–Srisawat Highway, either take a tour bus from Kanchanaburi or use the public bus. Buses (No. 8170) leave every hour for the 90-minute journey; it's a 1½-km (1-mi) walk or taxi ride to the foot of the falls.

Allow two hours to climb up all seven levels of the Erawan Waterfall, and you'll need to wear tennis shoes or similar footwear. The rock at the top of the falls is shaped like an elephant, hence the name Erawan, which means elephant in Thai.

Five km (3 mi) farther up the road from the Erawan Waterfall is the 91-m (300-ft) **Sri Nakharin Dam** and a hydroelectric power station. Behind the dam is a vast reservoir. A tour boat makes a two-hour excursion from here to the **Huay Khamin Falls.**

Another nearby waterfall is **Sai Yok Noi** (also called Kao Phang), about 1½ km (1 mi) from Nam-Tok Station, or 77 km (46 mi) from Kanchanaburi. A train makes the two-hour run from Kanchanaburi each day at 10:33 AM. From the sleepy village of Nam-Tok, formerly a major hospital camp for POWs, it's a 1½-km (1-mi) walk to the Sai Yok Noi Waterfall. A lot smaller than Erawan, this waterfall offers pools for swimming during the rainy season (May–Aug.), the best time to visit. On weekends, the area is packed with Thai families. The memorable train ride from Bangkok passes lush jungle landscape and rushing waterfalls, but it also hugs the cliffs en route; so it's not for the faint-hearted.

Dining and Lodging

Most of the restaurants for tourists are situated by the River Kwai Bridge or farther downstream at the confluence of the Kwai Noi and Kwai Yai rivers. The most attractive—and most crowded—is the open-air **River Kwai Floating Restaurant** (tel. 034/512–595), to the right of the bridge. Fish dishes, either cooked with Thai spices or lightly grilled, dominate the menu. The specialty is *yeesok*, a fish found in the Kwai Yai and Kwai Noi rivers. Try to arrive before the tour groups, and request a table alongside the river. For more authentic Thai food, try the **Pae Karn Floating Restaurant** (tel. 034/512–548) at the river confluence. The food is better, though the decor is plain.

Most of the area hotels are located along the riverbanks. A few of the resorts also offer thatched bungalows on the river. These raft houses offer a river view during the day, but tend to be hot and muggy at night. Most foreign visitors only spend a day in Kanchanaburi; so the hotels are designed primarily for Thai families who have come for an inexpensive vacation.

Kwai Yai Garden Resort. Located 15 minutes by ferry from Tha Kradan Pier, this small resort offers thatched bungalows, a few raft houses, a small restaurant, and a friendly staff. *125 Moo 2, Tambon Tamakham, Amphoe Muang, Kanchanaburi 71000, tel. 034/513–611; Bangkok reservations: 02/513–5399. 12 rooms and 4 rafts. Facilities: restaurant, bar, tour desk. MC, V. Moderate.*

River Kwai Hotel. Across the bridge on the banks of the Kwai Yai, this hotel is a small complex of thatched bungalows, including some on rafts. On one raft, the dining room and lounge offer a picturesque view of the bridge. *Amphoe Muang, Kanchanaburi 71000, tel. 034/511–313. 7 rooms and 9 raft houses. Facilities: restaurant, tour desk. MC, V. Moderate.*

River Kwai Village. Nestled in the heart of the jungle in the River Kwai Valley, this resort village consists of five one-story log cabins. A few guest rooms are also located on rafts. All guest rooms have air-conditioning and are simply furnished with teak and colored stones embedded in the walls. The cafeteria-style restaurant offers a combination of Thai and Western dishes. More enjoyable is the casual restaurant on one of the anchored floating rafts. The resort will supply transportation from Bangkok and arrange tours of the area. *Amphoe Sai Yok, Kanchanaburi 71150. No telephone. Reservations should be made in Bangkok at 1054/4 New Petchburi Rd., Bangkok 10400, tel. 02/251–7552. 60 rooms and 7 raft houses. Facilities: 2 restaurants, outdoor pool, conference rooms. Tours arranged. AE, DC, V. Moderate.*

Ayutthaya and Bang Pa-In

Toward the end of the 16th century, Europeans described Ayutthaya, with its 1,700 temples and 4,000 golden images of Buddha, as more striking than any capital in Europe. Certainly the Ayutthaya period was also Thailand's most glorious.

Ayutthaya became the kingdom's seat of power in 1350. For the next 400 years, relations between Ayutthaya and Burma vacillated between all-out war and hostile peace. After 32 kings and five dynasties, the Ayutthaya court had become self-indulgent. Sensing weakness, the Burmese attacked. After a 15-month siege, the city fell in 1767, and the Burmese vented their pent-up anger. In their fury, they killed or enslaved all but 10,000 of the million inhabitants, and they ransacked the temples with such vengeance that little remained standing.

Ayutthaya never recovered from the Burmese invasion. Today, it is a small provincial town with partially restored ruins; if you use your imagination, you can re-create some of the magnificent architecture and fabulous statuary that were the glory of Ayutthaya. The site is particularly striking at sunset, when the silhouetted ruins glow orange-brown and are imbued with a melancholy charm.

Guided Tours

Ayutthaya and Bang Pa-In. This visit to Thailand's former glorious capital and the royal palace of Bang Pa-In takes a full day. Tours may travel the 75 km (46 mi) to Ayutthaya either both ways by coach or in one direction by cruise boat and the other by coach. The most popular trip is aboard the *Oriental Queen*, managed by the Oriental Hotel (tel. 02/236–0400, ext. 3133; cost B900). The *Oriental Queen* now has some stiff competition, however. The *Ayutthaya Princess* (tel. 02/255–9200), a new boat with an exterior design resembling a royal barge, offers the *Oriental Queen*'s itinerary for the same fare. It departs from both the Shangri-La and Royal Orchid Sheraton piers. To book either of these cruises, contact the respective hotels or any travel agent.

The **Bang Pa-In Summer Palace** is a popular Sunday excursion for Thais. A tour boat departs from Bangkok's Maharat Pier at 8:30 AM and travels up the Chao Phraya River to Bang Pa-In in time for lunch. On the downriver trip, the boat stops at the Bang Sai Folk Arts and Craft Centre before returning to Bangkok by 5:30 PM. The tour is operated by the Chao Phraya Express Boat Co. (2/58 Aroon-Amarin Rd., Maharat Pier, Bangkok, tel. 02/222–5330).

Getting There

Ayutthaya, 72 km (45 mi) north of Bangkok, may be visited either as an excursion from Bangkok or on the way from Bangkok to Thailand's northern provinces. Try to get an early start for Ayutthaya in order to visit as many of the sights as possible before 1 PM, when the heat becomes unbearable. Then take a long lunch and, if you have time, continue sightseeing in the late afternoon and catch the sunset before you leave.

By Train Between 4:30 AM and late evening, trains depart frequently from Bangkok's Hualamphong station, arriving in Ayutthaya 80 minutes later. Halfway between the two cities (in time, not distance) is Don Muang Airport. Many travelers on their way south from Chiang Mai stop at Ayutthaya and then continue by train only as far as the airport, from which they fly to their next destination instead of going all the way back into Bangkok.

By Bus Buses leave Bangkok's Northern Terminal on Phaholyothin Road (tel. 02/271–0101) every 30 minutes between 6 AM and 7 PM.

Getting Around

For a three-hour tour of the sights, tuk-tuks can be hired within Ayutthaya for approximately B100; a four-wheel samlor can be rented for about B300. English-speaking guides can be hired around the station.

Exploring

Ayutthaya Ayutthaya is situated within a large loop of the Chao Phraya River, where it meets the Nam Pa Sak and Lopburi rivers. To completely encircle their capital by water, the Thais dug a canal along the northern perimeter, linking the Chao Phraya to the Lopburi. Although the new provincial town of Ayutthaya, including the railway station, is on the east bank of the Nam Pa Sak, most of Ayutthaya's ancient glory is on the island. An exception is Wat Yai Chai Mongkol, about a B20 tuk-tuk ride southeast of the railway station.

Wat Yai Chai Mongkol was built in 1357 by King U-Thong for meditation. After King Naresuan defeated the Burmese by killing the Burmese crown prince in single-handed combat on elephants in 1582, he enlarged the temple. The complex was totally restored in 1982; with the contemporary images of Buddha lining the courtyard and the neatly groomed grounds, it looks a little touristy, an impression not helped by a souvenir shop, beverage stand, and a host of tour buses from Bangkok. *Admission charge. Open daily 8–5.*

The road continues to **Wat Phanan Choeng,** a small temple on the banks of the Lopburi. The temple predates the time when Ayutthaya became the Thai capital. In 1324, one of the U-Thong kings, who had arranged to marry a daughter of the Chinese emperor, came to this spot on the river; instead of entering the city with his fiancée, he arranged an escort for her. But she, thinking that she had been deserted, threw herself into the river in despair and drowned. The king tried to atone for his thoughtlessness by building the temple. The story has great appeal to Thai Chinese, many of whom make romantic pilgrimages here. *Admission charge. Open daily 8–6.*

Returning to the main road, go left and cross over the bridge to the island. Continue on Rojana Road for about 1½ km (1 mi) to the **Chao Phraya National Museum.** Ayutthaya's more important historical masterpieces are in Bangkok's National Museum, but if you do visit the Chao Phraya Museum, find a guide who can highlight the evolution of Ayutthaya art over four centuries. *Admission charge. Open Wed.–Sun. 9–noon and 1–4.*

Just beyond the Chao Phraya National Museum, turn right onto Si Samphet Road. Pass the city hall on the left and continue for 1 km (½ mi) to **Wat Phra Si Samphet,** easily recognizable by the huge parking lot. The shining white marble temple nearby not only looks modern, it is. Built in 1956, **Viharn Phra Mongkol Bopitr** houses one of Thailand's largest bronze images of Buddha, one of the few that escaped the destruction wrought by the Burmese.

Wat Phra Si Samphet was the largest wat in Ayutthaya and the temple of the royal family. Built in the 14th century, in 1767 it lost its 15-m (50-ft) Buddha, Phra Sri Samphet, to the Burmese, who melted it down for its gold—170 kilograms (374 pounds) worth. The chedis, restored in 1956, survived and are the best examples of Ayutthaya architecture. Enshrining the ashes of Ayutthaya kings, they stand as eternal memories of a golden age. Beyond these monuments is a grassy field where the royal palace once stood. The field is a cool, shady place in which to walk and picnic. The foundation is all that remains of the palace that was home to 33 kings. *Open daily 8–5.*

Before you leave, visit some of the stalls in the market behind the souvenir stands; you'll find a marvelous array of vegetables, fruits, and other foods. After wandering around, stop at the café at the viharn end of the market for refreshments—try the chilled coconut in its shell.

From the large coach park, Naresuan Road crosses Si Samphet Road and continues past a small lake to nearby **Wat Phra Mahathat,** on the corner of Chee Kun Road. Built in 1384 by King Ramesuan, the monastery was destroyed by the Burmese, but a buried treasure chest was found during a 1956 restoration project. The chest contained a relic of Lord Buddha, golden Buddha images, and other objects in gold, ruby, and crystal that are now housed in Bangkok's National Museum. If you climb up what is left of the monastery's 42-m (140-ft) *prang* (Khmer-style pagoda with an elliptical spire), you'll be able to envision just how grand the structure must have been. You can also admire the neighboring **Wat Raj Burana,** built by the seventh Ayutthaya king in memory of his brother.

Continue down Naresuan Road, now called Chao Phnom Road, to the Mae Nam Po Sak River. Either go left up U-Thong Road to **Chandra Kasem Palace** or right to the bridge that leads to the mainland. The reconstructed 17th-century palace is used as Ayutthaya's second national museum. If you're hungry, take a right on U-Thong Road; at the bridge over the Mae Nam Po Sak are two floating restaurants. If you have a train to catch, try **Tevaraj,** a good Thai restaurant near the railway station, for tasty freshwater lobster.

For an educational overview of the 400 years of the Ayutthaya period, stop in at the new Ayutthaya Historical Study Centre, located near the Teacher's College and the U-Thong Inn. Financed by the Japanese government, the center functions as a place of national research and as a museum. Models of the city as a royal capital, as a port city, as an administrative and international diplomatic center, and as a rural village depicting lifestyles in the countryside are displayed. *Rotchana Rd., tel. 035/ 245–124. Admission charge. Open Tues.–Sun. 9–4:30.*

About 5 km (3 mi) north of Ayutthaya is the **Elephant Kraal,** the only intact royal kraal in the country. A stockade of massive teak logs, it was formerly used to hold wild elephants picked to be trained for martial service. The kraal was last used in May 1903, during King Chulalongkorn's reign.

Bang Pa-In A popular attraction outside Ayutthaya is **Bang Pa-In Summer Palace,** 20 km (12 mi) to the south. Minibuses leave Chao Prom Market in Ayutthaya regularly, starting from 6:30 AM. The 50-minute trip costs B10. Boats also make the 40-minute run between Ayutthaya and Bang Pa-In; the fare is B150. Trains regularly travel the 70 km (42 mi) from Bangkok to Bang Pa-In railway station, from which a minibus runs to the palace.

The original palace, built by King Prusat (who ruled from 1630 to 1655) on the banks of the Mae Nam Pa Suk, was used by the Ayutthaya kings until the Burmese invasion. Neglected for 80 years, it was rebuilt during the reign of Rama IV (1851–1868) and became the favored summer palace of King Chulalongkorn (Rama V, 1868–1910) until tragedy struck. Delayed in Bangkok on one occasion, the king sent his wife ahead by boat. The boat capsized and she drowned. She could easily have been saved, but the body of a royal personage was sacrosanct and could never be touched by a commoner, on pain of death. King Chulalongkorn could never forgive himself. He built a pavilion in her memory; be sure to read the touching inscription engraved on the memorial.

King Chulalongkorn was fascinated by Europe and its architecture, and many Western influences are evident in Bang Pa-In. The area's most beautiful building, however, is the **Aisawan Thippaya,** a Thai pavilion that seems to float on the lake. Featuring a series of staggered roofs leading to a central spire, the pavilion has represented the country at worldwide expositions.

In addition to Aisawan Thippaya, four other buildings and well-tended gardens make up this striking architectural complex. **Phra Thinang Warophat Piman,** nicknamed the Peking Palace, stands to the north of the Royal Ladies Landing Place in front of a stately pond. Constructed from materials custom-made in China as a replica of a palace of the Chinese imperial court, it was a gift from Chinese Thais eager to demonstrate their loyalty and persuade the king to look more favorably on them. An exquisite collection of jade and Ming-period porcelain is on display inside.

Take the cable car across the river to the unique wat south of the palace grounds. In his fascination with Western architecture, King Chulalongkorn built this Buddhist temple, **Wat Nivet Thamaprawat,** in the Gothic style. Complete with a belfry and stained-glass windows, it looks as much like a Christian church as a wat. *Admission charge to Bang Pa-In Palace. Open 8–3, closed Mon. and Fri.*

Bang Sai Folk Arts and Craft Centre is 24 km (14½ mi) south of Bang Pa-In on the Chao Phraya River. Set up by the queen in 1976 to employ families with handicraft skills, the center makes products that are sold throughout Thailand at the Chirlada handicraft shops. The handicrafts on sale include fern-vine basketry, wood carvings, dyed silks, and handmade dolls. The park is a pleasant place for a picnic, although it is crowded on weekends with Thai families. It also has a small restaurant.

Dining and Lodging

Romantics may want to stay overnight in Ayutthaya to see the ruins at night. Since most tourists arrive from Bangkok around 10 AM and depart at 4 PM, those who stay are treated to genuine Thai hospitality. Don't expect deluxe accommodations or restaurants, however: Ayutthaya boasts only simple Thai hotels.

Dining **Pae Krung Kao.** If you want to dine outdoors and watch the waters of the Mae Nam Pa Sak, this is the better of the two floating restaurants near the bridge. The food is Thai; you can also come here for a leisurely beer. *4 U-Thong Rd., tel. 035/241–555. Dress: very casual. No credit cards. Moderate.*
Tevaraj. For good Thai food that does not spare the spices, it's worth heading to this unpretentious restaurant behind Ayutthaya's railway station. The restaurant is short on decor, but the fish dishes and the *tom khaa* (soup made with coconut milk) are excellent. *74 Wat Pa Kho Rd., no phone. Dress: casual. No credit cards. Inexpensive.*

Lodging **U-Thong Inn.** This is the most comfortable hotel in town. Rooms are simply furnished, but include carpeted floors and private bathrooms. The staff is accustomed to foreign guests and can make arrangements for tours. The hotel's dining room, serving Thai and Chinese food, is the most congenial place to eat in Ayutthaya. (Don't confuse this hotel with the U-Thong Hotel, which is not quite as commodious.) *210 Moo 5, Tambon Rotchana Rd., Amphoe Phra Nakhon Si, Ayutthaya 13000, tel. 035/251–136. 100 rooms. Facilities: restaurant, coffee lounge, bar, tour desk, gift shop. MC, V. Moderate.*

Lopburi

Lying 150 km (94 mi) north of Bangkok is Lopburi, one of Thailand's oldest cities. The first evidence of inhabitants in this city dates from the 4th century AD. After the 6th century, Lopburi's influence grew under the Dvaravati rulers, who dominated northern Thailand until the Khmers swept in from the east. From the beginning of the 10th century until the middle of the 13th century, when the new Thai kingdom drove them out, the Khmers used Lopburi as the chief provincial capital to control the region. During the Sukhothai and early Ayutthaya periods, Lopburi's importance declined until, in 1664, King Narai (of Ayutthaya) made the city his second capital to escape the heat and humidity of Ayutthaya. French architects were employed to build King Narai's palace; consequently, Lopburi is a strange mixture of Khmer, Thai, and Western architecture.

Lopburi is relatively off the beaten track for tourists. Few foreigners stay overnight, which perhaps explains why the locals are so friendly and eager to show you their town—and to practice their English!

Getting There

Lopburi is another 75 km (47 mi) north of Ayutthaya from Bangkok. While it's possible to visit both towns in one day, the journey would be strenuous. You can spend a night in either Ayutthaya or Lopburi, but don't expect deluxe accommodations. Another option is to visit Lopburi on a day's excursion out of Bangkok or en route to Phitsanulok and/or Chiang Mai. Luggage storage is available at the train station.

By Train Three morning and two afternoon trains depart from Bangkok's Hualamphong station on the three-hour journey to Lopburi. The journey from Ayutthaya takes just over an hour. Trains to Bangkok run in the early and late afternoon. The express sleeper train to Chiang Mai from Bangkok comes through Lopburi at 8:20 PM.

By Bus Buses leave Bangkok's Northern Terminal on Phaholyothin Road (tel. 02/271–0101) every 30 minutes between 6 AM and 7 PM.

Getting Around

Although bicycle samlors are available, most of Lopburi's attractions are within easy walking distance.

Exploring

At the back of the railway station is **Wat Phra Si Mahathat.** First built by the Khmers, it underwent so many restorations during the Sukhothai and Ayutthaya periods that it's difficult to discern the three original Khmer prangs—only the central one has survived intact. Several Sukhothai- and Ayutthaya-style chedis are also within the compound. *Admission charge. Open 8:30–4:30.*

Walk diagonally through Wat Phra Si Mahathat to **Narai Ratchaniwet Palace.** The preserved buildings, which took 12 years (1665–1677) to complete, have been converted into a museum. Surrounding the buildings are castellated walls and triumphant archways grand enough to admit an entourage mounted on elephants. The most elaborate structure is the **Dusit Mahaprasat Hall,** built by King Narai to receive foreign ambassadors. The roof is gone, but you'll be able to spot the mixture of architectural styles: The square doors are Thai and the dome-shaped arches are Western. *Admission charge. Open Wed.–Sun. 9–noon and 1–4.*

The next group of buildings in the palace compound—the **Chan Phaisan Pavilion** (1666), the **Phiman Monghut Pavilion** (mid-19th century), and the row of houses once used by ladies of the court—are now all museums. The latter houses the **Farmer's Museum,** which exhibits regional tools and artifacts seldom displayed in Thailand.

Heading north across the road from the palace (away from the station), you'll pass through the restored **Wat Sao Thong Thong.** Notice the windows of the viharn, which King Narai changed in imitation of Western architecture. Beyond the wat and across another small street is **Vichayen House,** built for Louis XIV's personal representative, De Chaumont. The house was later occupied by King Narai's infamous Greek minister, Constantine Phaulkon, whose political schemes eventually caused the ouster of all Westerners from Thailand. When King Narai was dying in 1668, his army commander, Phra Phetracha, seized power, attacked these residences, and beheaded Phaulkon. In the attack, the Vichayen House and its ancillary buildings, including a Roman Catholic church, were nearly destroyed. *Admission charge. Open Wed.–Sun. 9–noon and 1–4.*

Walk east along the road separating Wat Sao Thong Thong and Vichayen House to **Phra Prang Sam Yot,** a Khmer Hindu shrine and Lopburi's primary landmark. The three prangs symbolize the sacred triad of Brahma, Vishnu, and Siva. King Narai converted the shrine into a Buddhist temple, and a stucco image of the Lord Buddha sits serenely before the central prang once dedicated to Brahma.

Walk about 250 yards down the street facing Phra Prang Sam Yot, and cross over the railway tracks to the **San Phra Kan shrine.** The respected residents of the temple, Samae monkeys, often perform spontaneously for visitors. These interesting animals engage in the human custom of burying their dead.

Dining and Lodging

Accommodations in Lopburi are very Spartan, and restaurants are simply places in which to eat rather than culinary experiences.

Lopburi Inn. Located in the new part of town, this is the only hotel in Lopburi with air-conditioning and modern facilities. Even so, don't expect your room to have much more than a clean bed and a private bath. The dining room serves Thai and Chinese food. The staff doesn't speak English, but communicates with smiles and gestures. *28/9 Narai Maharat Rd., Lopburi, tel. 036/412–300; fax 036/411–917. 142 rooms. Facilities: dining room, coffee lounge. DC, V. Moderate.*

5 Northern Thailand

Chiang Mai

Introduction

by Nigel Fisher

Chiang Mai is the second most popular city to visit in Thailand. Its rich culture stretches back 700 years. Under King Mengrai, several small tribes banded together to form a new "nation" called Anachak Lanna Thai, and made Chiang Rai (north of Chiang Mai) their capital. In 1296, they moved the capital to the fertile plains between Doi Suthep mountain and the Mae Ping River and called it Napphaburi Sri Nakornphing Chiang Mai.

Lanna Thai eventually lost its independence to Ayutthaya and later, Burma. Not until 1774—when General Tuksin (who ruled as king before Rama I) drove the Burmese out—did the region revert to Thailand. After that, the region developed independently of southern Thailand. Even the language is different, marked by its relaxed tempo.

Only in the last 50 years have communications between Bangkok and Chiang Mai opened up. No longer a small, provincial town, it has exploded beyond its moat and gates. Some of its innocence has gone, but except for the hustling of *samlor* (trishaw) cyclists and tuk-tuk drivers, Chiang Mai has few of the big-city maladies that engulf Thailand's capital.

Chiang Mai serves as Thailand's northern capital and, for the tourist, the gateway to the north. Many travelers take lodging for a month or longer and make several excursions, returning to Chiang Mai to rest. The hill tribes around Chiang Mai have been visited so frequently by tourists that they have lost some of their character. Travelers in search of villages untainted by Western commercialism need to go farther afield to areas around Tak to the west and Nan to the east.

Even Mae Hong Son, northwest of Chiang Mai, is developing its tourist trade. A paved highway from Chiang Mai opened up the region in 1965, and now daily flights connect the two towns. Mae Hong Son is known for its sleepy, peaceful pace of life and the regular gathering of the area's hill tribes, which exchange goods at the town's market. By road the shortest route is the northern route through Mae Thaeng and Hual Nam Dang that takes about six hours. The road twists and turns and should not be negotiated at night.

An adventurous excursion, especially if you are traveling independently, is the 369 km (231 mi) from Chiang Mai to Mae Hong Son, stopping en route at Don Inthanon National Park. The park's scenic beauty is characterized by trees, flowers, waterfalls, and tremendous views from Thailand's highest mountain (2,565 m/8,464 ft). The turnoff for the park is 57 km (36 mi) from Chiang Mai. From that point, you're faced with a 48-km (30-mi) stiff climb on a paved toll road to the top. If you don't feel like making the drive yourself, you can rent a minibus from Chom Thong, beyond the park's turnoff. It's a good idea to rent a minibus if you wish to see the Mae Ya waterfall. The road to the waterfall, consisting of 12 km (7½ mi) of unpaved tracks, can be impassable. An easier waterfall to reach is Mae Klang, which has three tiers of falls. The turnoff for Mae Klang is 6 km (3½ mi) after the entrance to the park. The main road then continues on to Mae Hong Son through Mae Sariang and Khun Tuan and is easier driving than the northern route.

Other, less-strenuous excursions from Chiang Mai are to the ancient town of Lamphun, 26 km (16 mi) south of Chiang Mai, and to Lam Pang, which is farther to the south.

Arriving and Departing by Plane

Thai Airways International has seven or more flights daily between Chiang Mai and Bangkok, and direct daily flights between Phuket and Chiang Mai. The flight takes about an hour and costs approximately B1,335. During the peak season, flights are heavily booked. The airport is about 10 minutes from the downtown area, about a B70 taxi (fixed price) ride away.

Arriving and Departing by Train and Bus

By Train The State Railway links Chiang Mai to Bangkok and points south. Trains depart from Bangkok's Hualamphong Railway Station and arrive at Chiang Mai Depot (Charoenmuang Rd., tel. 053/244–795). As the journey from Bangkok takes about 13 hours and there is little to see but paddy fields, the overnight sleeper (departs Bangkok 6 PM, arrives Chiang Mai 7:25 AM) is the best train to take. For the return trip, the train departs Chiang Mai at 5:15 PM and arrives in Bangkok at 6:25 AM. Not only is this train the cleanest of the State Railways, but the bunks in second class, in either the air-conditioned or the fan-cooled coaches, are comfortable. First class has only the advantage of two bunks per compartment for twice the price. There is also the Nakhonphing Special Express that departs Bangkok at 7:40 PM and arrives at Chiang Mai at 8:25 AM (return trip departs at 7:30 PM and arrives Bangkok at 8:25 AM). This train does not have first-class compartments. Most of the Bangkok–Chiang Mai trains stop at Phitsanulok and Lam Pang. There are hotel booking agents at Chiang Mai railway station. The tuk-tuk fare to the center of town ranges from B20 to B30.

By Bus Numerous companies run buses both day and night between Bangkok and Chiang Mai. The buses are slightly faster than the trains (time is about 11 hours) and less expensive—approximately B240 for an air-conditioned bus. State-run buses leave from Bangkok's Northern Terminal (Phahonyothin Rd., Bangkok, tel. 02/279–4484). Direct buses also connect Chiang Mai with Phitsanulok and Sukhothai.

Private tour coach operators have more luxurious buses and cost B30–B60 more. Try **Top North** (tel. 02/252–2967) or **Chan Tour** (tel. 02/252–0349).

Getting Around

The city itself is compact and can be explored easily on foot or by bicycle, with the occasional use of public or other transport for temples, shops, and attractions out of the city center.

By Car A car, with a driver and guide, is the most convenient way to visit three of the five key temples located outside Chiang Mai as well as the Elephant Camp and hill tribe villages. For a morning's visit to the 6-km- (3.8-mi-) long craft factory/shopping area, the price for a car should not be more than B100, as the driver will be anticipating commissions from the stores you visit. You can also make private arrangements with a taxi for a day's transportation. The cost for a day is approximately B1,000–B1,400, depending on mileage. Be sure to negotiate the price before you step in the car or, better yet, establish the price the evening before and have the driver collect you from your hotel in the morning. Do not pay until you have completed the trip.

By Motorcycle Motorcycles are popular. Rental agencies are numerous, and most small hotels have their own agency. Shop around to get the best price and a bike in good condition. Remember that any damage to the bike that can be attributed to you will be. This includes theft of the vehicle.

By Samlor Most trips in a tuk-tuk within Chiang Mai should cost less than B30.

By Songthaew These red minibuses follow a kind of fixed route, but will go elsewhere at a passenger's request. Name your destination before you get in. The cost is B5.

By Bus The Arcade bus terminal serves Bangkok, Sukhothai, Phitsanulok, Udorn Thani, and Chiang Rai (and towns within the province of Chiang Rai). The other terminal, Chiang Phuak, serves Lamphun, Fang, Tha Ton, and destinations within Chiang Mai province.

Important Addresses and Numbers

Tourist Information **TAT** (105/1 Chiang Mai-Lamphun Rd., tel. 053/248–604) recently moved to the far side of the river and lost some of the helpful brochures it used to give to travelers. Contact **Thai International Airways** (Phra Poklao Rd., tel. 053/241–044), to arrange domestic and international bookings.

Emergencies **Police** and **ambulance** (tel. 191). **Tourist Police** (105/1 Chiang Mai-Lamphun Rd., tel. 053/248–974 or 053/248–130). **U.S. Consulate** (387 Wichayanom Rd., tel. 053/252–657).

Hospitals **Lanna Hospital** (103 Superhighway, tel. 053/211–037) has 24-hour service and up-to-date equipment.

English-Language Bookstores **D.K. Books** (234 Tapae Rd., opposite Wat Buparam, tel. 052/235–151) has one of the best selections of English-language books, including guidebooks. **Suriwongse Centre** (54/1–5 Sri Douchai Rd., tel. 053/252–052) also carries a range of English-language books, with a large selection of Thai/English dictionaries.

Travel Agencies For plane, train, or bus tickets, one efficient and helpful agency is **ST&T Travel Center** (193/12 Sridonchai Rd., Amphur Muang, tel. 053/251–922), on the same street as the Chiang Plaza Hotel.

Guided Tours

Every other store seems to be a tour agency here; so you'd be wise to pick up a list of TAT-recognized agencies before choosing one. Also, each hotel has its own travel desk and association with a tour operator. **World Travel Service** (Rincome Hotel, Huay Kaeo Rd., tel. 053/221–1044) is reliable, but it is the guide who makes the tour great; so meet yours before you actually sign up. This is particularly important if you are planning a trek to the hill tribe villages. Prices vary quite a bit, and so shop around, and carefully examine the offerings.

For trekking, unless you speak some Thai, know the local geography, understand the local customs, and are stricken with the romance of adventure, use the services of a certified guide. Dozens of tour operators, some extremely unreliable, set up shop on a Chiang Mai sidewalk and disappear after they have your money. Obtain a list of trekking tour agencies from TAT. **Top North** (Chiang Mai Hill Hotel, 18 Huay Kaeo Rd., tel. 053/221–254) and **Summit Tour and Trekking** (Thai Charoen Hotel, Tapas Rd., tel. 053/233–351) offer good tours at about B350 a day (more for elephant rides and river rafting). However, it is not so much the tour agency as the individual guide who determines the quality of the tour and the villages visited. Be sure yours knows several hill tribe languages, as well as good English.

Because areas quickly become overtrekked and guides come and go, the only way to select a tour is to obtain the latest information by talking to travelers in Chiang Mai. What was good six months ago may not be good today. It is imperative, also, that you discuss with your proposed guide the villages and route before setting out. You usually can tell whether the guide is knowledgeable and respects the villagers. It can become very cold at night; so take something warm as well as sturdy hiking shoes. You may also want to take along some strong soap, preferably with disinfectant, in case the sleeping huts are grubby. Otherwise, travel light.

Exploring Chiang Mai

Numbers in the margin correspond to points of interest on the Chiang Mai map.

Tour 1: The Outer City

❶ **Wat Prathat Doi Suthep** is perched high up—1,080 m (3,542 ft)—on Doi Suthep, a mountain that overlooks Chiang Mai. It is a 30-minute drive (16 km, or 10 mi) from Chiang Mai, and then a cable car ride or a steep climb up 290 steps beside a marvelous balustrade in the form of *nagas* (mythical snakes that bring rain to irrigate the rice fields, and then cause the waters to retreat so the crop may be harvested), with scales of inlaid brown and green tiles, to the *chedi* (Thai pagoda where holy relics are kept).

❷ Across from Wat Prathat is **Phuping Palace,** the summer residence of the Thai Royal Family. Though the palace may not be visited, the gardens are open on Friday, Sunday, and public holidays. The blooms are at their best in January.

❸ On Suthep Road is **Wat Suan Dok,** one of the largest of Chiang Mai's temples, said to have been built on the site where some of Lord Buddha's bones were found. Some of these relics are reportedly housed in the chedi; the others went to Wat Prathat on Doi Suthep. At the back of the *viharn* (large hall where priests perform religious duties) is the *bot* (main chapel) housing Phra Chao Kao, a superb bronze Buddha made in 1504. In a graveyard alongside the wat, Chiang Mai nobility are buried in stupas.

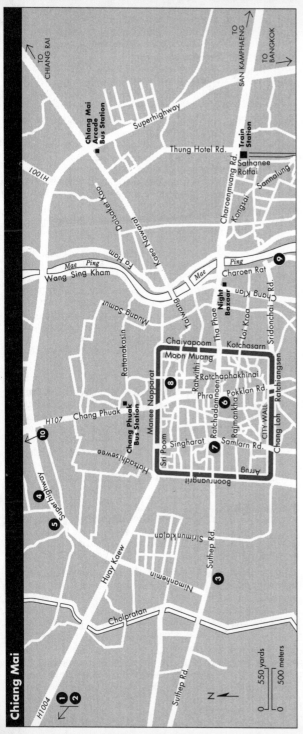

Chiang Mai

Elephant Training
Centre, **10**
National Museum, **4**
Phuping Palace, **2**
Wat Chaimongkol, **9**
Wat Chedi Luang, **6**

Wat Chiang Man, **8**
Wat Photharam
Maha Viharn, **5**
Wat Phra Singh, **7**
Wat Prathat Doi
Suthep, **1**
Wat Suan Dok, **3**

4 On the superhighway, between its intersection with Huay Kaew Road and Highway 107, is the **National Museum.** In this northern Thai-style building are numerous statues of the Lord Buddha, as well as a huge footprint of Buddha's made from wood and inlaid with mother-of-pearl. The upper floor houses collections of archaeological items, including a bed with mosquito netting used by one of the early princes of Chiang Mai. *Admission charge. Open weekdays 8:30–noon and 1–4:30.*

5 From the museum, you can walk to **Wat Photharam Maha Viharn,** more commonly known as Wat Chedi Yot (Seven-Spired Pagoda). Built in 1455, it is a copy of the Mahabodhi temple in Bodh Gaya, India, where the Lord Buddha achieved enlightenment. The seven spires represent the seven weeks that Lord Buddha spent in Bodh Gaya after attaining enlightenment. The sides of the chedi have marvelous bas-relief sculptures of celestial figures.

Tour 2: The Inner City

Three of the most important temples are within Chiang Mai's city walls, all in easy walking distance of one another. The first **6** is **Wat Chedi Luang** on Phra Pokklan Road just before it crosses Rajmankha Road. In 1411, a vision commanded King Saen Muang Ma to build a chedi to a "height as high as a dove could fly." He died before it was finished, as did the next king, and, during the third succeeding king's reign, an earthquake knocked down 100 feet of the 282-foot-high chedi. It is now a superb ruin. Don't miss the naga balustrades flanking the entrance steps to the viharn—they are considered the finest of their kind.

Nearby at the junction of Ratchadamnoen and Singharat roads, **7** in the middle of town, is Chiang Mai's principal monastery, **Wat Phra Singh,** with the Buddha image Phra Singh. The serene and benevolent facial expression of this statue has a radiance enhanced by the light filtering into the chapel. Be sure to note the temple's facades of splendidly carved wood, the elegant teak beams and posts, and the masonry. In a large teaching compound, student monks often have the time and desire to talk.

8 **Wat Chiang Man,** Chiang Mai's oldest (1296) monastery, typical of northern Thai architecture, has massive teak pillars inside the bot. Two important images of the Buddha sit in the small building to the right of the main viharn. Officially, they are on view only on Sunday, but sometimes the door is unlocked.

Each of Chiang Mai's multitude of temples has merit, but the one that counts is the one that inspires you. One that may, for **9** example, is **Wat Chaimongkol,** along the Mae Ping River, near the Chiang Mai Plaza Hotel. It's small, with only 18 monks in residence, and foreigners rarely visit. Though the little chedi is supposed to contain holy relics, its beauty lies in the quietness and serenity of the grounds.

If you have not visited an "elephant camp" elsewhere in Thai-**10** land, visit the **Elephant Training Centre** about 20 km (12 mi) from Chiang Mai at **Mae Sa.** As commercial and touristy as it is, elephants are such magnificent beasts that the show cannot fail to please. Action begins at 9:30. The mahouts bring their beasts to the river for a thorough wash down. The elephants frolic in the water, loving every moment of it. They then stage a dull demonstration of dragging 30-m- (100-ft) long teak logs into the "camp," where the strongest nudge the logs onto a pile. At the end of the show, some tourists choose to ride an elephant around the camp. Far better is riding the elephant on a 2½-hour trek through the jungle to the Mae Sa Valley waterfall (reserve ahead—price is B300), where your driver-guide will meet you with the car. In the valley, lunch at the Mae Sa Valley Resort (tel. 053/251–1662) with well-appointed thatched cottages among beautiful landscaped and flower-filled gardens. Ask the owner for the honey-cooked chicken with chili.

Shopping

Always negotiate prices. Even if the shop lists prices, there is room for negotiation. Most of the shops honor major credit cards. A further discount for cash is often possible. One excursion you will surely want to make is along the 16-km (10-mi) stretch of road from Chiang Mai to San Kamphaeng. On both sides, large emporiums sell crafts and goods for which the region has particular expertise—silverware, ceramics, cottons and silks, wood carvings, hill tribes crafts and artifacts, lacquerware, bronzeware, and hand-painted umbrellas. Most of these emporiums include a factory workshop where you can watch the goods being made, an experience worth the trip whether you buy anything or not. Any taxi driver will happily spend a couple of hours taking you around for about B50 to B100, depending on the level of your intent to make purchases. If you make purchases, he receives a commission.

Markets One of Thailand's fullest and most exciting markets is the **Night Bazaar** in the center of town. On the sidewalk on the main street and inside the covered building is a congestion of stalls selling anything from intricately woven Burmese rugs to designer-label shirts made in Thailand. The clothing can be very inexpensive, and, at times, good quality. The "Dior" and "Lacoste" shirts can be excellent at a third of the price of their cousins in the West. Some objets d'art are instant antiques. If you are careful and inspect the goods thoroughly, this is a shopper's heaven for crafts made in the rural villages throughout Burma, Laos, and northern Thailand.

Specialty Stores **Borisooki Antiques** (15/2 Chiang Mai–San Kamphaeng Rd., tel. *Antiques* 053/351–777) has a reputation for expertise in Thai and Burmese antiques, though it is always recommended that you have some expertise yourself before you settle on a purchase. Borisooki also manufactures Ming Dynasty–style furniture.

Ceramics **Siam Celadon** (40 Moo 6, San Kamphaeng Rd., Km 10, tel. 053/ 331–526) has the largest collection of Thai Celadon. Celadon is a type of ceramicware modeled on the Sawankholoke pottery that was much in demand throughout Thailand hundreds of years ago. Its character comes from the mixture of Chiang Mai and Lumpang clays. The deep, cracked, glazed finish is achieved with a wood-ash formula developed a thousand years ago. Celadon tends to be expensive, but prices are better here than in Bangkok.

Handicrafts **Prempracha's Collection** (224 Chiang Mai–San Kamphaeng Rd., tel. 053/331–540). In a single 2,000-sq-m (21,600-sq-ft) complex next to Bo Sang (the umbrella village) is displayed an array of products from ceramics, instant antiques, batik, and

Thai silk, to wood carvings and bronze statues. Prices tend to be high here, though, and bargaining is discouraged.

Hilltribe and Handicraft Centre, Co, Ltd. (172 Moo 2, Bannong Khong, Chiang Mai-San Kamphaeng District, tel. 053/331-977). Handicrafts and fabrics from the six hill tribes (Meo, Yao, Lisu, Igo, Muser, and Karen) are on display. Goods range from dolls, dressed in multicolored traditional costumes, to elaborate half-moon necklaces and clothes made from natural hemp.

Pen's House (267/11 Chang Klarn Rd., Ampher Muang, tel. 053/252-917). To the side, somewhat artificially, are hill-tribe-style houses where craftsmen "perform" their craft. There are also musical instruments, including antique Karen elephant bells, which go for B30,000. Shoulder bags in traditional hill-tribe designs make especially good gifts.

Jewelry Chiang Mai is fast becoming Thailand's major jewelry center for trinkets, precious stones, and hill tribe ornaments. **PN Precious Stones** (Nai Thawan Arcade, opposite the Rincome Hotel, 95/6-7 Nimmanhemin Rd., tel. 053/222-395) has quality gems. For hill tribe jewelry and ornaments, visit the **Hill Tribe Products Promotion Centre** (21/17 Suthep Rd., near Wat Suan Dok, tel. 053/277-743, and a branch at 100/51-52 Huay Kaew Rd., opposite Chiang Mai University, tel. 053/212-978).

Lacquerware **Chiang Mai Laitong** (80/1 Moo 3, Chiang Mai–San Kamphaeng Rd., tel. 053/331-178). This shop offers a vast array of lacquerware, ranging from small boxes to tables, and is a good place to see what is available. The shop attendants explain the seven-step manufacturing process, and visitors can watch the artists at work.

Leather **BU Leather** (Boonkrong Leather Chiang Mai, 919 Chiang Mai–San Kamphaeng Rd., tel. 053/242-753). The offering here is a variety of bags (including Vuitton) and shoes made from a range of skins, particularly cow and elephant.

Silk and Cotton **San Kamphaeng** (toward the end of the Golden Mile) has the best Thai silk at good prices. **Shinawatra** (on the Golden Mile) has the most stylish silk clothing and fabrics. For cotton, the best merchandise is south of Chiang Mai at **Passang,** near Lamphun.

Jolie Femme (8/3 Chiang Mai–San Kampaeng Rd., 500 m beyond the superhighway intersection, tel. 053/247-222) has Thai silk garments designed in the United Kingdom or will custom-make clothes in 24 hours. **Anongpoin** (208-19 Thepae, tel. 053/236-654) has a wide selection of fabrics and handicrafts from the hill tribes. It is especially good for colorful cloth shoulder bags.

Silverwork The silverwork along the Golden Mile is delicate, using close to 100% pure silver (look for the marks certifying percentage). The silversmiths here are known for their bowls with intricate hammered designs depicting stories from the life of the Buddha or scenes from *Ramayana*.

Hill-tribe jewelry is chunky but attractive and can be bought at the villages (that of the Meos has the most variety) or at **Thai Tribal Crafts** (208 Bamrung Rd., tel. 053/233-493, closed Sun.), a nonprofit store run by church groups.

Umbrellas A fascinating traditional craft still continues at **Baw Sang** (off the Golden Mile). Here villagers make paper umbrellas, beginning by soaking mulberry wood and ending by hand-painting with colorful designs.

SA Paper and Umbrella Handicraft Centre (999/16 Ban Nongkhong, Chiang Mai–San Kamphaeng Rd., tel. 053/331–973). At one of the largest manufacturers of handmade paper, umbrellas, and fans, the selection is extensive—the hand-painted fans make an attractive gift.

Umbrella Making Centre (111/2 Basang, Chiang Mai, tel. 053/331–324). This manufacturer and retailer has some of the most colorful displays of hand-painted umbrellas and fans.

Wood Carvings　Modern carvings of all sorts abound, most of which are suitable for the woodpile. An inexpensive, but useful souvenir is a teak salad bowl. Some furniture stores on the Golden Mile have teak furniture carved in incredible detail with jungle and other scenes in deep relief. These *must* be seen. Some also have "antique" wood carvings of the Buddha, but religious carvings need an export certificate.

Dining

In all the top hotels, restaurants serve Continental and Thai cuisines. For Thai food, though, some of the best dining in Chiang Mai is in its restaurants. A new area with several good bistro-style restaurants, most of which serve northern Thai cuisine, is across from the Rincome Hotel on Nimanhaemin Road (off Huay Kaew Road), about 1½ km (1 mi) from downtown. The **Hong Tauw Inn** (tel. 053/215–027), for example, has excellent spicy dishes and is adjacent to a beer garden.

Arun Rai. This is one of Chiang Mai's best restaurants for northern Thai cuisine. Don't expect great ambience at this open-air garden restaurant; the focus is on the food. Try the *phak nam phrik* (fresh vegetables in pepper sauce), *tabong* (bamboo shoots boiled then fried in batter), *sai owa* (sausage filled with minced pork and herbs). The menu is available in English. The Arun Rai often has the delicacy *jing kung* (an insect much like a cricket) that you may want to try. *45 Kotchasarn Rd., tel. 053/236–947. No reservations. Dress: casual. No credit cards. Moderate.*

Baen Suan. This delightful restaurant is off the San Kamphaeng Road (the shopping/factory street) and a B40 tuk-tuk ride from downtown. The northern-style teak house sits in a peaceful garden, and the excellently prepared food is from the region. Try the hot Chiang Mai sausage (the recipe originally came from Burma), broccoli in oyster sauce, green curry with chicken, and a shrimp-and-vegetable soup. *51/3 San Kamphaeng Rd., tel. 053/242–116. Reservations suggested. Dress: casual. No credit cards. Moderate.*

Nung Nual. Though this large restaurant has tables indoors, it's pleasant to sit at a table on the terrace facing the Mae Nam Ping. Located 3 km (2 mi) south of Chiang Mai, you'll need a tuk-tuk or taxi to reach it, but the *kai tom khaa* (chicken soup with coconut milk) and the *yam nua* (beef salad) are worth the trip. Grilled charcoal steaks and fresh seafood (from display tanks) are also on the menu. *27/2 Ko Klang Rd., Nonghoy, tel. 053/241–274. Reservations accepted. Dress: casual but neat. AE, DC, MC, V. Moderate.*

Riverside. On the banks of the Mae Nam Ping, in a 100-year-old teak house, this restaurant serves primarily Western food given zest by the Thai chef. In the casual, conversation-laden atmosphere with lots of beer flowing, the food receives only partial attention. The choice tables are on the terrace over the river. Bands play light jazz or popular music after 7 PM. *9–11 Charoen Rat Rd., tel. 053/243–239. No reservations. Dress: casual. No credit cards. Moderate.*

Ta-Krite. This small, intimate restaurant opens onto the street and is patronized by local Thais. The service and ambience are casual. Cheerful blue tablecloths, wooden beams, and a veranda facing a garden set the tone for the food, which ranges from spicy hot to gently mild. Try the watercress sweet-and-sour soup and the crispy sweet rice noodles with shrimp and egg in a taro basket. For curry, choose the duck for its seasoned sauce, which is tasty without being too hot. *Off Samkarn Rd., tel. 053/ 216–333. No reservations. Dress: casual. No credit cards. Moderate.*

Whole Earth. On the road leading to the Chiang Plaza Hotel, this long-established restaurant serves delicious vegetarian and health foods. On the second floor of an old, attractive Thai house, the dining room takes full advantage of any breezes. *88 Sridonchai Rd., tel. 053/232–463. No reservations. Dress: informal. No credit cards. Moderate.*

Lodging

With Chiang Mai on every tourist's itinerary, hotels of every persuasion flourish, with new construction making possible many new choices. In high season, however, the better hotels are booked in advance, and some add a surcharge to room rates during January and February. Hotels cluster in four main Chiang Mai districts. The commercial area, between the railway station and the city walls, offers modern accommodations, but in a region that holds little interest for most tourists. The area between the river and the old city walls has the largest concentration of hotels and has the advantage of being close to most of the evening street activity. Within the old city walls are small hotels and guest houses offering inexpensive and simple accommodations, centrally located between markets and temple sites. The west side of town, near Doi Suthep, has attracted the posh hotels, which are quietest but also farthest from points of interest. A considerable amount of hotel and condominium construction is under way in Chiang Mai.

Expensive **Chiang Mai Orchid Hotel.** The change of management in 1989
★ has led to improvements in this leading hotel. The goal is to become the only four-star hotel in the northern capital. So far the new management has added new facilities and renovated the guest rooms. An additional 200 rooms are scheduled to be completed by the end of 1991. This is a grand hotel in the old style, with teak pillars in the lobby. Rooms are tastefully furnished and trimmed with wood. You can choose among the formal Continental restaurant, Le Pavillon, the new Japanese restaurant, or the informal Thai coffee shop, and find entertainment in the lobby bar or the cozy Opium Den. The suites include the Honeymoon Suite, which, we are told, is often used by the Crown Prince. The drawback is that the hotel is a 10-minute taxi ride from Chiang Mai center. *100–102 Huay Kaeo Rd., Chiang Mai 50000, tel. 053/222–099; Bangkok reservations, tel. 053/245– 3973. 267 rooms, including 7 suites, with a proposed addition of 200 rooms. Facilities: 3 restaurants, 2 bars, disco, business*

center, *Clark Hatch fitness center, sauna, outdoor pool with poolside bar, meeting room, beauty salon, drugstore, doctor on call 24 hours. AE, DC, MC, V.*

Dusit Inn. If you like to wander the streets and soak up the atmosphere, the Dusit Inn is well located. Step out of its front door and you are in the heart of Chiang Mai, just a few minutes' walk from the Night Bazaar. Formerly the Chiang Mai Palace, it has undergone two years of refurbishing. The rooms are considerably more attractive now, but their relatively small size and rectangular shape can be confining. The Garden Café serves Thai and Western fare, there is a pianist in the cocktail lounge, and the Jasmine restaurant has some of the best Cantonese food in town. *112 Chang Khan Rd., Chiang Mai 50000, tel. 053/251–033; Bangkok reservations, tel. 02/233–1130. 200 rooms. Facilities: 2 restaurants, small outdoor pool with poolside service, airport shuttle service, meeting room. AE, DC, MC, V.*

Mae Ping Hotel. This high-rise hotel opened in 1988. Its advantage is the newness of the rooms, decorated in ever-popular pastels. An executive club floor offers escape from the tour groups massing in the remainder of the hotel. The service staff could use more training. Two restaurants serve Thai and Western food and Italian specialties, respectively. *153 Sridonchai Rd., Changklana Muang, Chiang Mai 50000, tel. 053/270–160; Bangkok reservations, tel. 02/232–7712. 400 rooms. Facilities: 2 restaurants, outdoor pool with poolside bar, garden terrace, meeting rooms. AE, DC.*

Moderate   **Chiang Inn.** Behind the Night Market and the center of Chiang Mai, the Chiang Inn has offered well-kept guest rooms for the last 14 years. As the hotel is set back from the main street, the rooms are quiet (the higher the better). Appealingly decorated in light pastels with locally handwoven fabrics produced from homegrown cotton and dyed with purely natural herbs, the rooms are reasonably spacious. For dining, La Grillade serves Thai-influenced French cuisine in a formal atmosphere, or, more casual, the Ron Thong Coffee House serves Thai and Western dishes. The only problem is that the Chiang Inn is usually swamped with tour groups arriving and departing, and its facilities are geared to that kind of traffic. *100 Chang Khlan Rd., Chiang Mai 50000, tel. 053/235–655; Bangkok reservations, tel. 02/251–6883. 170 rooms, including 4 suites. Facilities: 2 restaurants, disco, outdoor pool with poolside service, meeting room, travel/tour desk. AE, DC, MC, V.*

Novitel Suriwongse. Located around the corner from the Dusit Inn and near the Night Bazaar, this hotel has recently undergone a refurbishment that brings it up to first-class standards. Its association with the French hotel chain attracts European tour groups, and the staff makes a game attempt to speak French using some English words and a Thai accent! The Suriwongse offers all tourist facilities, including a pickup point for the airport shuttle bus. The rooms, redecorated in pastels, are bright and cheery. Centrally located, the hotel compares favorably with the Dusit Inn. *110 Chang Khlan Rd., Chiang Mai 50000, tel. 053/236–733, Bangkok reservations, tel. 02/251–9883, U.S. reservations, tel. 800/221–4542. 170 rooms, including 4 suites. Facilities: restaurant, coffee shop, tour desk, airport shuttle bus stop. AE, DC, MC, V.*

Inexpensive   **Grand Apartments.** In the old city, this new building offers rooms by the day or by the month, making it a useful place for an extended stay at very reasonable rates (B4,000 per month). The rooms are efficient and clean, and guests have access to telex and fax machines. *Phra Pok Kico Rd., Chang Pluck Gate, Chiang Mai 50000, tel. 053/217–291. 36 rooms. Facilities: café for breakfast and snacks. MC, V.*

★ **River View Lodge.** Facing the Mae Nam Ping and within an easy 10-minute walk of the Night Bazaar, the hotel is tastefully furnished with Thai furniture and rust-colored clay floor tiles. The more expensive rooms have private balconies overlooking the river. The small restaurant is better for breakfast than for dinner, and the veranda patio is good for relaxing with a beer or afternoon tea. The owner speaks nearly fluent English and will assist in planning your explorations. Some seasoned travelers to Chiang Mai say this is the best place to stay in the city. Avoid making long-distance telephone calls from here if you can: The hotel surcharge is exorbitant. *25 Charoen Prathet Rd., Soi 2, Chiang Mai 50000, tel. 053/271–110. 36 rooms. Facilities: restaurant. AE, DC, MC, V.*

Budget **Galor Guest House.** On the Mae Ping riverfront, this guest
★ house has many advantages: its good location, within five minutes' walk of the Night Bazaar; friendly service from its staff; small but clean rooms with air-conditioning or fan; and a restaurant. Even though this hotel is in the budget category, it offers more charm and personal service than many of the other city hotels. It is also the best value in town. *7 Charcoplathat Rd., Chiang Mai 50000, tel. 053/232–885. Facilities: restaurant. No credit cards.*

Lai Thai. On the edge of the old city walls, and a 10-minute walk from the Night Bazaar, this friendly guest house offers rooms around a garden courtyard and a casual open-air restaurant that serves Thai, European, and Chinese food. The rooms are either air-conditioned or cooled by fan. Bare, polished floors and simple furniture give them a fresh, clean look. The rooms farthest back from the road have less traffic noise. *111/4–5 Kotchasarn Rd., Chiang Mai 50000, tel. 053/271–725. 80 rooms. Facilities: restaurant, laundry, tour/travel desk, motorbike rental. MC.*

The Arts and Nightlife

No first visit to Chiang Mai should be without a Khantoke dinner, which usually consists of sticky rice (molded into balls with your fingers for eating), delicious *kap moo* (spiced pork skin), a super spicy dip called *nam prink naw* with onions, cucumber, and chili, and *kang kai*—a chicken-and-vegetable curry. All this is to be washed down with Singha beer.

Often the Khantoke dinner includes performances of Thai and/ or hill-tribe dancing. One such "dinner theater" is at the back of the **Diamond Hotel** (tel. 053/234–155), which offers a commercial repertory of Thai dancing in a small, comfortable restaurant-theater setting. The other place for a Khantoke dinner and dance is at the **Old Chiang Mai Cultural Centre** (tel. 053/ 235–097), a complex of buildings just out of Chiang Mai designed as a hill tribe village. Both places charge B200 per person. The show at the Cultural Centre is the more elaborate and is authentic in its dance.

For more mundane evening entertainment, aside from the "love palaces," of which Chiang Mai has its share, there are several pub restaurants. The **Riverside** (*see* Dining, above) is one of the most popular, especially for its location next to the Mae Ping and the small bands that drop in to perform throughout the evening. For a casual evening, with a jazz trio, you may want to stop off at the European-style **Rikker Pub** (84/5–6 Sridonchai Rd., no phone).

At the **Black Cat Bar** (25 Moon Muang Rd., tel. 053/216–793) the pub atmosphere, chatty hostesses, and beer garden with a waterfall are all popular with the patrons, who come for hamburgers and beer. For those who want to visit each branch of the famous chain, there is a **Hard Rock Café** (6 Kotchasern Rd., Soi 1, near Thape Gate, tel. 053/216–432) in Chiang Mai. Described by *Newsweek* as "one of the world's best bars," **The Pub** (88 Huay Kaew Rd., tel. 053/211–550) can get a little crowded. Still, for draft beer, good grilled steak, and a congenial atmosphere, this place is hard to beat.

Excursions from Chiang Mai

To the south and west of Chiang Mai are Lamphun, Pa Sang, and Lam Pang. A trip to Lamphun, only 26 km (16 mi) from Chiang Mai, is an easy morning or afternoon excursion. Include Pa Sang, and the excursion will take the whole day. If you continue on to Lampang, 100 km (62 mi) southwest of Chiang Mai, you will probably want to stay in Lamphun overnight.

Lamphun

Lamphun claims to be the oldest existing city in Thailand (but so does Nakhon Pathom). Originally called Nakorn Hariphunchai, it was founded in AD 680 by the Chamdhevi dynasty, which ruled until 1932, when Thailand changed from a system of city rulers to provincial governors. Unlike Chiang Mai, which has experienced rapid growth over the past two decades, Lamphun remains a sleepy town. Its architectural prizes are two temple monasteries, Wat Phra That Hariphunchai and Wat Chama Devi.

Getting There
By Train Local trains running between Bangkok and Chiang Mai stop at Lamphun. Local trains are slow, however, and the Lamphun station is 3 km (2 mi) out of town. Bicycle samlors can take you into town for B30.

By Bus The easiest way to reach Lamphun from Chiang Mai is to take the minibus songthaew (fare is B10), which leaves about every 20 minutes from the new TAT office on Lamphun Road.

Getting Around Lamphun is a small town; all sights are within a B20 bicycle samlor ride.

Exploring Lamphun Located 2 km (1¼ mi) west of the town's center is **Wat Chama Devi**—often called Wat Kukut (topless chedi) because the gold at its top has been removed. You'll probably want a samlor to take you down the narrow residential street to the wat. Since it is not an area where samlors generally cruise, you may want to ask the driver to wait for you.

Despite the modern viharn to the side of the complex, the beauty of this monastery is in its weathered look. Suwan Chang Kot, to the right of the entrance, is the most famous of the monastery's two chedis. Built by King Mahantayot to hold the remains of his mother, the legendary Queen Chama Devi, the first ruler of Lamphun, the five-tier, sandstone chedi is square; on each of its four sides, and on each tier, are three Buddha images. The higher the level, the smaller the images. All are in the Dvaravati style—8th and 9th century—though many have obviously been restored over the centuries. The other chedi was probably built in the 10th century, though most of what we see today is the work of King Phaya Sapphasit in the 12th century.

The other major attraction, **Wat Phra That Hariphunchai,** is dazzling. Enter the monastery from the river, passing through a large coach park lined with stalls selling mementos. Once through the wat's gates, which are guarded by two ornamental lions, you'll encounter a traditional, three-tier, sloping-roof viharn. This is a replica (built in 1925) of the original, which burned to the ground in 1915. Inside, note the large Chiang Saen–style bronze image of Buddha, Phra Chao Thongtip, and the carved *thammas* (Buddhist universal principals) to the left of the altar.

Leave the viharn by walking to the right past what is reputedly the largest bronze gong in the world, cast in 1860. The 50-m (165-ft) Suwana chedi, covered in copper plates and topped by a golden spire, dates from 847. A century later, King Athitayarat, the 32nd ruler of Hariphunchai, raised its height and added more copper plating to honor the relics of Lord Buddha inside. On top of the chedi, he added a nine-tier umbrella, gilded with 6½ kilograms (14 pounds) of pure gold. The monk who brought the relics from Lamphun is remembered by a gold statue in a nearby chamber. He's also remembered for his potbelly—legend has it that he made himself obese so his youthful passion for women wouldn't prevent him from concentrating on Buddha's teachings.

At the back of the compound—which leads to a shortcut to the center of town—is another viharn with a standing Buddha, a *sala* (an assembly hall in a Buddhist monastery) housing four Buddha footprints, and the old museum. The new museum, just outside the compound, has a fine selection of Dvaravati stucco work and Lamma antiques. *Admission charge. Museum open Wed.–Sun. 8:30–4.*

Downtown Lamphun, a sleepy town where the locals are in bed by 10 PM, consists of a main street with stores, several food stalls, and not much else. For lunch or cold drinks, go back through Wat Hariphunchai to the main road along the Kwang River and choose any one of the string of cafés. Lamphun is also known for its lamyai fruit (a sweet cherry-sized fruit with a thin shell). (In the nearby village of Tongkam, a B10,000 lamyai tree nets its owner that sum in fruit every year.) Buy yourself a jar of lamyai honey; you'll be in for a treat.

Many visitors go to **Pa Sang,** 12 km (7½ mi) down Highway 106, for the cotton weaving. Songthaews (fare is B10) ply the route all day long. Once in town, you'll find one main street with numerous stores selling cotton goods produced locally. However, in recent years, the better stores have relocated to Chiang Mai, and the selection of goods is not as great as it once was. Most of the shops have clothing with traditional designs and good prices; a shirt with a batik pattern is about B100, while dresses run about B175. More contemporary clothing and household items may be found at **Nandakwang Laicum,** on the right-hand side of the street as you arrive from Lamphun. Five km (3 mi) south of Pa Sang on Highway 106 is **Phra Bhat,** commonly known as the Temple of Buddha's Footprint. While the energetic may mount the 152 steps to the chedi at the top of the hill for the view, the main attraction is the huge imprint of the Lord Buddha's footprint inside the temple that is located to the right of the car park. As you enter the temple, purchase a piece of gold leaf (B20), which you can paste in the imprint and make a wish.

On the return trip to Chiang Mai, about 20 km (12 mi) from Lamphun, is a small road off to the left marked by a Shell station on the corner. Down this road is **Wat Chedi Liem,** a five-tier wat built by King Mengrai in the 13th century and probably copied from Wat Chama Devi in Lamphun. Approximately 3 km (2 mi) past this monastery is the **McKean Leprosarium.** Occupying a small island in the Mae Nam Ping River, the institute was created in 1908 to treat sufferers of leprosy, and it has since become internationally recognized as a model of a self-contained community clinic. Don't worry about catching the disease—it requires multiple contacts with a leper to acquire leprosy. The community itself is inspiring: Some 200 patients have their own cottages on 160 secluded acres. In addition to the medical facilities, there are occupational therapy workshops, stores, and a church. A visit here is an ennobling experience. *Donations requested. Open weekdays 8–noon and 1–4, Sat. 8–noon.*

Lam Pang

During the reign of Rama VI, horses were imported from England to draw the carriages through the streets of Lam Pang. This charming image, combined with quaint streets, is still promoted by tourism officials. The 20th century has come to Lam Pang, however, and a superhighway connects it to Chiang Mai and Bangkok. Concrete houses and stores have replaced the wooden buildings, and cars and buses have taken over the streets, leaving only a few remaining horses. Today, Lam Pang is a busy metropolis, built on both sides of the Wang River. The confusion and congestion of its streets may deter you from spending the night here, but a few hours visiting the city's impressive temples makes for a pleasant stopover between Chiang Mai and Phitsanulok.

Getting There   Lam Pang is 100 km (62 mi) southeast of Chiang Mai and 602 km (373 mi) north of Bangkok.

By Plane   **Thai International Airways** has one morning flight between Bangkok and Lam Pang.

By Train   From Chiang Mai, the train takes approximately 2½ hours to reach Lam Pang. From Bangkok, it takes 11 hours, and from Phitsanulok, five hours.

By Bus   Both air-conditioned and nonair-conditioned buses connect Lam Pang to Thailand's northern and northwestern cities. Buses also travel directly to Bangkok's Northern Bus Terminal. The bus ride actually takes less time than the train. The bus station is 3 km (2 mi) out of town—take a samlor into the city—but you can book your ticket at the bus companies' offices in town.

Getting Around Horse-drawn carriages are available for tourists. The carriage rank is outside the government house, although some carriages are usually waiting for tourists at the train station. The price for a 15-minute tour of central Lam Pang is B30. The hourly rate is approximately B100. The easiest and least expensive way to get around, however, is by samlor.

Exploring Lam Pang Despite its rush into the 20th century, Lam Pang has some notable Burmese architecture remaining. Two particularly noteworthy wats are in the center of town; two others are to the north off Chiang Mai Road; and 20 km (12 mi) to the south is Wat Phra That, a particularly fine monastery built in the northern style.

Opposite the Thai International Airways office is **Wat Phra Fang,** easily recognizable by the green corrugated-iron roof on the viharn. The monastery's primary attraction is the tall white chedi, decorated with gold leaf, at the top. Surrounding the chedi are seven small chapels, one for each day of the week. Inside each chapel is a niche with images of the Lord Buddha.

The next stop is **Wat Sri Chum,** a well-preserved example of Burmese architecture. Pay particular attention to the viharn: The roof eaves have beautiful carvings, and its doors and windows have elaborate decorations. Inside, gold-and-black lacquered pillars support a carved-wood ceiling, and to the right is a bronze Buddha cast in the Burmese style. Red-and-gold panels on the walls depict country temple scenes.

To the north of town, on the right bank of the River Wang, is **Wat Phra Kaeo Don Tao.** The dominating visual element here is the tall chedi, built on a rectangular base and topped with a rounded spire. Two buildings of more interest, however, are the Burmese-style shrine and the adjacent Thai-style *sala* (assembly hall). The 18th-century shrine has a multitier roof rising to a point; inside are masterfully carved walls with colored-stone inlays, and an ornately engraved ceiling inlaid with enamel. The Thai sala next door has the traditional three-tier roof and carved-wood pediments, which house a Sukhothai-style reclining Buddha. Legend suggests that the sala was also home to the famous Emerald Buddha (Phra Keo). In 1436, King Sam Fang Kaem was transporting the statue from Chiang Rai to Chiang Mai; when his elephant reached Lam Pang, it refused to go any farther. The statue remained in Lam Pang for the next 32 years until the succeeding king managed to bring it into Chiang Mai.

Farther along the road toward Chiang Mai is **Wat Chedi Sao,** a charming, peaceful monastery named after its 20 small white chedis. It's only worth coming here if you are driving to Chiang Mai or you want a tranquil rural escape.

South of Lam Pang is **Wat Phra That Lampang Luang,** one of the most venerated temples in the north. You'll spot the chedi towering above the trees, but it is the viharn to the left that is most memorable. The carved-wood facade and two-tier roof complement the harmonious proportions of the structure. The intricate decorations around the porticoes are the painstaking work of Thai artisans. The temple compound was once part of a fortified city, which has long since disappeared. Originally founded in the 8th century by the legendary Princess Chama Dewi of Lopburi, the city was destroyed about 200 years ago when the Burmese occupied the city and monastery. Inside the temple museum are excellent wood carvings, but the most revered treasure is a small emerald Buddha, which some claim was carved from the same stone as its counterpart in Bangkok's Royal Palace. *Admission charge. Open 9–4, closed Mon.*

Shopping Lam Pang is known for its blue-and-white pottery. You'll find shops selling the pottery in the city center, or you can visit any of the 60 factories located throughout Lam Pang. A store with a good selection of ceramics is **Ku Ceramic** (167 Mu 6, Phahonyothin Rd., tel. 054/218–313). Generally, a samlor driver will be happy to take you to these factories for a few baht, hoping you'll give him a commission on what you buy. These goods are sold in Bangkok and Chiang Mai with hefty markups; so do your shopping here.

Lodging While Lam Pang has lost some of its quaint charm, the city's wats, shops, and few old-style Thai wooden houses are sufficiently pleasant that you may wish to spend the night. Hotels in Lam Pang are the best that you will find between Chiang Mai and Phitsanulok.

Thip Chang. This is the most comfortable hotel in Lam Pang; most rooms have two small double beds, a coffee table, and a couple of chairs. Rooms are kept clean, though the furnishings are basic. The hotel boasts the only swimming pool in town. A few of the staff members speak some English. The coffee shop stays open until 1 AM, and the restaurant serves respectable Thai and Chinese food. *54/22 Thakraw Noi Rd., Amphoe Muang, Lam Pang 52000, tel. 054/218–078. 120 rooms. Facilities: restaurant, coffee shop, bar, outdoor pool. AE, MC. Inexpensive.*

Phitsanulok and Sukhothai

For a brief span, Phitsanulok was the capital of Siam after the decline of Sukhothai and before the consolidation of the royal court at Ayutthaya in the 14th century. Further back in history, before the Kwae Noi River changed its course, Phitsanulok was a Khmer outpost called Song Kwae—now only an ancient monastery remains. The new Phitsanulok, which had to relocate 5 km (3 mi) from the old site, is a modern provincial administrative seat with few architectural blessings. Two outstanding attractions in Phitsanulok, however, merit a visit: Phra Buddha Chinnarat and the Pim Buranaket Folklore Museum. Phitsanulok is also the closest city with modern amenities and communications to Sukhothai—Siam's first royal capital—making the city a good base for exploring the region.

An hour from Phitsanulok by car, Sukhothai has a unique place in Thailand's history. Until the 13th century, most of Thailand consisted of many small vassal states under the suzerainty of the Khmer Empire in Angkor Wat. But the Khmers had overextended their resources, allowing the princes of two Thai states to combine forces against their overlords. In 1238, one of the two princes, Phor Khun Bang Klang Thao, marched on Sukhothai, defeated the Khmer garrison commander in an elephant duel, and captured the city. Installed as the new king of the region, he took the name Sri Indraditya, founding a dynasty that ruled Sukhothai for nearly 150 years. His youngest son became the third king of Sukhothai, Ram Khamhaeng, who ruled from 1279 to 1299 (or possibly until 1316). Through military and diplomatic victories, he expanded the kingdom to include most of present-day Thailand as well as the Malay peninsula.

The Sukhothai period was relatively brief—a series of only eight kings—but it witnessed lasting accomplishments. The Thais gained their independence, which has been maintained to the present day despite the empire building of Western powers. King Ram Khamhaeng formulated the Thai alphabet by adapting the Khmer script to suit the Thai tonal language. And, first under the patronage of Ram Khamhaeng and later under his successor, King Lö Thai, Theravada Buddhism was established and later became the dominant national religion. In addition, a distinctive Thai art tradition was established toward the end of the Sukhothai dynasty that was so impressive that the period has become known as Thailand's Golden Age of Art.

By the mid-14th century, Sukhothai's power and influence had waned, permitting its dynamic vassal state of Ayutthaya to become the capital of the Thai kingdom. Sukhothai was gradually abandoned to the jungle, and a new town of Sukhothai was founded 10 km (6 mi) away. In 1978, a 10-year restoration project costing more than $10 million saw the creation of the Sukhothai Historic Park.

Important Addresses and Numbers

Tourist Information
Phitsanulok

The **TAT office** has useful brochures, including one describing a walking tour. The office is also responsible for tourist information on Sukhothai. *209/7–8 Boromtrailokanat Rd., Amphoe Muang, Phitsanulok 65000, tel. 055/252–742. Open weekdays 9–4:30.*

Sukhothai

Sukhothai doesn't have a tourist information office. If you need information, try the **Chinawat Hotel** in the center of New Sukhothai (tel. 055/611–385). It has a travel and tour desk, and the staff members volunteer information about the area.

Emergencies
Phitsanulok

Phitsanulok doesn't have a Tourist Police office, but the local police (tel. 055/240–199) are helpful in an emergency. For medical attention, try the **Phitsanuwej Hospital** (Khun Piren Rd., tel. 055/252–762).

Sukhothai

There is no Tourist Police, but the local police (tel. 055/611–199) are accustomed to helping foreigners. For medical emergencies, contact the **Sukhothai Hospital** (tel. 055/611–782).

Arriving and Departing

Phitsanulok
By Plane

With three direct flights each day, **Thai Airways International** connects Phitsanulok with Bangkok and Chiang Mai. Taxis meet incoming flights.

By Train

Phitsanulok is about halfway between Bangkok and Chiang Mai. On the rapid express, it takes approximately six hours from either city. Some trains between Bangkok and Phitsanulok stop at Lopburi and Ayutthaya, enabling you to visit these two historical cities en route. A special express train between Bangkok and Phitsanulok takes just over five hours. Tickets for this service, which cost 50% more than those for regular second-class travel, may be purchased at a separate booth inside the Bangkok and Phitsanulok stations; reservations are essential.

By Bus   Buses run frequently to Phitsanulok from Chiang Mai, Bangkok, and Sukhothai. Bus service also connects Phitsanulok to eastern Thailand. Long-distance buses arrive and depart from the intercity bus terminal, 2 km (1¼ mi) northeast of town.

Sukhothai
By Plane   The closest airport and railway station to Sukhothai is at Phitsanulok, a 45-minute taxi ride or an hour's bus ride (B16) away. Taxis, which can be rented for the day for about B900, are available at the airport.

By Bus   Buses depart from Phitsanulok's intercity bus terminal, located on the northeast edge of town. The Sukhothai bus, however, makes a stop just before the Naresuan Bridge. These buses end their journey in New Sukhothai; you can take the minibus at the terminal to Old Sukhothai.

Buses also travel directly to Sukhothai from Chiang Mai's Arcade Bus Station (tel. 053/242–664); the trip takes five hours and costs B100. The bus trip from Bangkok's Northern Bus Terminal (tel. 02/279–4484) takes seven hours and costs B140.

Getting Around

Phitsanulok   Most sights in Phitsanulok are within walking distance, but bicycle samlors are easily available. Bargain hard for a proper fare—most rides should cost between B10 and B20. Taxis are available for longer trips; you'll find a few loitering around the station.

Sukhothai   Bicycle samlors are ideal for getting around New Sukhothai, but take either a taxi (B120) or a local bus (B5) to travel the 10 km (6 mi) from New Sukhothai to Old Sukhothai (Muang Kao) and the Historical Park. Buses depart from the local terminal, located 1 km (½ mi) on the other side of Prarong Bridge.

The best means of transportation around the Historical Park is a rented bicycle (B20 for the day). If you don't have much time, you can hire a taxi from New Sukhothai for B250 for a half day. The drivers know all the key sights. Within the Historical Park, a tourist tram takes visitors to the major attractions for B20.

Exploring Phitsanulok and Sukhothai

Phitsanulok   A major street runs from the railway station to the Kwae Noi River. The newer commercial and office area is found along this street and a little farther south, where the TAT office is located. North of this main street is the market and Phitsanulok's most treasured statue of the Lord Buddha. Phra Buddha Chinnarat sits in majesty at the Wat Phra Si Ratana temple, commonly known as **Wat Yai**.

Use a samlor to reach Wat Yai from the railway station or the major hotels, but pay no more than B15. The temple is close to the river, on the city side of Naresuan Bridge. Built in 1357, the temple has developed into a large monastery with typical Buddhist statuary and ornamentation. Particularly noteworthy are the viharn's wooden doors, inlaid with mother-of-pearl at the behest of King Boromkot in 1756. Behind the viharn is a 30-m (100-ft) *prang* (Khmer-style pagoda) that you can climb, though you cannot see the Buddha relics, supposedly resting in a vault.

All this is secondary, however, to what many claim is the world's most beautiful image of the Buddha, **Phra Buddha Chinnarat.** Cast during the late Sukhothai period in the position of subduing evil, the statue was covered in gold plate by King Eka Thossarot in 1631. According to folklore, the king applied the gold with his own hands. The statue's grace and humility have an overpowering serenity. The black backdrop, decorated with gilded angels and flowers, further increases its strength. It's no wonder that so many copies of this serene Buddha image have been made, the best known of which resides in Bangkok's Marble Temple. The many religious souvenir stands surrounding the *bot* (main chapel) make it hard to gain a good view of the building itself, but the bot has a fine example of the traditional three-tier roof, with low sweeping eaves. This design has the effect of diminishing the size of the walls, accentuating the nave, and emphasizing the image of the Lord Buddha. *Admission free. Open daily 8–6.*

From Wat Yai, walk south along the river past numerous tempting food stalls lining the bank, particularly in the evening. On the far side of the bank are many houseboats, still popular among the Thais, who have an affinity for rivers and fish. The Naresuan Bridge crosses the river, but some Thais still paddle from one bank to another in sampan ferries. Two blocks after the post office and communications building—from which you can make overseas calls—is a small park. Turn left and the railway station is straight ahead.

Wat Yai may hold Thailand's most sacred image of the Lord Buddha, but Phitsanulok also has an unheralded folk museum that alone justifies a visit to the city. The **Pim Buranaket Folklore Museum** is about a 15-minute walk south of the railway station, on the east side of the tracks. Since the museum is not well known, here are the directions: Turn left at the traffic circle 50 yards in front of the railway station; go down this street (there's a pleasant coffee shop on the right-hand side) and make another left onto the first main road, about 500 yards farther on; cross the railway tracks and turn right at the first traffic light. The museum will be on your right, about 1 km (½ mi) down the road, but there is no sign and seldom any attendant, either. If no one is around, continue for 50 yards to a private house on your left, where Khun Thawee lives. His compound also contains the Burananthai Buddha Image Factory. Ask at the house to visit the folk museum, and you will be let in. Eight years ago, Sergeant-Major Khun Thawee traveled to small Thai villages collecting traditional tools, cooking utensils, animal traps, and crafts that are rapidly disappearing. His consuming passion for the past is seen in the array of items he has crammed into a traditional Thai house and barn. Nothing has been properly documented, and so you stumble through a Thailand of tiger traps and cooking pots. Thawee is bashful; so encourage him to demonstrate the instruments. He loves to do so, especially the simple wood pipes used by hunters to lure their prey. *Donations requested. Open daily 9–5.*

Sukhothai *Numbers in the margin correspond to points of interest on the Old Sukhothai map.*

New Sukhothai, where all intercity buses arrive, is a small, quiet market town where most inhabitants are in bed by 11 AM. The new town has more restaurants and lodgings, however, than does the area near the Historical Park. None of the hotels are deluxe, so many tourists make Phitsanulok their base.

The old historical site of Sukhothai *(Sukhothai* means "the dawn of happiness") is vast—an area of 70 square km (27 sq mi) with 193 historic monuments, though many of these are little more than clusters of stones. Only about 20 monuments can be classified as noteworthy, of which six have particular importance.

❶ Most of the significant pieces of Sukhothai art are in Bangkok's National Museum, but the **Ramkhamhaeng National Museum** has a sufficient sampling to demonstrate the gentle beauty of this period. The display of historical artifacts helps visitors form an image of Thailand's first capital city, and a relief map gives an idea of its geographical layout. *Admission charge. Open Wed.–Sun. 9–noon and 1–4.*

The restaurant across the street from the museum is your last chance for refreshment until you reach the food stalls at the center of the Historical Park. It's a good idea to take a bottle of water with you into the park—cycling in the sun is hot work.

❷ For the modern Thai, Sukhothai represents the utopian state, in which man is free, land is plenty, and life is just. The magical and spiritual center of this utopia is **Wat Mahathat.** Sitting amid a tranquil lotus pond, Wat Mahathat is the largest and quite possibly the most beautiful monastery in Sukhothai. Enclosed in the compound are some 200 tightly packed chedis, each containing the funeral ashes of a nobleman. Towering above these minor chedis is a large central chedi, notable for its bulbous, lotus-bud prang. Around the chedi are friezes of 111 Buddhist disciples, hands raised in adoration, walking around the chedi's base. Though Wat Mahathat was probably built by Sukhothai's first king, Sri Indradita, it owes its present form to a 1345 remodeling by Sukhothai's fourth ruler, King Lö Thai. He erected the lotus-bulb chedi to house two important relics— the Hair Relic and the Neck Bone Relic—brought back from Ceylon by the monk Sisatta. Despite its Singhalese origins, the lotus-bulb chedi became the symbol of Sukhothai. Copies of it were made in the principal cities of its vassal states, signifying a magic circle emanating from Sukhothai, the spiritual and temporal center of the empire.

The image of Sukhothai's government is that of a monarchy that served the people, stressing social needs and justice. Slavery was abolished, and people were free to believe in their local religions, Hinduism and Buddhism (often simultaneously), and to pursue their trade without hindrance.

❸ In the 19th century, the famous stone inscription of King Ram Khamhaeng was found among the ruins of the **Royal Palace** across from Wat Mahathat. Sometimes referred to as Thailand's Declaration of Independence, the inscription's best-known quote reads: "This Muang Sukhothai is good. In the water there are fish, in the field there is rice. The ruler does not levy tax on the people who travel along the road together, leading their oxen on the way to trade and riding their horses on the way to sell. Whoever wants to trade in elephants, so trades. Whoever wants to trade in horses, so trades." No other political platform appeals to the Thais as much as this one.

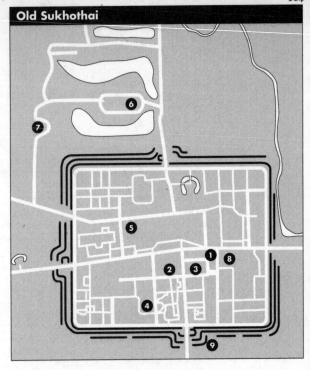

Old Sukhothai

4 Possibly the oldest structure of Sukhothai is **Wat Sri Sawai.** The architectural style is Khmer, with three prangs—similar to those found in Lopburi—surrounded by a laterite wall. (Laterite, made from red porous soil that hardens when exposed to air, is the building material used most in Sukhothai.) The many stucco images of Hindu and Buddhist scenes suggest that Sri Sawai was probably first a Hindu temple, later converted to a Buddhist monastery. Brahmanism probably played an important role throughout the Sukhothai period. Certainly, King Ram Khamhaeng would have used Brahman astrological advisers. And King Lö Thai tried to win back vassal states lost during the reign of his predecessor by having several statues of Vishnu and Brahma sculpted to appease the powerful Brahman faction in his kingdom.

5 Another one of Sukhothai's noteworthy attractions is the striking and peaceful **Wat Sra Sri,** which sits on two connected islands encircled by a lotus-filled lake; the rolling, verdant mountains beyond add to the monastery's serenity. The lake, called Traphong Trakuan Pond, supplied the monks with water and served as a boundary for the sacred area. In classical Sukhothai style, a Singhalese chedi dominates six smaller chedis. A large, stucco, seated Buddha looks down a row of columns, past the chedis, and over the lake to the horizon. Even more wondrous is a walking Buddha by the Singhalese-style chedi. The walking Buddha is a Sukhothai innovation and the most ephemeral of Thailand's artistic styles. The depiction of Buddha is often a reflection of political authority and is modeled after the ruler. Under the Khmers, authority was hierarchical, but the kings of Sukhothai represented the ideals of serenity, happiness, and justice. The walking Buddha is the epitome of Sukhothai's art: Lord Buddha appears to be floating on air, neither rooted on this earth nor placed on a pedestal above the reach of the common people. Later, after Ayutthaya had succeeded as the kingdom's capital, statues of Buddha took on a sternness that characterized the new dynasty.

6 Just beyond the northern city walls is **Wat Phra Phai Luang,** second in importance to Wat Mahathat. This former Khmer Hindu shrine was also converted into a Buddhist temple. Surrounded by a moat, the sanctuary is encircled by three prangs, similar to those at Wat Sri Sawai. Only one of the laterite prangs has remained intact, decorated with stucco figures. In front of the prangs are the remains of the viharn and a crumbling chedi with a seated Buddha on its pedestal. Fronting these structures is the *mondop* (square structure with a stepped pyramid roof, built to house religious relics), once decorated with standing Buddha images in four different poses. Most of these are now too damaged to be recognizable; only the reclining Buddha still has a definite form.

7 The **Wat Si Chum,** southwest of Wat Phra Phai Luang and 1½ km (1 mi) west of Wat Mahathat, is worth visiting for its sheer size. Like other sanctuaries, it was originally surrounded by a moat serving as a perimeter to the mondop. The main sanctuary is dominated by Buddha in the posture of subduing Mara. The huge stucco image is one of the largest in Thailand, measuring 11¼ m (37 ft) from knee to knee. Enter the mondop through the passage inside the left inner wall. Keep your eyes on the ceiling: More than 50 engraved slabs illustrate scenes from the *Jakata* (stories about the previous lives of Lord Buddha).

8 On the east side of the park, the most notable temple is **Wat Traphang Thong Lang.** The square mondop is the main sanctuary, the outer walls of which boast beautiful stucco figures in niches—some of Sukhothai's finest art. The north side depicts episodes of Buddha returning to preach to his wife; on the west side, Buddha is preaching to his father and relatives. Note the figures on the south wall, where the story of Buddha is accompanied by an angel descending from Tavatisma Heaven.

9 Also on the east side of the park is **Wat Chang Lom.** The Ceylonese-style bell-shaped chedi is raised on a square base atop now damaged elephant buttresses. A few of these elephant sculptures have been reconstructed to give visitors an idea of how impressive these supports looked. In front of the chedi is a viharn and solitary pillars; the remains of nine other chedis have been found within this complex.

Off the Beaten Track

With its expanse of mown lawns, Sukhothai Historical Park is sometimes criticized for being too well groomed—even the ruins are neatly arranged. **Si Satchanalai,** 57 km (35 mi) north of Sukhothai, offers a complete contrast. Si Satchanalai may be reached either as part of a tour from Sukhothai—Chinawat Hotel offers a day minibus tour—or by local bus. Si Satchanalai was a sister city to Sukhothai, usually governed by a son of Sukhothai's reigning monarch. The compactness of Si Satchanalai makes the ancient city easier to explore than Sukhothai, and its setting on the right bank of the Mae Yom River adds to the site's attraction.

Dining and Lodging

Neither Phitsanulok nor Sukhothai has smart restaurants, and so most travelers eat at their hotels. If you've grown accustomed to Thai food, however, you can choose from numerous cafés and food stalls in both towns. The food stalls around Naresuan Bridge in Phitsanulok are particularly tempting, and most items cost only a few baht. In New Sukhothai, across from the bus station, there are a number of good Thai restaurants. Sukhothai also has wonderful ice cream; the **Rainbow Cafe**, in particular, has delicious sundaes. For the best coffee in the province, visit the **Dream Coffee Shop** across from Sawat Phong Hotel on Singhawat Road. For formal meals, especially for Western food, the choice is limited to major hotels.

Phitsanulok has a wider range of hotels than Sukhothai. Most travelers staying in Sukhothai more than one night prefer New Sukhothai to Muang Kao (Old Sukhothai) because it offers more evening entertainment. In Si Satchanalai, accommodations are available only at bungalow-type guest houses.

Phitsanulok
★

Rajapruk Hotel. Of the two best hotels in town, this one is quieter and more refined, and has newer furnishings. The owner's wife is American, and many staff members speak a few English words. Guest rooms are decorated with wood and warm colors that accentuate the hotel's feeling of intimacy. The small restaurant off the lobby is good for dining and light meals; a formal restaurant serves Thai and Chinese food. The hotel's main drawback is its location, away from the town center on the east side of the railroad tracks. *99/9 Pha-Ong Dum Rd., Phitsanulok, tel. 055/258–477. For reservations in Bangkok, tel. 02/251–4612. 110 rooms. Facilities: coffee shop; restaurant serving Thai, Chinese, and Western food; outdoor pool; nightclub; beauty salon; car-rental desk. AE, DC, MC, V. Moderate.*

Amarin Nakhon. If a central location is a priority, this is Phitsanulok's best offering. The hotel is a bit dark and worn, but the staff members are helpful and the rooms are clean. Rooms have two queen-size beds, leaving little space for other furniture. The coffee shop stays busy 24 hours a day, serving late-night customers from the hotel's basement disco. U.S. Army personnel use this hotel during visits to the Thai military base on the outskirts of town. *3/1 Chao Phraya Rd., Phitsanulok, tel. 055/258–588. 130 rooms. Facilities: Chinese restaurant, coffee shop, disco. AE, DC, MC, V. Moderate.*

Hotel Phitsanulok. A commercial traveler's hotel next to the station, this hotel can only be recommended for its low price. The rooms are fan-cooled and clean, even though snakes have, on occasion, been found basking in the sunlight next to the bed. Quieter rooms face the inner courtyard. The large reception counter on the ground floor serves as a place to drink beer and watch television. *82 Naresuan Rd., Phitsanulok, tel. 055/258–425. 65 rooms. No credit cards. Inexpensive.*

Sukhothai

Rajhanee Hotel. Just across the Yom River from the center of the new town, this modern hotel is Sukhothai's best. Rooms have twin beds and are furnished in drab greens and browns. Everything is clean, however. The staff speaks a little English, and the bar serves as an evening gathering spot. The dining room offers superior Chinese and Thai food. Western food is served in the coffee shop. *229 Charodwithithong Rd., Amphoe Muang, Sukhothai 64000, tel. 055/611–031. 81 rooms. Facilities: restaurant, coffee shop, souvenir shop. MC, V. Moderate.*

Thai Village House. This compound of thatched bungalows is usually fully booked with tour groups. Consequently, the staff is impersonal and unhelpful. The hotel's advantage is its location—a five-minute bicycle ride from the Historical Park. Guest rooms have two queen-size beds and little else except for private bathrooms. The open-air dining room is pleasantly relaxing when tour groups aren't around. *2/4 Jarodvithitong Rd., Muang Kao, Sukhothai 64000, tel. 055/611–049. 45 rooms with bath. Facilities: restaurant, souvenir shops. MC, V. Moderate.*

Chinawat Hotel. Steps away from the private bus terminal in the center of the new town, this glorified guest house goes the extra mile to help travelers see the region. (Tours to Si Satchanalai are offered.) The restaurant area includes a bake shop and serves Thai food with Western additions. The rooms are Spartan, small, and rather depressing, except for the air-conditioned ones in the newer block; they are clean, however. *1–3 Nikorn Kasem Rd., Sukhothai, tel. 055/611–385. 43 rooms, a few with private bath. Facilities: dining room, tours arranged. No credit cards. Budget.*

No. 4 Guest House. In a small Thai home located down a narrow *soi* (lane) on the south side of the river, this guest house is run by a couple of friendly, helpful women. The wood floors and beams and the small garden add to the feeling that this could be your home away from home. No food is offered, but tea and coffee are always available. *234/6 Jarodwitheethong Rd. and Soi Panison, Sukhothai 64000, tel. 055/611–315. 14 rooms, a few with bath. No credit cards. Budget.*

6 The Golden Triangle

Introduction

by Nigel Fisher

The Golden Triangle (Sop Ruak in Thai), the area where Thailand, Laos, and Burma meet, has long captivated the Western imagination. The opium poppy grows here, and the hill tribes that cultivate it are semiautonomous, ruled more by warlords such as Khun Sa than by any national government. Today, the tribes of Laos and Burma retain their autonomy, but Thailand's Corner of the Golden Triangle has become a tourist attraction, with the tribes caught up in the tide of commercialism. Guest houses and sophisticated hotels accommodate travelers spilling out of crowded Chiang Mai, and well-worn tracks lead into the tribal villages. The opium trade still flourishes—a record yield was expected in 1990—flowing illegally into southern Thailand en route to the United States. For the tourist, however, the attractions are forested hills laced with rivers, the cultures of the hill tribes, and the cool weather.

Chiang Rai, 180 km (112 mi) northeast of Chiang Mai, is the closest city to the hill tribes and the Golden Triangle. A year ago Chiang Rai had only one luxury hotel; now, two additional resort complexes have opened and more are planned. A deluxe resort has even been built at the heart of the Golden Triangle, overlooking Laos and Burma.

Essential Information

Arriving and Departing

By Plane
Thai Airways International offers two direct flights into Chiang Rai from Bangkok (B1,420) and two from Chiang Mai (B230).

By Bus
Buses run throughout the day from Chiang Mai to Chiang Rai, departing from the Chiang Mai Arcade Bus Station (tel. 053/242–664). The express bus takes 2½ hours, while the local bus takes 3½ hours.

By Bus and Boat
The most exciting way to reach Chiang Rai is via a combination bus and boat trip. Passengers depart from Chiang Mai at 6:30 AM for a four-hour trip on a local bus to Tha Ton. An alternative to the bus is to hire a car and driver for about B1,200 and have him pick you up from your Chiang Mai hotel at 8 AM. In Tha Thon, take lunch at the restaurant opposite the landing stage. Long-tailed boats depart at 12:30 PM. Purchase your passage beforehand at the kiosk. These public boats hold 10 passengers, and the fare is B160 per person. You may hire your own personal boat for B1,600, something you will have to do if you arrive after 12:30 PM. The trip down the Mae Kok River to Chiang Rai takes five hours and passes through rapids and by a few hill-tribe villages. Bringing bottled water and a sun hat is recommended. The more adventurous visitors can travel to Chiang Rai by unmotorized raft. These raft trips are best taken during October and November, when the water flows quickly; participants stay overnight in small villages on the three-day journey.

Getting Around

Taxis and bicycle samlors are always available in Chiang Rai and in the surrounding small towns. Buses depart frequently for nearby towns (every 15 minutes to Chiang Saen or to Mae Dai, for example), or you can commission a taxi for the day.

Important Addresses and Numbers

Tourist Information The **Tourist Authority of Thailand** (TAT) in Chiang Mai handles the region, but Chiang Rai also has a small **Tourist Information Center** (Singhakhlai Rd., tel. 053/711–313). Information and a good local map are also available at the **Thai Airways International office** (tel. 053/711–464).

Emergencies The local police (tel. 053/711–444) provide assistance to visitors. For medical services, call either the **Chiang Rai Hospital** (tel. 053/711–300) or the **Over Brook Hospital** (tel. 053/711–366).

Guided Tours

The four major hotels in Chiang Rai (*see* Dining and Lodging, below) and the Golden Triangle Resort in Chiang Saen organize minibus tours of the area. Their travel desks will also arrange treks to the hill-tribe villages with a guide. Should you prefer to deal directly with a tour/travel agency, try *Golden Triangle Tours* (590 Phahotyothin Rd., Chiang Rai 57000, tel. 053/711–339).

Exploring Chiang Rai and the Golden Triangle

King Mengrai, who founded the Lammu kingdom, built his capital in Chiang Rai in 1256. According to legend, a runaway royal elephant stopped to rest on the banks of the Mae Kok River. Believing the elephant's actions to be auspicious, King Mengrai built his capital where the elephant stopped. In the 15th century, the area was overrun by the Burmese, and the Thais were unable to recover the region until 1786. Architecturally, little can be said for this city of two-story concrete buildings. Most of the city's famous old structures are gone: Wat Phra Keo once housed the Emerald Buddha that is now in Bangkok's Royal Palace, and a precious Theravada Buddha image in the 15th-century Wat Phra Singh has long since disappeared. Today, Chiang Rai is a market town that works during the day and is fast asleep by 10 PM. Chiang Rai's raison d'être is as a base for exploring. The Akha, Yao, Meo, Lisu, Lahu, and Karen tribes all live within Chiang Rai province. Each tribe has a different dialect, different customs, handicrafts, costumes, and a different way of venerating animist spirits. Only in the past two decades have the tribes been confronted with 20th-century internationalism and tourism. Now, the villages are learning to produce their handicrafts commercially for eager buyers in exchange for blue jeans and other commodities. Visits to these villages can be done as day trips or as two- to five-day treks to more remote villages. A guide is necessary for these treks. It's important to pick a guide who's familiar with the languages spoken in the villages and who knows which villages are least frequented by tourists. Question a guide thoroughly about his experience before you sign up.

Remarkable for its natural beauty and friendly inhabitants, the Golden Triangle is relatively easy to explore on your own. The following itinerary passes from Chiang Rai to Chiang Saen and up to the focal point of the Golden Triangle, Ban Sop Ruak. Then, following the Burmese border, the route continues to Mae Sai and back to Chiang Rai. You can travel either by hired taxi or public bus, though many people rent Jeeps or motorbikes.

An hour outside Chiang Rai, on the banks of the Mae Khong River, is **Chiang Saen.** Buses from Chiang Rai depart every 30 minutes, or you can take a taxi. Chiang Saen is only a small, one-street town, but in the 12th century, it was home to the future King Mengrai. Only fragments of the ancient ramparts destroyed by the Burmese who dominated northern Thailand after 1588 survived. The remainder was ravaged by fire in 1786, when the Thai army ousted the last Burmese intruders.

Only two ancient chedis are standing. Just outside the city walls is Chiang Saen's oldest chedi, **Wat Pa Sak.** Its name (*sak* means teak) reflects the fact that 300 teak trunks were used to build the structure. The stepped pyramid, which narrows to a spire, is said to enshrine holy relics brought here when the city was founded. Inside the city walls is an imposing octagonal 14th-century chedi, **Wat Luang.** Next door, the **National Museum** houses artifacts from the Lamma period (Chiang Saen style), as well as some archaeological finds dating to Neolithic times. The museum also has a good collection of carvings and traditional handicrafts from the hill tribes, and Burmese lacquerware. *Admission charge. Open Wed.–Sun. 9–4.*

Continuing past the museum, the road comes to the Mae Khong River. Turn right onto an unsurfaced road and drive 57 km (35 mi) to the town of **Chiang Khong.** Probably by 1992 the road will be paved, but to date, the trip can be extremely rugged and a four-wheel drive jeep is essential. Not too many tourists make the journey to these villages, and the tribes—Hmong and Yao—seem less affected by visitors. Across the river is the Laotian town of Ban Houie Sai, from which beautiful antique Lao textiles and silver jewelry are smuggled to Thailand. After a long period of border confrontation, Laos recently opened the country to Western tourists (with the appropriate visa), but they are only permitted to cross the Mae Khong at Nong Khai, opposite Vietiane. Only locals are permitted to cross over to Ban Houie Sai; they bring back tiger skins and deer antlers in exchange for salt, sugar, and soap.

A left turn at the *T* junction in Chiang Saen leads 8 km (5 mi) to **Bop Sop Ruak,** the village in the heart of the Golden Triangle where the opium warlord Khun Sa ruled. A decade ago, Thai troops forced him back to Burmese territory, but visitors still flock here to see this notorious region. Now the village street is lined with souvenir stalls to lure tourists from their buses. Worse yet, on a small island in the river, a casino is being built.

Some of the best views over the confluence of the Mae Ruak and Mae Khong rivers, and into the lush hills of Burma and Laos, are from the new **Golden Triangle Resort Hotel.** Even if you are not staying at the hotel, visit to check out the view. Another good viewing point is the pavilion along the path leading from behind the police station.

From Bop Sop Ruak, take a minibus—or your car or motor-bike— to **Mae Sai**, 60 km (37 mi) west along the Mae Ruak River (its name changes to the Mae Sai). The road is semipaved, dusty, and easy to travel. Mae Sai is a border market town where merchants trade goods with the Burmese from Tha Kee Lek village, on the other side of the river. Thais and Burmese are free to cross the bridge, but visitors are not. Thais take across household goods and consumer products, and the Burmese bring sandalwood, crafts, raw jade, and rubies. Prices here are better than those in Chiang Mai. A good store is **Mengrai Antique** (tel. 053/731–423), located close to the bridge. On the east side of Phaholyothim Road, opposite the Tourist Police, is the **Thong Tavee Jade** factory. If you are in Mae Sai during December or January, be sure to try the area's famous strawberries.

Time Out To the side of the bridge, the **River Side Restaurant** (tel. 053/731–207) has an open terrace above the Mae Sai that overlooks Burma. The Thai food is good, but you can also admire the view with just a Singha beer. Leave time to climb up to **Wat Phra That Doi**—the 207-step staircase starts from behind the Top North Hotel—for the best view of the Mae Sai River and Burma.

From Mae Sai, it is a two-hour local bus ride back to Chiang Rai (B14), or you can take an express, air-conditioned bus to Chiang Mai (via Chiang Rai) that takes about five hours. If you are traveling back by car or motorbike, drive 5 km (3 mi) from Mae Sai to the **Cheng Dao Cave Temple,** known for its Buddha carvings and monstrous stalactites. Farther up the dirt road is the **Monkey Temple,** where playful monkeys will snatch any-thing that sparkles with silver.

Back on the road toward Mae Chan and Chiang Mai, look for the right-hand turnoff for Highway 149, a steep, rough road that runs 17 km (11 mi) up to **Phra That Chedi** on Doi Tun, the high-est peak in northern Thailand. En route, stop at the Akha Guest House to inquire about road conditions up to Doi Tun. The drive is awe-inspiring; at the summit, mist cloaks monks chanting at the temple, which was built in 911. If you don't feel like driving, you can arrange in Ban Hui Kai (farther down the road toward Mae Chan) for a car to take you.

Dining and Lodging

For Western food, stick to the luxury hotels; countless small restaurants serve Thai food. The local staple is sticky rice, which you will inevitably eat if you stay in any of the hill-tribe villages. The luxury hotels are in Chiang Rai and in Chiang Saen (Bop Sop Ruak). Wang Thong, a 150-room, four-star hotel facing the river, is under construction at Mae Sai and is sched-uled to be completed in 1992. Elsewhere, accommodations are in guest houses, usually separate thatched bungalows consist-ing of a small room (most without bath) and an eating area. Lam Pang has no tourist hotels, though there are several Thai ho-tels.

Chiang Rai

Dusit Island Resort. Of the three luxury hotels that have recently opened in Chiang Rai, the Dusit Island has the most enviable location. Sitting on an island in the Kok river, which skirts the northern edge of town, the hotel offers guests quick access to town with all the space and amenities of a resort hotel. The 10-story building has three wings permitting all of the guest rooms to have a stunning view of the river. The spacious rooms are decorated in warm pastel colors, and the furniture is a modern rendition of traditional Thai. Bedside control panels, air-conditioning and television. The large bathrooms are marble tiled. The high-ceilinged and spacious lobby/lounge/reception area enhances the hotel's appeal. The formal dining room offers Western cuisine and a panoramic view; a chinese restaurant offers Cantonese food; and the Cattleya Garden, where a buffet breakfast is served, has Thai and Continental food throughout the day. *1129 Kraisorasit Rd., Amphur Muang, Chiang Rai 57000, tel. 053/715–777, fax 053/715–801. Bangkok reservations, tel. 02/238–4790. 271 rooms. Facilities: 3 restaurants, bar, nightclub, in-room safes, fitness center, pool, games room, shops, Avis car rentals, airport shuttle service, and banquet facilities. AE, DC, MC, V. Expensive.*

Little Duck Hotel. The first luxury resort in Chiang Rai, this hotel screams modernity. Guests, often salespeople on an incentive trip, mill around the huge lobby among the imitation marble pieces, far removed from the world outside. The rooms are bright and cheery, with light-wood fixtures and large beds. Service is brisk and smart, and the travel desk is ready to organize excursions into the neighboring hills. *450 Super Highway Rd., Amphoe, Muang, Chiang Rai 57000, tel. 053/715–620; fax 053/712–083. Bangkok reservations, tel. 02/255–5960. 350 rooms. Facilities: 2 restaurants, 24-hr coffee shop, outdoor pool, tennis, travel desk, meeting and banquet rooms. AE, DC, MC, V. Expensive.*

Rimkok Resort. Though this hotel opened in early 1991, work was still being done on its extensive grounds. Because of its location, across the Mae Kok river from Chiang Mai and a 10-minute drive from town, the hotel has more appeal for tour groups than for the independent traveler. The main building is designed in modern Thai style with palatial dimensions—a long wide lobby lined with boutiques leading to a spacious lounge and dining area. Guest rooms are in wings on both sides of the main building. Rooms have twin or double beds on one side, a table/desk on the other, and a picture window at the far end. *6 Moo 4 Chiang Rai Tathorn Rd., Rimkok Muang, Chiang Rai 57000, tel. 053/716–445, fax 053/715–859. Bangkok reservations: tel. 02/279–0102. 248 rooms. Facilities: 4 restaurants, bar, pool, shops, car rental, and banquet facilities. AE, DC, MC, V. Moderate–Expensive.*

Wiang Inn. In the heart of town, this comfortable, well-established hotel features a small outdoor pool, a pleasant sitting area, and a restaurant. Spacious bedrooms, now slightly worn, made this the top hotel in Chiang Rai until the two resort hotels opened; it is still the best hotel within the town itself. *893 Phaholyothin Rd., Chiang Rai 57000, tel. 053/711–877; fax 053/711–533. 260 rooms. Facilities: restaurant with Chinese, Thai, and Western food; outdoor pool; nightclub; health club; travel desk. AE, DC, V. Moderate–Expensive.*

Golden Triangle Inn. Don't confuse this hotel with the resort at

Ban Sop Ruak. This guest house is a backpackers' base for trips into the hills. Rooms have private bathrooms and are either air-conditioned or fan-cooled. The restaurant/lounge offers Thai and Western fare. The owners arrange trips to Chiang Klong, where they have another guest house. *590 Phaholyothin Rd., Chiang Rai 57000, tel. 053/711–339. 20 rooms. No credit cards. Budget.*

Chiang Saen

Baan Boran Hotel. The newest entry in the Golden Triangle is this distinctive resort hotel, located off the Mae Sai road two miles out of Chiang Saen. Situated on a hill, the hotel has panoramic views over the confluence of the Ruak and Mekong rivers and beyond into Laos. All the guest rooms share the view, and feature rust-red fabrics and carpet, a corner table/desk, a couch, a coffee table, and a picture window opening onto a balcony. Bedside panels control the television and lights. The central building houses the Yuan Lue Lao restaurant serving Thai and Western fare. For more serious dining, the Suan Fin offers elaborate Thai and European dishes. A lounge and cocktail bar are the evening meeting venues. *Chiang Saen, Chiang Rai 57150, tel. 053/716–678, fax 053/716–702. Bangkok reservations: tel. 02/251–4707. 106 rooms. Facilities: 3 restaurants, bar, in-room safes, pool, tour desk, car hire, airport shuttle, and banquet facilities. AE, DC, MC, V. Expensive.*

★ **Golden Triangle Resort Hotel.** The views of the forested hills across the rivers are splendid from this new resort, located on a rise at the outskirts of Bop Sop Ruak. The architecture is northern Thai, utilizing plenty of wood throughout its 66 rooms and seven suites. The superior (termed "executive") rooms have private balconies overlooking the Golden Triangle, third-floor rooms have the best view. (Another 130 rooms are planned for 1991.) The hotel also has an elegant dining room called the Border View, but it's more fun sitting out on the deck, sipping Mekong whiskey and imagining the intrigues in the villages across the border. Classical Thai dances are performed in the evening. *222 Golden Triangle, Chiang Saen, Chiang Rai, tel. 053/714–801. Bangkok reservations, tel. 02/512–0392, fax 02/ 512–0393. 74 rooms. Facilities: 2 restaurants, evening entertainment, outdoor pool, tennis, travel/tour desk. AE, DC, MC, V. Moderate–Expensive.*

Chiang Saen Guest House. One of several guest houses in Chaen Saen and Ban Sop Ruak, the Chiang Saen was among the first on the scene and is still a gathering point for travelers. Rooms are clean and simple, and guests can eat and socialize in the dining room. The owner is well informed on trips in the area and is always eager to help. *45 Tambon Wiang, Amphoe Chiang Sean, Chiang Rai 57150. No phone. 18 rooms. No credit cards. Budget.*

Mae Sai

Mae Sai Guest House. This is ranked by backpackers as the best guest house in Mae Sai. On the river, 1 km (½ mi) west of the bridge, the guest house offers clean bungalows and some river views. A small garden area surrounds the bungalows, and a casual dining area is located in the office building. *688 Wiengpangkam, Mae Sai, Chiang Rai, tel. 053/732–021. 20 cottages. No credit cards. Budget.*

Northern Guest House. When the Mae Sai Guest House is full, this is a good second choice. Located on the way back to town from the Mae Sai, the guest house offers small (there's just enough room for a bed) but clean rooms. A few cottages have their own shower and toilet. The veranda-style dining room is pleasant in the evenings, and the Mae Sai flows at the edge of the garden. The owner of the guest house is always eager to please. *402 Tumphajom Rd., Mae Sai, Chiang Rai, tel. 053/ 731–537. 26 cottages, a few with bath. Facilities: dining room. No credit cards. Budget.*

7 The Southern Beach Resorts

Phuket

by Nigel Fisher

Backpackers discovered the beauty of Phuket less than 20 years ago. The word got out about its long, white sandy beaches, cliff-sheltered coves, waterfalls, mountains, fishing and seafood, clear waters and excellent scuba diving, rainbow colors shimmering off the turquoise Andaman Sea, and fiery sunsets. Entrepreneurs were quick to see Phuket's potential. They built massive developments, at first clustering around Patong, and then spreading out to other tranquil bays and secluded havens. Most formerly idyllic deserted bays and secluded havens now have at least one hotel impinging on the beauty.

Phuket's popularity continues because, despite the tourist development and commercialism, the island is large enough (so far) to absorb the influx.

When to Go

Phuket has two seasons. During the monsoon season, from May until October, hotel prices are considerably lower. Though the rain may be intermittent during this time, the seas can make some of the beaches unsafe for swimming. The peak season is the dry period from November to April.

Important Addresses and Numbers

Tourist Information
The **TAT office** (73–75 Phuket Rd., Phuket Town, tel. 076/212–213), located near the bus terminal, has information on all Phuket hotels, as well as free maps. The TAT desk at the airport offers limited help.

Emergencies
Police (tel. 076/212–046); **ambulance** (tel. 076/212–297). **Tourist police** (tel. 076/212–115) are the best officials to seek in an emergency. They are located next to the TAT office.

Arriving and Departing by Plane

Thai Airways International has daily 70-minute flights from Bangkok and 30-minute flights from Hat Yai. The airline also has direct flights from Chiang Mai, from Penang (Malaysia), and from Singapore. **Bangkok Airways** now offers two flights daily between Bangkok and Phuket. A departure tax of B200 on international flights and B20 on domestic flights is charged.

Between the Airport and the Beaches/ Center City
Phuket's airport is at the northern end of the island. Phuket Town is 32 km (20 mi) to the south. Most of the hotels are on the west coast, south of the airport. Many send their own limousine minivans to meet arriving planes. These are not free, just convenient. For Phuket Town, take a Thai Airways minibus—buy the B75 ticket at the transportation counter in the terminal. Sporadically, songthaews run between the airport and Phuket Town for B20.

Arriving and Departing by Train and Bus

By Train
The closest station is on the mainland at Surat Thani, where trains connect to Bangkok and Singapore. A bus/coach service links Phuket with Surat Thani. Traveling time between Phuket and Bangkok is five hours on the bus and nine hours on the over-

night train (with sleeping bunks). The State Railway of Thailand, in conjunction with Songserm Travel, issues a combined train and bus ticket.

By Bus   Nonair-conditioned buses leave throughout the day from Bangkok Southern Bus Terminal. One air-conditioned bus leaves in the evening. Tour companies also run coach service. These are slightly more comfortable, and often the price of a one-way fare includes a meal. **Songserm** (121/7 Soi Chapermla, Phyathai Rd., Bangkok 10400, tel. 02/252–9654) is one such company. The bus trip from Bangkok to Phuket takes 13 to 14 hours.

Getting Around

By Taxi   Fares are, to a large extent, fixed between different destinations. If you plan to use taxis frequently, obtain a fare listing from the TAT office because drivers are not above charging more. A trip from Phuket Town to Patong Beach is B100 and to Promthep Cape is B120.

By Bus   Songthaews, the minibuses that seat six people, have no regular schedule, but all use Phuket Town as their terminal. Songthaews to the beaches leave from Rangong Road near the day market and Fountain Circle. They ply back and forth to most beaches, and a few make the trip to the airport. Should you want to travel from one beach to another along the western shore, you will probably have to go into Phuket Town first and change songthaew. Fares range from B10 to B40, depending on the length of the trip.

By Rental Car and Scooters   As Phuket has so many different types of beaches, your own transport offers the most convenience for exploring. Driving poses few hazards, except for the motor scooter—potholes and gravel can cause a spill, and some minor roads are not paved.

Many hotels have a car/Jeep/scooter rental desk, but their prices are 25%–40% higher than those in Phuket Town. Try the **Phuket Car Centre** (Takuapa Rd., Phuket Town, tel. 076/212–671). Prices for Jeeps start at B620 per day. Motor scooters range up from B150. The larger, 150-cc scooters are safer. Both **Avis** (tel. 076/311–358) and **Hertz** (tel. 076/311–162) have offices at the airport, as well as at some hotels.

Guided Tours

You may want to take advantage of a set tour to visit some of the attractions. These can be arranged through your hotel or by any travel agent and can be enjoyed privately or by joining a group.

Two reputable tour operators on the island are **New World Travel Service** (Hotel Phuket Merlin, tel. 076/212–866, ext. WTS) and **Songserm** (64/2 Ressada Rd., Phuket Town 83000, tel. 076/216–820), which, in addition to standard tour bookings, operates several cruise boats, air-conditioned buses to Bangkok, and minibuses to Surat Thani, Hat Yai, Penang, and Singapore.

Orientation Tour   A half-day Phuket sightseeing tour includes Wat Chalong, Rawai Beach, Phromtrep Cape, and Khao Rang.

Excursions   A full-day boat tour goes from Phuket to Phang Nga Bay on the mainland with visits to other islands. Another full-day tour visits the Phi Phi Islands for swimming and caving. The full-day

Ko Hav (Coral Island) tour features snorkeling and swimming. The nine islands of the Similan group offer some of the world's clearest waters and most spectacular marine life. Full-day cruises, costing B1,500, operated by Songserm (tel. 076/216–820), are often available. The luxury cruise ship *Andaman Princess* (Siam Cruise Co., 33/10–11 Chaiyod Arcade, Sukhumvit Soi 11, Sukhumvit Rd., Bangkok 10110, tel. 02/255–8950), operates two- and three-night cruises to the islands.

Special-Interest Tours A half-day tour features the Thai Cultural Village, for folk dances, Thai boxing, and Thai martial arts (Krabea-Krabong). The half-day Naga pearl tour visits cultured pearl farms on Naga Noi Island.

Exploring Phuket

Shaped like a teardrop pendant with many chips, Phuket is linked to the mainland by a causeway. The airport is at the northern end of the island. Phuket Town is in the southeast, and the best beaches are on the west coast. Typically, tourists go directly to their hotels on arrival and then make day trips to various other beaches. Hence, the exploring section below is less an itinerary than an overview of places to visit.

Numbers in the margin correspond to points of interest on the Phuket map.

Tour 1: Phuket Town

❶ About one-third of the island's population lives in **Phuket Town,** the provincial capital, but very few tourists stay here. The town bustles as the island's administrative and commercial center, though drab modern concrete buildings have replaced the old Malay-Colonial-influenced architecture. A few hours of browsing through the tourist shops are not wasted, however.

Most of the shops and cafés are along Phang-Nga Road and Rasda Road. By bus, you arrive in Phuket on the eastern end of Phang-Nga Road at the Phuket Bus Terminal.

Time Out Sidewalk tables in front of the **Thavorn Hotel** on Rasda Road provide a good place to do a little people-watching while sipping a cold beer.

East of the Thavorn Hotel, Phuket Road forks right off Rasda Road. On the left are the TAT office and the Tourist Police. In the opposite direction (west) along Rasda Road, crossing the traffic circle (Bangkok Circle), is Ranong Road. Here, on the left, is the **local market,** Phuket Town's busiest and most colorful spectacle—a riot of vegetables, spices, meats, sellers and buyers, and rich aromas. On the next block down Ranong Road is the Songthaew Terminal for minibus service to Patong, Kata, Kamala, Karon, Nai Harn, and Surin beaches. Songthaews for Rawai and Nai Harn beaches stop at Bangkok Circle. Diagonally across town from Phuket's market is the Provincial Town Hall, which was used as the French Embassy in the movie *The Killing Fields*. Perhaps the most relaxing way to see Phuket is

❷ from the top of **Khao Rang** (Rang Hill) in the northwest of the town. The elevation permits a view of both Phuket Town and the island's interior.

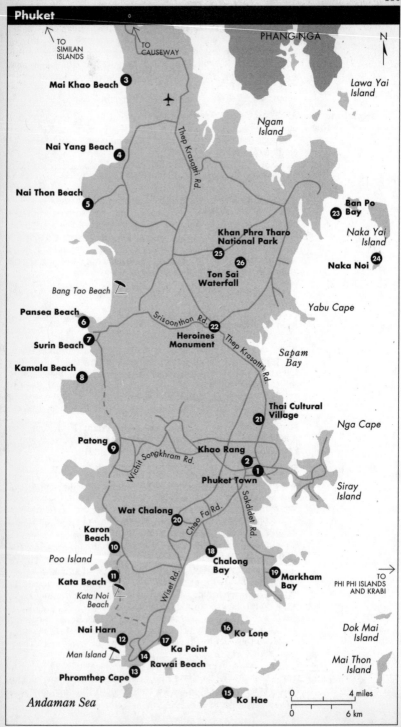

Phuket

TO
SIMILAN
ISLANDS

TO
CAUSEWAY

PHANG-NGA

N

*Lawa Yai
Island*

Mai Khao Beach **3**

*Ngam
Island*

Thep Krasattri Rd.

Nai Yang Beach **4**

Nai Thon Beach
5

**Ban Po
Bay**
23

*Naka Yai
Island*

Khan Phra Tharo
National Park
25   **26**

Naka Noi **24**

Ton Sai
Waterfall

Bang Tao Beach

Pansea Beach
6

Srisoonthon Rd.   **22**

Thep Krasattri Rd.

Yabu Cape

Surin Beach
7

Heroines
Monument

*Sapam
Bay*

Kamala Beach
8

Thai Cultural
Village

Nga Cape

21

Patong **9**

Wichit Songkhram Rd.

Khao Rang

2 **1**

Phuket Town

*Siray
Island*

Wat Chalong

20

Chao Fa Rd.

Sakdidet Rd.

TO
PHI PHI ISLANDS
AND KRABI

Karon
Beach
10

Poo Island

18

Wiset Rd.

Chalong
Bay

19 Markham
Bay

Kata Beach **11**

*Kata Noi
Beach*

16 Ko Lone

*Dok Mai
Island*

Nai Harn

12

17 Ka Point

14 Rawai Beach

13

Phromthep Cape

Man Island

*Mai Thon
Island*

Andaman Sea

15 Ko Hae

0   4 miles
0   6 km

Time Out While enjoying the view from Khao Rang, try the **Tunka Café** (tel. 076/311–5000), which serves good Thai food for lunch and dinner.

But don't come to Phuket Island for its town. It is an island of beaches, sand cliffs, and hypnotic colors of the Andaman Sea. These are the places to explore.

Tour 2: The Beaches

❸ Starting from the north and working down the west coast, the first beach is **Mai Khao Beach,** just 5 km (3 mi) from the airport. This beach is the island's largest, often ignored by Western tourists because at low tide it turns slightly muddy, and its steep drop-off makes it unpopular with swimmers. The absence of farangs attracts the Thais, who appreciate the peacefulness of the beach. Giant sea turtles like it, too. They come between November and February to lay their eggs.

❹ **Nai Yang Beach** is really a continuation of Mai Khao—making a 10-km (6-mi) stretch of sand. It curves like a half-moon, with casuarina trees lining the shore. It is also popular with Thais, and now a new resort, Pearl Village, has opened here.

❺ Tucked in the center of a headland is **Nai Thon Beach.** Its rough waters keep swimmers away, and the village remains a peaceful fishing port. South of the headland, the shore curves in to form **Bang Tao Beach,** which, with the exception of the posh new Dusit Laguna Hotel, has been left undisturbed.

❻ ❼ Next in line are **Pansea Beach** and **Surin Beach,** with the island's most elegant resort, Amanpuri. Tucked in a small cove with a complete feeling of privacy, the hotel blends into the cliffside. Surin Beach, despite a long stretch of golden sand, is not good for swimming because of strong currents. On the headland south of Surin are several small intimate and romantic coves. Each requires a climb down a cliff. Surrounded by palms and rocks, the tiny beach is, with luck, your personal haven.

❽ After the headland is **Kamala Beach,** a small curving strip of sand with coconut palms and a few bungalows rented by Krathomtip Cottages. Unfortunately, a new Sheraton Hotel has been built here. A small dirt road leads on from Kamala Beach to Patong—passable, but very tricky and not advised if it's your first time on a motor scooter. If you don't use this dirt road, drive inland to join the main road before turning west again for Patong.

❾ **Patong** is Phuket's mini-Pattaya, complete with German restaurants, massage parlors, hustlers selling trinkets, or places like Tatum's, a combined coffeehouse, disco, and go-go dance floor. The abundance of hotels, ranging from deluxe to small cottages, attests to Patong's popularity among the charter groups flying into Phuket. Most tourists seek it out for at least one night's revelry, and the long, white sandy beach still justifiably attracts swimmers to its safe waters.

Time Out In the evening, check out **Doolie's Place** (82/51 Soi Bangla, Patong, tel. 076/321–275), where an American proprietor serves steaks, hamburgers, barbecued chicken, and pizza. For entertainment, the restaurant's garden is a minizoo, with monkeys in the majority.

⑩ Beyond Patong is **Karon Beach,** which is divided into two areas. Karon Noi is a small bay surrounded by verdant hills. It is truly beautiful, but virtually taken over by Le Meridien Hotel. Occasionally, cruise ships anchor offshore from this beach, doubling the crowds. Because of its good swimming and surfing, the other part of Karon, Karon Yai, is becoming increasingly popular, and several hotels and a minitown have sprung up to join the first of the luxury hotels.

⑪ **Kata Beach** is the next beach south, 17 km (10.2 mi) due west of Phuket Town. The sunsets are as marvelous as ever, but the peace and quiet are fading fast. Club Meditérranée has moved in, but there are still stretches of sand with privacy, and the center of town has only a modest number of bars. Nearby is **Kata Noi Beach** (*noi* means small) in the shelter of a forest-clad hill. A few inexpensive bungalows share the quiet beach with the Kata Thani Hotel that's popular with tour groups.

The road beyond Kata cuts inland across the hilly headland to
⑫ drop into yet another gloriously beautiful bay, **Nai Harn.** Protected by Man Island, the deep-water bay has been a popular anchorage for international yachtsmen. On the north side, a huge, white stucco, stepped building, the Phuket Island Yacht Club, rises from the beach in stark contrast to the verdant hillside. From the Yacht Club's terrace, the view of the sun, dropping into the Andaman Sea behind Man Island, is superb. The beach is good for sunning and swimming in the dry season, but beware of the steep drop-off.

From Nai Harn, the road swings around to climb up to
⑬ **Phromthep Cape.** Its panorama includes Nai Harn Bay, the island's coastline, and the far-off horizon of the Andaman Sea. At sunset, the view is supreme. This evening pilgrimage has become so popular that policemen organize parking, and a row of souvenir stands lines the parking lot. But, once away from this congestion, you can find space enough to enjoy the colors of the setting sun in contemplative solitude.

⑭ Down from Phromthep is **Rawai Beach.** The shallow, muddy beach is not so attractive, but the shoreline, with a small fishing village set in a coconut grove, has the charm you may have expected in all of Phuket.

⑮ Cruise boats leave Rawai for **Ko Hae** (Coral Island), 30 minutes
⑯ from shore. Slightly farther out is **Ko Lone.** Both are choice islands for snorkeling and sunbathing. Ko Hae has a couple of cafés and receives more visitors than Ko Lone. *Boat fare: B750.*

At the southern end of Rawai Beach is a small gypsy village. The inhabitants are descendants of the original tribes living on Phuket. Called Chao Nam (Water People) by the Thais, they tend to shy away from the modern world, preferring to stay among their own. They are superb swimmers, able to fish at 27-m (90-ft) depths in free dives. One of the three tribes of the Chao Nam is believed to have been the sea gypsies who pirated 17th-century trading ships entering the Burmese-Singapore waters. Though there are two other Chao Nam villages on Phuket, the one at Rawai Beach is the easiest to visit.

⑰ South of Rawai is **Ka Point,** where most of the promontory is owned by the huge Phuket Island Resort, virtually a small township, with several restaurants, two swimming pools, and a minibus to take guests from one facility to another. Along the
⑱ southern coast is **Chalong Bay,** with several good inexpensive outdoor seafood restaurants—try Kanning II for delicious crabs and prawns. To the southeast of Chalong Bay is the pen-
⑲ insula with **Markham Bay,** the place to catch the ferry boat to the Phi Phi Islands and Krabi.

Tour 3: Inland and Pearl Island

Turning inland from Chalong Bay, rather than take the main
⑳ road to Phuket Town, take the road at the traffic circle to **Wat Chalong.** Phuket has 20 Buddhist temples—all built since the 19th century—but Wat Chalong is the largest and most famous. It enshrines the gilt statues, wrapped in saffron robes, of two revered monks who helped quell an 1876 rebellion by Chinese immigrants.

㉑ North of Phuket Town, toward the airport, is the **Thai Cultural Village.** In a 500-seat amphitheater, it presents various aspects of southern Thai culture, including classical Thai dance, shadow puppets, exhibition Thai boxing, sword fighting, an "elephants-at-work" show, and more. *Admission charge. Show times: 10:15, 11, 4:45, 5:30.*

Farther north on the airport road, you'll notice a statue of two women; they rallied the Thais in 1785 to ward off a siege by the Burmese, who had sacked Ayutthaya four years earlier. A
㉒ right turn (east) at this crossroads of the **"Heroines Monu-**
㉓ **ment"** leads to **Ban Po Bay,** where you can take a 20-minute
㉔ boat ride over to **Naka Noi,** the Pearl Island. A small restaurant offers refreshment after you tour the facilities. The tour demonstrates how pearls are formed by placing an irritant inside an oyster—the same method perfected by the Japanese.

㉕ Turning inland from Ban Po, the road traverses **Khan Phra Tharo National Park,** the last remaining virgin forest on Phu-
㉖ ket. You may want to stop at **Ton Sai Waterfall,** a few minutes off the road. It's a popular picnic spot all year, but the falls are best during the rainy season.

After a few miles, the road joins the main island road, with the airport 10 km (6 mi) to the north, and Phuket Town 22 km (14 mi) to the south.

Dining

Restaurants abound on Phuket and serve all types of cuisines, including versions of Western cooking. Fresh seafood is the specialty.

Expensive **Amanpuri.** The dining room here is beautiful, with a thatched Thai roof and modern bamboo furniture. The once-French cuisine is now really more Continental with a definite Italian accent, though the good use of the local produce, especially the seafood, plus the idyllic setting, still makes a meal here a treat. Try the fresh fish on a bed of vegetables topped with a sauce sparked with fresh ginger and lemongrass. If you aren't staying at the hotel, make a special effort to visit even if only for a drink at this split-level Thai building perched above the beach with spectacular sea views. *Pansea Beach, Phuket, tel. 076/311–394. Reservations advised. Dress: casual but neat. AE, DC, V. Open 11:30–2 and 6–10.*

Phuket Yacht Club. Though the exterior of this hotel may be an eyesore, the main restaurant, the Chart Room, is lovely. With one side completely open, the restaurant has a panoramic view of the bay and islands. The menu now has the choice of European and Thai dishes with an emphasis on seafood, though steaks are available. Try the baked fresh fish stuffed with prawns in a tasty mixture of Thai spices. For entertainment, classical Thai dancers perform. *Nai Harn Beach, Phuket, tel. 076/214–020. Reservations advised. Dress: casual but neat. AE, DC, V.*

Moderate **Coral Beach Hotel.** Perched on a bluff overlooking the Andaman Sea and the beach at Patong, the Chao Lay open-front restaurant is in an ideal location to enjoy fantastic views and Thai cooking. Dishes include *tom kha gai* (slightly spicy chicken soup made with coconut milk), *mae krob* (Thai noodles), spring rolls, and grilled seafood. Should you prefer Italian fare, the hotel has recently opened La Gritta, one floor down from the Chao Lay, also with spectacular views. *104 Moo 4, Patong Beach, tel. 076/321–106. Reservations advised. Dress: casual but neat. AE, DC, MC, V.*

Kan Eang. Some of the best seafood in town is served at this beachside restaurant in Chalong Bay. The cooking is Thai, perhaps a little too bland in order to accommodate Western taste, but the fish is fresh and the spices Thai. Choose a mild evening to eat outdoors under the coconut palms and indulge in the crabs. *9/3 Chaofa Rd., Chalong Bay, Phuket, tel. 076/216–288. No reservations. Dress: casual. AE, V.*

Mallee's Seafood Village. An international array of cuisines is offered at this restaurant in the center of Patong. Two Thai dishes worth trying are the charcoal-grilled fish in banana leaves and the steamed fish in a tamarind sauce. If you want Chinese food, try the shark steak in a green-pepper sauce; for European fare, consider the veal sausage with potato salad. On the other hand, you may simply want to sit at one of the sidewalk tables and indulge in pancakes with honey. *94/4 Taweewong Rd., Patong, tel. 076/321–205. No reservations. Dress: casual. AE, DC, MC, V.*

Lodging

Phuket has accommodations of every variety in virtually all of its main beach areas. You can choose from the most elegant resorts, such as Amanpuri, to modest, thatch-roof bungalows that are a fraction of the price. In all, approximately 100 hotels or cottages offer various levels of hospitality. Hotel tariffs fluctuate widely, depending on high and low season, weekend or weekday, and holiday periods, when they can more than double.

Very Expensive **Amanpuri.** For relaxation amid tasteful and elegant surround-
★ ings, there is no finer place in Thailand—nor is any place quite as expensive. The main building is completely open, with polished floors, modern bamboo furniture and pitched, thatch roofs. Individual pavilions, staggered up the hillside back from the beach, house guests. The architectural style is distinctly Thai, adapted with flair to accommodate modern creature comforts and to maximize cooling breezes from the sea. Furnishings are handcrafted with local woods, and each suite has its

private sun deck. A split-level bar perches on the hill, affording a romantic view of the sun setting into the Andaman Sea. Meals are prepared by an enthusiastic French chef, whose culinary delights will tempt you to return again and again. The swimming pool is up from the beach, and the beach itself is secluded and private. Should you wish even more privacy, arrangements may be made for an overnight stay on one of the uninhabited islands. Guests are greeted and cared for individually by personally assigned staff. *Pansea Beach, Phuket 83110, tel. 076/311–394; Bangkok reservations, tel. 02/250–0746. 40 guest cottages. Facilities: 2 restaurants, bar, outdoor pool, 2 tennis courts, water sports, custom tours arranged, gift shop, and drugstore. AE, V.*

★ **Phuket Yacht Club.** Set in an extremely picturesque westward-facing bay, this stepped, modern luxury hotel looks like an ambitious condominium complex. The architectural inappropriateness aside, its comfort, service, amenities, and secluded location make the Phuket Yacht Club extremely pleasant. Whether you stay here or not, make a point of dining in the open-sided restaurant that overlooks the bay. Furnishings in the guest rooms are modern and stylish, but, like the exterior, lack any identification with the environment. Guest rooms are large and have separate sitting areas and private balconies overlooking the beach and the small offshore islands. *Nai Harn Beach, Phuket 83130, tel. 076/214–020; Bangkok reservations, 02/251–4707. 108 rooms, including 8 suites. Facilities: 2 restaurants, outdoor pool and poolside bar, 2 tennis courts, fitness center, water sports arranged, and tour desk. AE, DC, MC, V.*

Expensive **Boathouse Inn & Restaurant.** With all 33 rooms looking on to Kata Beach, an excellent Thai restaurant facing the Andaman Sea, and a relaxing beach bar, this small hotel is a very comfortable retreat. The Thai-style architecture adds a traditional touch to the otherwise modern amenities, such as bedside control panels and a Jacuzzi pool. Guest rooms are furnished in reds and browns and have individually controlled air-conditioning, private safes, and bathrooms with bath and a massage shower. *Kata Beach, Phuket 83100, tel. 076/381–557, Bangkok reservations: tel. 02/253–9168. 33 rooms. Facilities: restaurant, bar, beauty salon, tour desk. AE, DC, MC, V.*

Diamond Cliff Hotel. North of town, away from the crowds, this is one of the smartest and architecturally most pleasing resorts in Patong. The beach across the road has mammoth rocks that create the feeling of several private beaches. The swimming pool is built on a ledge above the main part of the hotel, providing an unobstructed view of the coast and the Andaman Sea. Rooms are spacious, full of light, and decorated in pale colors to accentuate the open feel of the hotel. Dining is taken seriously, with the fresh seafood cooked in European or Thai style. Guests may dine indoors or on the restaurant's terrace looking out to sea. *61/9 Kalim Beach, Patong, Kathu District, Phuket 83121, tel. 076/321–501; Bangkok reservations, tel. 02/246–4515. 140 rooms. Facilities: restaurant, cocktail/tea lounge, outdoor pool, pool bar, water sports arranged, tour desk, and pharmacy. AE, MC, V.*

Dusit Laguna. Facing a mile-long beach and flanked by two lagoons, this resort hotel is off by itself on the northwestern part of the island, on beautiful Bang Thao Bay. The rooms, with picture windows opening onto private balconies, have modern pastel decor and commodious bathrooms. The hotel is popular with upmarket Thais seeking refuge from the more commercial areas of Patong. It offers barbecue dining on the terrace, and after dinner, dancing to the sounds of the latest discs. European fare is served at the Junkcelyon; Thai cuisine, to the tune of traditional Thai music, is served in the Ruen Thai restaurant. Business groups also come here to mix work and pleasure. *390 Srisoontorn Rd., Cherngtalay District, Amphur Talang, Phuket 83110, tel. 076/311–320; Bangkok reservations, tel. 02/236–0450. 240 rooms, including 7 suites. Facilities: 4 restaurants, outdoor pool, 2 tennis courts, water sports, putting green, tour desk, meeting rooms. AE, DC, MC, V.*

Moderate **Phuket Cabana.** This hotel's attraction is its location, in the middle of Patong, fronting 300 m (1,000 ft) of beach. Laid-back and casual describe guests as well as staff, but the basic resort amenities are here, with a good tour desk and a reputable dive shop to arrange outings. Modest rooms are in chalet-type bungalows furnished with rattan tables and chairs. The restaurant serves a hybrid Western-Thai cuisine. *94 Taveewong Rd., Patong Beach, Phuket 83121, tel. 076/321–138; Bangkok reservations, tel. 02/278–2239. 80 rooms. Facilities: restaurant, outdoor pool, airport bus, tour desk, dive shop. AE, MC, V.*

Budget **Friendship Bungalows.** In Kata, a four-minute walk from the
★   beach, two rows of single-story buildings house modest, sparsely furnished, but spotlessly clean rooms, each with its own bathroom (there is usually hot water). The owners are extremely hospitable and encourage guests to feel at home. The small restaurant/bar on a terrace offers good Thai food; Western food is also available. What you leave will probably be enjoyed by the two monkeys on the restaurant's wall that play throughout the day. *6/5 Patak Rd., Kata Beach, Phuket 83130, no phone. 30 rooms. Facilities: restaurant. No credit cards.*

Excursions from Phuket

The two best excursions from Phuket are to the Similan Islands, where you can view some of the world's most interesting marine life, and Phang Nga Bay, where the weird and fascinating shapes of tiny islets rise vertically from the sea. Both of these excursions may be taken as organized boat trips arranged through your hotel's travel desk or directly through a tour operator (*see* Getting There, below).

The Similan Islands

The Similan Islands are renowned for snorkeling and diving. No hotels are permitted on the islands, though there are camping facilities. The most comfortable way to visit the islands and to enjoy the marine life is to take a cruise boat with sleeping cabin. Phang Nga Bay may be reached by day-long boat trips from Phuket or by road and then hiring a boat. The former is recommended unless you embark on the following excursion that makes a loop via Ko Phi Phi and Krabi to return to Phuket via Phang Nga Bay.

Ko Phi Phi

The Phi Phi islands are idyllic retreats, with secret silver-sand coves, unspoiled beaches, and limestone cliffs that drop precipitously into the sea. Ten years ago, one could sling a hammock between two coconut trees and spend the night under the stars for B10. Now, tourists come over from Phuket to escape its commercialism only to bring that very commercialism to Phi Phi. Several comfortable air-conditioned hotels have been built, and a number of more modest bungalow accommodations are available for the budget traveler. In some ways, Phi Phi has become the poor man's Phuket.

Tourist Information — There is no TAT office in Phi Phi, although a dozen or more travel/tour shops can help plan trips and excursions.

Getting There — From Phuket, boats leave Markham Bay at approximately 8:30 AM and 2:30 PM. The cost is B250 for the two-hour journey. **Songserm Travel Agency** (64/2 Rasada Rd., Phuket Town, tel. 076/216–820) is the best company to use. Two boats also make the daily trip from Krabi. Phi Phi is 48 km (29 mi) from Phuket Town and 42 km (25 mi) from Krabi.

Exploring Ko Phi Phi — Ko Phi Phi consists of two main islands, Phi Phi Don and Phi Phi Lae; only Don is inhabited. Shaped like a butterfly, Phi Phi Don has two hilly land portions linked by a wide sandbar, 2 km (1¼ mi) long. Except for two moderately priced deluxe hotels, all accommodations and the main mall with its shops and restaurants are on this sandbar; no vehicles are allowed on the island. On either side of the sandbar are two bays, Ton Sai and Lohdalum. Boats come into Ton Sai.

The most popular way to explore the islands is by boat, either a cruise boat or on a long-tailed boat that seats up to six people. One of the most visually exciting trips is to Phi Phi Lae. The first stop along the way is **Viking Cave,** a vast cavern of limestone pillars covered with what look like prehistoric drawings. The cave drawings are actually only a few centuries old, depicting either Portuguese or Dutch cutters. The boat continues on, gliding by cliffs rising vertically out of the sea, for an afternoon spent in **Maya Bay.** Here the calm, clear waters, sparkling with color from the live coral, are ideal for swimming and snorkeling. Another worthwhile trip is the 45-minute journey by long-tailed boat to **Bamboo Island.** The island is roughly circular and has a superb beach around its circumference. The underwater colors of the fish and the coral are brilliant—reds, yellows, greens, and blues. The island is uninhabited, but you can spend a night under the stars if you like.

In the evening, visitors stroll up and down the pedestrian walkway along the sandbar. Here, numerous small restaurants serve the catch of the day, displayed on ice in big bins outside the restaurants. There are no bars or discos on the island. Even though it has been discovered, Ko Phi Phi is still very laid-back. It's popular with backpackers and others searching for nothing more than sea, sand, and sun.

Dining and Lodging — Restaurants on Phi Phi consist of a row of closely packed one-room cafés down the narrow mall. The menus consist mostly of fish dishes—you choose your fish from the ice bin outside, and the chef cooks it according to your instructions. Prices are well under B200 for two people, including a couple of Singha beers.

More expensive dining can be found at the open-air restaurants to the left of the pier, but the food is essentially the same.

Hotels and bungalow guest houses are congregated on the isthmus where the ferries arrive. The two more luxurious accommodations are off by themselves, 15 minutes by boat or a stiff 45-minute hike from the isthmus.

P.P. International Resort. On the north cape of Laemthong, this is the most expensive resort on the island. Accommodations at this isolated retreat range from standard double rooms to larger deluxe rooms in bungalows with sea views at twice the price. All rooms are air-conditioned, have small refrigerators, and come with a color TV. The terraced restaurant has splendid views of the sea, and the fish is absolutely fresh. *Cape Laemthong, Phi Phi. Reservations: in Bangkok, tel. 02/250–0768; in Phuket, tel. 076/214–297; in Ko Samui, tel. 077/421–228. 120 rooms. Facilities: restaurant serving Thai and European cuisines, water sports and island tours arranged. AE, V. Expensive.*

Pee Pee Cabana and Ton Sai Village. Facing the sea amid coconut palms, these two adjacent hotels are owned by the same management company and offer the best accommodations in the center of Phi Phi. Abutting cliffs, Ton Sai Village is about a 10-minute walk from the ferry docks, and it is the quieter of the two. Rooms are slightly larger than those at Pee Pee Cabana. Both have either air-conditioned or fan-cooled rooms, and their outdoor restaurants offer food similar to that found in the village, but costing twice as much. *Reservations: Pee Pee Marina Travel Co., 201/3–4 Uttarakit Rd., Amphoe Muang, Krabi 81000, tel. 075/612–196; fax 075/612–251. 100 rooms. Facilities: restaurant. No credit cards. Moderate.*

Pee Pee Island Village. In the same vicinity as P.P. International Resort, this hotel offers more modest accommodations in small thatched bungalows. It provides the same water sports and tours as its neighbor, but the service is more casual and the atmosphere more laid-back. Views from the hotel are less impressive, however, although guests do have panoramas of the sea and palm-clad hills. *Cape Laemthing, Phi Phi. Reservations in Bangkok, tel. 02/277–0038; in Phuket, tel. 076/215–014. 65 rooms. Facilities: restaurant, water sports, island tours arranged. AE, V. Moderate.*

Krabi Pee Pee Resort. In the center of the isthmus, this collection of small bungalows in a coconut grove offers clean, simple, fan-cooled rooms with private Asian-style squat toilets and showers. The complex faces Lohdalum Bay, though only a few of the thatched, palm-woven bungalows have views. Guests don't seem to frequent the restaurant, but they do hang around the bar, which faces the bay. Compared with the overpriced costs of other accommodations on the island, this "resort" is the best value. *Lohdalum Bay, Phi Phi. Reservations in Krabi, tel. 075/611–484. 60 rooms. Facilities: restaurant, bar, dive shop. No credit cards. Inexpensive.*

Pee Pee Resort. One of the cheapest places to stay in, this hotel consists of two rows of huts facing the beach. The rooms, each with its own Asian-style toilet, are in these tiny, thatched, palm-woven units. A mosquito net is supplied. A small café, attractively located on a small headland, offers basic Thai food. *Phi Phi. No phone. 40 rooms. No credit cards. Budget.*

Krabi and Ao Phra Nang

On the mainland, 43 km (27 mi) east of Ko Phi Phi, is Krabi, the provincial capital of the region. Once a favorite harbor for smugglers bringing alcohol and tobacco from Malaysia, it has become a fishing port and gateway to the province's offshore islands and famed beaches, particularly Ao Phra Nang Bay.

Tourist Information There is no TAT office in Krabi, although an unofficial tourist information center is located at **Tip House** (49 Prachachem Rd., Krabi, tel. 075/612–015), where you can obtain a free map and make hotel bookings.

Guided Tours No guided tours are offered from Krabi, but customized trips of the area can be made at **Tip House** (*see* above), **Lao Ruam Kij** (11 Khongka Rd., Krabi, tel. 075/611–930), or from one of the many travel shops on Uttarakit Road.

Getting There *Krabi* Two to four ferries a day make the two-hour run between Krabi and Phi Phi. Bookings can be made on Phi Phi Don; the fare is B150. Air-conditioned buses depart from Bangkok's Southern Bus Terminal at 7 PM and 8 PM for the 290-km (180-mi) journey to Krabi. The fare is B290.

Ao Phra Nang To reach Ao Phra Nang, take a songthaew for B20 from Krabi. If you book accommodations for Ao Phra Nang in Krabi, transportation will probably be arranged for you.

Exploring Krabi is a pleasant, low-key town. Most visitors, however, only stop here to do some shopping, cash traveler's checks, arrange onward travel from one of the travel shops, and catch up on the news with fellow travelers idling at the many restaurants on main street, Uttarakit Road. If you have more time, stop off for lunch at the waterfront restaurant, Isouw. Take a table overlooking the estuary; you'll get the best meal in Krabi and a view of all the boat activity in the estuary.

Ao Phra Nang, less than 20 minutes by road from Krabi, is just in the process of being discovered by land speculators. Only one deluxe hotel, the Krabi Resort, is on the island. Unfortunately, it has just extended what was a pleasant, attractive thatched bungalow complex with a new concrete eyesore that professes to have all the modern amenities of Bangkok. Aside from this one hotel, accommodations consist solely of rustic bungalows, in which time is measured only by the sunrise and sunset.

The beaches have fine sand and calm waters, backed by verdant green jungles inland and sheltered by islands offshore. In fact, though windsurfers are available for rent at the Marine Sports Center, the waters are often too calm for enthusiastic sailors. Days are spent on the beach or exploring the islands by boat, particularly Turtle Island and Chicken Island for snorkeling. You can rent boats from the local fishermen or from the Krabi Resort.

Between Krabi and Ao Phra Nang is **Susan Hoi** (Shell Cemetery Beach), aptly named for the 75-million-year-old shells that have petrified to form bizarre-shaped rock slabs. Farther up from Ao Phra Nang Bay is another beach known as **Haad Noppharat Thara,** famed for its rows of casuarina trees. You can walk out to the little rocky island offshore at low tide, but don't linger there too long. When the tide comes in, so does a current. For total seclusion, hire a long-tailed boat to take you the 15 minutes to the empty beaches of Pai Pong or Rai Lee.

Sometime in 1991, the Siam Group of Hotels plans to open a 300-room deluxe hotel tentatively named Paradise Cove Hotel. Facilities will include five restaurants, outdoor pool, tennis, and water sports. Beachcombers may have to renew the search for another idyllic area untouched by developers!

Dining and Lodging In Krabi you have the choice of small Thai restaurants, European breakfast food at the cafés along main street, or more elaborate Thai food at the **Isouw,** a restaurant on stilts over the estuary. In Krabi Town, two basic Thai hotels serve the needs of visiting businessmen, while guest houses for tourists are mostly located around Ao Phra Nang Bay. At press time construction was under way on a new hotel, the **Paradise Cove,** owned and managed by the Siam Lodge Group (Bangkok reservation office, tel. 02/252–6087). When it opens in 1992, it should be the most luxurious hotel in the area.

Dining **Isouw.** Right on the main street of Krabi Town, this restaurant stands on stilts over the water. It is a wonderful place in which to sit, enjoy lunch, and watch the river traffic. The restaurant specializes in grilled fish with sweet-and-sour sauce, and the *mee krob* (fried Thai noodles) here has an abundance of fresh, sweet shrimp. *256/1 Uttarakit Rd., Krabi, tel. 075/611–956. No reservations. Dress: casual. No credit cards. Moderate.*

Lodging **Krabi Resort.** What started as a small collection of thatched cottages on Ao Phra Nang has now mushroomed into a large resort, including a concrete addition to provide another 55 air-conditioned rooms. Modernly furnished, rooms in the new addition are often preferred. The pool is also new, though the beach has greater attraction. Dinners are often feasts, with steaks or steamed fish in soy sauce; you can work off the calories later, in the disco lounge. *Ao Phra Nang. Reservations: 55–57 Pattana Rd., Amphoe Muang, Krabi 81000, tel. 075/611–389. Bangkok reservations: tel. 02/251–8094. 80 rooms. Facilities: restaurant, outdoor pool, disco, boat rental. DC, MC, V. Expensive.*
Emerald Bungalows. On the quiet sandy beach of Haad Noppharat, just north of Ao Phra Nang, this hotel offers the option of tiny bungalows with no bath or larger bungalows with a private bath. Those fronting the beach are the best and the most expensive (B500). The restaurant, which specializes in seafood, is open all day and serves as the gathering place for guests in the evening, not only to eat, but also to socialize and read under the lights. *Haad Noppharat Beach, Moo 4, Tambol Ao Phra Nang. Reservations: 2/1 Kongca Rd., Krabi 81000, tel. 075/611–106. 36 rooms. Facilities: restaurant. No credit cards. Inexpensive.*
Thai Hotel. This hotel in Krabi Town offers standard accommodations—bed, table, chairs, and a private bathroom. It could use a bucket or two of paint, but the staff is willing to help foreign guests. *3 Issara Rd., Amphoe Muang, Krabi 81000, tel. 075/611–389. 100 rooms. Facilities: restaurant. No credit cards. Inexpensive.*

Phang Nga Bay

Halfway between Krabi and Phuket is Phang Nga Bay, made famous by the James Bond movie *The Man with the Golden Gun.* Caves and outcroppings of limestone, some rising 270 m (900 ft) straight up from the sea, are a unique sight.

Getting There Frequent bus service links Phang Nga Town with Krabi and Phuket. Phang Nga Town is located 10 km (6¼ mi) from the bay; most people come here simply to arrange transportation to nearby islands.

Getting Around At the bay, hire a long-tailed boat to tour the islands. Most tourists come to the bay from Phuket and don't arrive until 11 AM. If you can get into the bay before then, it will be more or less yours to explore, with a boatman as your guide. In order to make an early start, you may want to stay overnight. A new hotel on the estuary of the bay, Phang Nga Bay Resort, is comfortable, but lacks atmosphere.

Guided Tours Guided tours of Phang Nga Bay usually begin from Phuket. With travel desks at several hotels, including the Phuket Yacht Club (tel. 076/214–020 ext. WTS) and the Phuket Merlin (tel. 076/212–866 ext. WTS), **World Travel Service** offers one of the most comprehensive tours.

Exploring Phang Nga Bay The key sights to visit are **Ko Panyi,** with its Muslim fishing village built on stilts; **Ko Phing Kan,** now known as James Bond Island; **Ko Tapu,** which looks like a nail driven into the sea; **Tham Kaeo grotto,** an Asian version of Capri; and **Tham Lot,** where a large cave has been carved into an archway large enough to allow cruise boats to pass through. You really need two days to see everything and to appreciate the sunsets, which are particularly beautiful on **Ko Mak.**

Lodging **Phang Nga Bay Resort.** This new hotel's sole raison d'être is as a base for exploring the offshore islands and rocks. Located on an estuary 1½ km (1 mi) from the coast, it does not have panoramic views, but the rooms are comfortable and modern, the bathrooms are clean and large, and the dining room offers reasonable Chinese, Thai, and European food. *20 Thaddan Panyee, Phang Nga 82000, tel. 076/411–067; fax 076/411–057. Bangkok reservations: tel. 02/259–1994. 88 rooms. Facilities: restaurant, coffee shop, tennis, outdoor pool, and boat hire. AE, MC, V. Moderate.*

Ko Samui

Thailand has become inundated with tourists, many of them searching for new destinations untouched by developers. Five hundred km (310 mi) from Bangkok and 30 km (18½ mi) offshore from Surat Thani, in the Gulf of Siam, lies Ko Samui. Backpackers discovered the island several years ago; now, vacationing tourists regard it as an alternative to Phuket. It has already become too commercialized for some people, but there are far fewer hotels, restaurants, and café-bars than on Phuket, and Ko Samui is a veritable haven of tranquillity compared with the seediness of Pattaya.

Ko Samui is half the size of Phuket, and it can be easily toured in a day. But tourists come for the sun and beach, not for sightseeing. The best beaches, those with glistening white sand and clear waters, are on the island's east coast. Beaches on the other coasts either have muddy sand or rocky coves. Already the waters around Ko Samui are less clear than they were years ago. The sea surrounding the small islands nearby is still crystal clear, however, and the tiny islets to the north of Ko Samui that make up the Angthong Marine National Park are superb for snorkeling and scuba diving. Ko Samui has a different weather pattern from Phuket, on the west coast. Typhoons hit Ko Samui in November and December; in Phuket, the monsoon season extends from May to November. Off-season prices are 40% lower than those during peak season (January–June).

Important Addresses and Numbers

Tourist Information
The provincial **TAT** is not on Ko Samui, but on the mainland at Surat Thani (5 Talat Mai Rd., Surat Thani 84000, tel. 077/281–828). The tourist office sells a useful map of Ko Samui (B35) and provides information about guest houses and ferry connections.

Many travel agencies operate out of Surat Thani and Ko Samui's main town, Na Thon. **Songserm Travel Center** (64/1-2 Na Thon, Ko Samui, tel. 077/421–228) operates many of the interisland boats. You can also contact Songserm at its offices in Bangkok (tel. 02/251–8994), Surat Thani (tel. 077/272–928), and Ko Pha Ngan (tel. 077/281–639). A useful travel agency on the east coast of Ko Samui is the **International Air Agency** (63/2 Chaweng Rd., Chaweng Beach, Ko Samui, tel. 077/421–551; fax 077/431–544). For fishing and diving trips, **Fantasia Diving and Yachting** (21 Nathon, Moo 3, Ko Samui, tel. 077/421–289) offers one- to three-day offshore excursions.

Emergencies
The **Tourist Police** (Surat Thani, tel. 077/281–300; Na Thon or Ko Samui, tel. 077/421–281) are the people to call should you encounter any trouble. The **Surat Thani Hospital** is on Surat-Phun Phin Road (tel. 077/272–231).

Warning: Be sure to wear something to protect your feet when wading among the coral. Nasty abrasions can result, and an element in the coral hinders the healing process. Rusty nails in planks of old wood are another hazard.

Arriving and Departing by Plane

Ko Samui has a small airport, served by the 37-seater planes of **Bangkok Airways** (in Bangkok, tel. 02/253–4014; in Ko Samui, tel. 077/421–196), which runs five flights daily between Bangkok and Ko Samui. The cost of a one-way flight is about B1,375. Reservations are crucial during peak periods. **Thai Airways International** flies to Surat Thani on the mainland, from which you must travel by car and then ferry to Ko Samui.

Between the Airport and the Beaches/ Center City
The airport is on the northwest tip of the island. Taxis meet arrivals; their price is fixed—with little room for negotiation—to various parts of the island. The most common price is B200. Some hotels have a limo/van service at the airport, but these cost the same as a taxi. Songthaews sporadically travel between the airport and Ko Samui's main town, Na Thon, for B30.

Arriving and Departing by Train, Bus, and Ferry

By Train
Many express trains from Bangkok's main railway station, Hualamphong (tel. 02/223–7461), pass through Surat Thani on their way south. The journey takes about 12 hours, and the best trains are the overnighters that depart Bangkok at 6:30 PM and 7:20 PM, arriving in Surat Thani soon after 6 AM. The State Railway of Thailand offers a combined ticket that includes rail fare, a couchette in air-conditioned second class, bus connection to the ferry, and the ferry ride for B514. Passengers arrive at Ko

Samui at about 10 AM the following day. First-class sleeping cabins are available only on the 7:20 PM train.

By Bus Buses leave Bangkok from the Southern Bus Terminal (tel. 02/411–0112 for air-conditioned buses; tel. 02/411–4978 for non-air-conditioned ones). Buses cost less than the train (about B225 for air-conditioned buses), and they're a bit faster (11 hours), but they are also less comfortable. Buses do have the advantage of going directly to the ferry terminal. Private tour companies use more comfortable, faster buses; try **Chok Anan** (Ratchadamnoen Klang Ave., tel. 02/281–2277). Express buses also travel between Surat Thani and Phuket.

By Ferry Two ferries cross to Ko Samui from Surat Thani. Songserm's express boat leaves from the town dock and travels downriver before making the 30-minute sea crossing. The other ferry leaves from the pier at Donsak at the mouth of the river, 45 minutes by bus from Surat Thani. This ferry takes about an hour to make the sea passage. A combined bus-ferry ticket is available from one of the many tour/bus companies in Surat Thani. The last ferry to Ko Samui leaves around 4 PM, and the last ferry from Ko Samui departs at 3 PM. Times vary, so be sure to check the schedule.

Scheduled to begin operation in late 1991 is the **Jumbo Ferry,** a 400-seat passenger-and-car ferry that will make the run from Bangkok to Ko Samui (and on to Songkla) in 14 hours. Reclining seats and bunk beds will be available, as well as a restaurant and snack bar. Contact **Navarkun Transport** (70/14 Soi Sukhumvit Rd., Bangna-Prakhanong, Bangkok 10260, tel. 02/398–1170) for reservations and information. Departures are set for Friday at 7 PM from Bangkok, and the fare will range from B450 to B7,000 (depending on if you take your car).

Getting Around

By Songthaew Na Thon on the west coast is the terminus for songthaews (minibuses), which seat eight people. They take either the north route around the island to Cheng Mon on the northwest coast and Chaweng on the northeast coast, or the southern route to reach Lamai on the southeast coast. Their routes never quite link up: From Lamai Beach, you have to travel all the way around the island to reach Chaweng, 1½ km (1 mi) up the coast from where you started! The fare depends on the distance traveled; from Na Thon to Chaweng, the longest journey possible, is B30. Songthaews making the northern trip start from the waterfront north of the pier; those making the southern trip start south of the pier.

Songthaews may also be rented as private taxis. The price from Na Thon to Chaweng is about B250.

By Rental Car and Scooters If you want to explore Ko Samui, it's best to rent your own transportation. Jeeps are expensive, but they're the safest vehicles. Nevertheless, most people choose motor scooters. Gravel, pot holes, and erratic driving make riding on the island dangerous, and each year some travelers return home with broken limbs.

Exploring Ko Samui

Numbers in the margin correspond to points of interest on the Ko Samui map.

❶ The ferry from Donsak on the mainland arrives at **New Port** in Aow Thong Yang, 5 km (3 mi) south of Ko Samui's main town, **❷** **Na Thon.** Unless a hotel van is waiting for you, take a songthaew first to Na Thon, and then another to reach your final destination. The express boat from Surat Thani docks at Na Thon.

Compared with the other sleepy island villages, Na Thon is a bustling town with its shops and restaurants. Most of the restaurants and travel shops are along the waterfront. Commercial shops and banks line the parallel street one block from the waterfront. Though Na Thon has a hotel, tourists seldom stay in town.

On the north coast east of Na Thon, the first major tourist area **❸** is **Maenam.** Its long, curving, sandy beach is lapped by gentle waters that are great for swimming. Inexpensive guest houses can be found along the 5-km (3-mi) stretch of sand. A small **❹** headland separates Maenam from the next bay, **Bophut** (Big Buddha). The sand is not as fine at Bophut and becomes muddy during the rainy season, but the fishing village has become a popular gathering spot for backpackers—numerous village homes have become crash pads, some of which might even be called guest houses. The dramatic sunsets attract photographers and romantics.

Rather than cutting across the island on the main, paved road **❺** to Chaweng, continue along the north shore to **Ko Fan,** a little island with a huge sitting Buddha image covered in moss. Try to visit at sunset, when the light off the water shows the Buddha at its best.

❻ Continue east along the north coast to **Haad Chengmon** (*haad* means beach), dominated by the headland Laem Rumrong. This is the end of the road for the few songthaews that take this route. Few tourists come here because it's off the beaten track. Several guest houses are scattered along the shoreline, as well as Ko Samui's most elegant retreat, the Tongsai Bay Cottages, but you can still find peace and tranquillity.

If you have your own transportation—and don't mind bumping over rutted unpaved roads—the road continues around the peninsula for 6 km (3¾ mi) to **Chaweng Beach.** Of the 11 beach areas of Ko Samui, Chaweng has the finest glistening white sand. It is also Ko Samui's most congested beach, crammed with guest houses and tourists. Chaweng is divided into four **❼** parts: Northern **Chaweng Yai** (*yai* means large) is separated **❽** from **Chaweng Noi** (*noi* means little) to the south by a small point, Laem Koh Faan. Chaweng Yai is further divided by a reef into two sections, of which the northern one is Ko Matland, a quiet area popular with backpackers. The main part of Chaweng Yai is congested with hotels and tanned, scantily clad youths. South of this busy beach is Chaweng Noi, which is only partially developed. It is quieter than Chaweng Yai, and the salt air has yet to be tainted by the odor of suntan oil. At the end of this beach is the island's second-smartest resort, the Imperial Samui Hotel.

Ko Samui

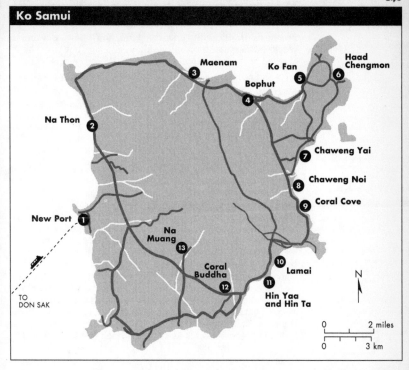

Na Thon

New Port ①

TO
DON SAK

Maenam ③

Bophut ④

Ko Fan ⑤

Haad Chengmon ⑥

Na Thon ②

Chaweng Yai ⑦

Chaweng Noi ⑧

Coral Cove ⑨

Na Muang ⑬

Coral Buddha ⑫

Lamai ⑩

Hin Yaa and Hin Ta ⑪

N

| 0 | | 2 miles |
| 0 | | 3 km |

⑨ Beyond the Imperial Samui Hotel is **Coral Cove,** popular among scuba diving enthusiasts. But you don't even have to be a diver to enjoy the underwater scenery: Just walk waist high into the water and look through a mask to see the amazing colors of the coral. For a Thai seafood lunch, walk up the rocks to Coral Cove Bungalows, where you also can rent snorkeling equipment.

⑩ A rocky headland separates Chaweng from Ko Samui's second most popular beach, **Lamai.** The beach does not have the glistening white sand of Chaweng, but its clear water and rocky pools made this attractive area the first to be developed on Ko Samui. Lamai has a different feel than Chaweng; tourists mingle freely with one another at the local restaurants and bars.

⑪ Every visitor to Ko Samui makes a pilgrimage to Lamai for yet another attraction. At the point marking the end of Lamai beach, two rocks have been named **Hin Yaa** (Grandmother's Rock) and **Hin Ta** (Grandfather's Rock). Erosion has shaped the rocks to resemble weathered and wrinkled grandparents.

⑫ Turn inland, heading back for Na Thon. Two km (1¼ mi) up this road is the **Coral Buddha,** carved by years of erosion. Continue farther on the main road to the village of **Baan Thurian,** where the road to the right climbs up into the jungle-clad hills to the ⑬ island's best waterfall, **Na Muang.** The falls are spectacular, especially after the rains, as they tumble from a limestone cliff to a small sandy pool. You can bathe in the pool, getting cooled by the spray and warmed by the sun. For a thrill, swim through the curtain of falling water; you can sit on a ledge at the back to catch your breath.

Back on the main highway, about 4 km (2½ mi) from Na Thon, the road turns off to the right, twisting for about a mile until it reaches a track leading up a steep hill. You'll have to walk this track, huffing and puffing, for about an hour, but you'll be rewarded at the top with magnificent views and refreshments.

At least one day should be given to a trip out to the 40 islets that make up the **Angthong Marine National Park,** which covers some 250 square km (90 sq mi). The waters, the multicolored coral, and the underwater life are superb. Above water, the rocky islets form weird and wonderful shapes. Songserm operates daily boat trips, departing from Na Thon at 8:30 AM, to the islands for snorkeling and scuba diving; the cost is B150.

Ko Samui is no longer off the beaten track. Travelers looking for the simple beach life with few signs of commercialism now head for **Ko Pha Ngan.** The morning Songserm express boat from Surat Thani continues from Na Thon for 25 km (15 mi) to **Thong Sala,** the main town on Ko Pha Ngan. The island doesn't have any fancy hotels, but guest houses are located on many of its beaches. Since the island's unpaved roads twist and turn, it's easier to beach-hop by boat. In fact, if you want to find the beach that most appeals to you, take a boat trip around the island on the ferries—it takes about nine hours. The southeast tip of the island is divided by a long promontory into **Haad Rin West** and **Haad Rin East,** the island's most popular and crowded areas. Boats from Thong Sala take 40 minutes to reach Haad Rin East; their departure is timed to meet arriving passengers from Songserm's interisland boat. If Haad Rin is too crowded, catch the onward boat up the east coast to **Thong Naay Paan.** Only a few guest houses are located here, and there's plenty of empty beachfront in the perfect horseshoe bay, which is split by a small promontory. The northern beach, Thong Naay Paan Noi, is the smaller and quieter of the two.

Farther north, two small islands, **Ko Tao** and tiny **Ko Nanyuan,** have neither paved roads nor electricity, but both have friendly residents. The boat for Ko Tao leaves three times a week from Thong Sala, and another boat travels daily between Ko Tao and Ko Nanyuan. It is also possible to reach Ko Tao via a boat that runs twice weekly from Chumphon on the mainland.

Dining and Lodging

Ko Samui has yet to establish notable restaurants. Visitors usually dine at their hotels or at one of the many local Thai restaurants. Most of the lodging options on Ko Samui are guest houses, but some resort hotels are located on Lamai, Chaweng, and Cheng Mon beaches. The TAT has a list of guest houses on the islands. Most travel agencies in Bangkok, Surat Thani, and Ko Samui can make reservations at the hotels and at some guest houses.

★ **Tongsai Bay Hotel.** Although the Imperial Samui Hotel is the leading hotel on the island, its sister property, Tongsai Bay, is the elegant resort retreat. Set on 25 acres overlooking Tongsai Bay, the hotel features rooms in whitewashed, red-tiled hillside cottages, each with its own balcony looking out to sea. The remaining 24 rooms are in the three-story main building. Rooms are stylishly furnished, and some of the split-level rooms incorporate the natural rock. The dining room is halfway up the hill, offering beautiful views over the bay. *Tongsai Bay,*

Ko Samui, tel. 077/421–451. Bangkok reservations: tel. 02/ 254–0023; fax 02/253–3190. 80 rooms. Facilities: restaurant, bar, outdoor pool, water sports. AE, DC, MC, V. Very Expensive.

The Imperial Samui. Ko Samui's best international resort hotel, this property is attractively laid out at the top of a landscaped garden terrace with steps leading down to the beach. Guest rooms, which fan out from the main building, are standard, with modern furnishings and little appeal except for the view of the beach. Attention is focused on the swimming pool adjacent to the sea; a small island sits in the pool, complete with three coconut trees. The hotel is located at the south end of Chaweng Noi, where the beach isn't crowded and the sea is clean. The restaurant tends to serve too many boring, albeit satisfying, buffets. *Chaweng Noi Beach, Ko Samui, tel. 077/ 421–390. Bangkok reservations: tel. 02/254–0023, fax 02/253– 3190. 77 rooms. Facilities: restaurant, bar, outdoor pool, water sports. AE, DC, MC, V. Expensive.*

Samui Pansea Hotel. The Pansea may not be quite as smart as its neighbor, the Imperial Samui, but it costs less and is the only other full-service hotel on Chaweng. Set back from the beach, rooms come with fans or, for a few more dollars, air-conditioning. Equipment for water sports is available, and the restaurant offers views over the gulf. *Chaweng Noi Beach, Ko Samui, tel. 077/421–384; fax 077/421–385. 50 rooms. Facilities: restaurant, coffee shop, bar, water sports, drugstore. AE, MC, V. Moderate.*

Fair House. Situated on the beach on Chaweng Noi, this hotel offers small, simple bungalows with air-conditioning or overhead fans, and rudimentary private bathrooms. Each bungalow has its own veranda, but only a few have a clear view of the beach. The open-fronted dining room has broad sea views, and the Thai cuisine—with a few Western dishes—is remarkably good. *Chaweng Noi Beach, Ko Samui, tel. 077/421–373. 26 rooms. Facilities: restaurant, bar. MC, V. Inexpensive.*

Pattaya

Three decades ago, Pattaya was a fishing village on an unspoiled natural harbor 147 km (88 mi) southeast of Bangkok. Discovered by affluent Bangkok residents, it became a weekend playground, replacing Hua Hin and Cha' Am on the southwest coast as vacation destinations. Then came the Vietnam War, when thousands of American soldiers sought release and recreation. With a large U.S. air base at nearby Utapano and a naval base at Cam Ranh, U.S. servicemen hit the beaches at Pattaya in droves and the resort became a boomtown, with a complete range of resort activities to cater to lonely soldiers looking for a good time.

After a few years in the doldrums, Pattaya is booming again. The highway traffic between Bangkok and Pattaya on weekends is congested, often stretching the two-hour trip to four. Pattaya has something tacky for everyone, the most obvious being its many bars and nightclubs catering to foreign males. Conveniently located on the side streets are dozens of clinics to treat venereal diseases. Raw sewage flows into the bay, threatening a dose of hepatitis for anyone foolish enough to swim in the once-crystal-clear waters.

If Pattaya were anywhere else but Thailand, it would be positively distasteful. But it is in Thailand, and somehow what is gross is made agreeable by the smiling Thais. Pattaya is Thailand's total beach resort, offering everything from deep-sea fishing to golf, from windsurfing to visits to elephant kraals.

Arriving and Departing

By Taxi Taxis make the journey from either Don Muang Airport or downtown Bangkok for a quoted B1,500, but the fare is quickly renegotiated to B1,200 or less. Coming back from Pattaya to Bangkok, the fare is only around B750.

By Limousine/Bus Direct buses make the three-hour drive between Pattaya's hotels and Bangkok's Don Muang Airport, leaving every two or three hours from 6 AM to 9 PM. **Thai Limousine Service** has the cleanest, most reliable buses, and they're also air-conditioned. A reservation-and-ticket desk is located in the International Arrivals terminal at Don Muang and at the Royal Cliff Beach Hotel (Jontien Beach, Pattaya, tel. 038/421–421). The cost is B200.

By Bus Buses depart every half hour from Bangkok's Eastern Terminal (Ekkamai) on Sukhumvit Road at Soi 63, about a B70 taxi ride from downtown. They arrive at Pattaya's bus station, in North Pattaya, just off Beach Road. The fare is B50 per person.

By Minibus Most hotels in Bangkok and Pattaya have a travel-agent desk that works directly with a minibus company. Minibuses leave approximately five times a day and cost B150 per person. There is also an Avis-operated minibus that departs from Bangkok's Dusit Thani hotel for its property in Pattaya.

By Ferry A new hydrofoil ferry, the *Thepsirinta*, operates daily departures from the Meanam Hotel pier on the Chao Phraya River, Bangkok to Pattaya. The journey takes three hours and costs B350 in second class, B450 in first class. The schedule varies, and so check departure times a few days in advance of your trip. For information, call: Thai Intertransport (2074/32–38 Thai Intertransport Bldg., New Rd., Yanawa, Bangkok 10200, tel. 02/291–9613).

Getting Around

By Minibus Songthaews cruise the two main streets of Pattaya, which run parallel to the beach. The fare is B5 in Pattaya town, and B10 between Naklua and Pattaya; for the Royal Cliff Resort, the fare is about B50 and at least B100 to Jontien Beach.

By Car/Motorbike Sedans and Jeeps can be rented in Pattaya for B700–B900 a day, with unlimited mileage. Be forewarned, however, that not all rental companies supply insurance. **Avis** (Dusit Resort Hotel, Pattaya, tel. 038/429–901) does offer insurance. Motorbikes may be rented for about B250 a day.

Important Addresses and Numbers

Tourist Information The **Tourist Authority of Thailand** (382/1 Beach Rd., South Pattaya, tel. 038/428–750) has free brochures and listings of festivities and events. The office is open daily 9–5.

Emergencies If you need the **police, fire department,** or an **ambulance,** dial 195, or contact the **Tourist Police** (North Pattaya Beach Rd., Pattaya, tel. 038/429–371).

Travel Agencies **Song Asawin Travel Service** (Beach Rd., Pattaya, tel. 038/423–704) in the South Pattaya Bus Terminal offers discounts on hotels and transportation. **Malibu Travel Co.** (183/82-84 Post Office La., Pattaya, tel. 038/423–180) arranges tours and travel around Pattaya, and to Ko Samet.

Exploring Pattaya

Pattaya can be divided into three sections, running from north to south. To the north, Naklua Beach attracts locals and has few tourist facilities. On a small promontory south of the Dusit Resort Hotel is the picturesque curving bay of Pattaya, which runs alongside Beach Road, lined with palm trees on the beach side and modern resort hotels on the other. At the southern end of the bay is the fun part of town—bars, nightclubs, restaurants, and open-front cafés dominate both the main street (Sunset Avenue) and the side streets.

Parallel to Beach Road is Pattaya 2 Road, with several inexpensive hotels and restaurants, as well as bowling alleys and large massage parlors. Pattaya's main commercial street, this road becomes more congested with traffic and local shops the farther south you go. Continuing through town, Pattaya 2 Road climbs a hill leading past Buddha Park on the left and then descends to quieter Jontien Beach. Relatively secluded in the past, Jontien Beach is now attracting condominium developers and hotels. In 1990 alone, six hotels and condominiums were slated to open, including the Ambassador City, which, when fully completed, will have 5,000 rooms.

The Pattaya resort district follows the bay along Beach Road and its extension, Sunset Avenue. The closer to Sunset Avenue you stay, the greater the number of shops, trinket sellers, and bar-cafés you'll see. Most of these places open soon after 10 AM, but business is slow until late afternoon, when tourists leave the beaches and swimming pools. Bars stay open until 1 AM or 2 AM, although some don't close until the last customer is carried out, shortly before dawn.

Many of Pattaya's diversions are designed more for the Thai family on vacation than for the foreign visitor. However, two attractions are worthwhile if you have not experienced them elsewhere in Thailand. The first is elephants. Since teak logging was restricted, this noble beast suffers from high unemployment, and only an estimated 4,000 of them live in Thailand now. At the **Elephant Kraal,** 14 pachyderms display their skill at moving logs in a two-hour show, twice daily. The show also includes demonstrations by war elephants, an enactment of ceremonial rites, and the capture of a wild elephant. Everything is staged, but it's always rewarding to see elephants at work and at play. *On the main highway 5 km (3 mi) out of Pattaya, tel. 038/428–640. Admission charge. Daily shows 2:30 and 4:30.*

For a more general overview of Thai culture, **Nong Nuch Village** offers a folk show, an exhibition of monkeys picking coconuts, elephants bathing, and a small zoo and aviary. Two restaurants, one Thai and one Western, offer refreshments on rolling grounds covered with coconut plantations. Despite its touristy nature, the village provides a pleasant break from sunbathing on the beach, particularly if you're traveling with children. Hotels will arrange transportation for morning and afternoon visits. *Located 15 km (9 mi) south of Pattaya, 163 km marker on Hwy. 1, Bang Saray, tel. 038/429–321. Admission charge. Open 9–5:30. Daily shows 10 AM and 3 PM.*

If Nong Nuch Village whets your appetite for more exhibits of Thai culture, **Mini Siam** is a miniature village that exhibits 80 models of well-known Thai tourist attractions, such as Wat Phra Keo, Phra Pathom Chedi, and the Victory Monument. *387 Moo 6, Sukhumvit Rd., tel. 038/421–628. Admission charge. Open daily 9–5.*

Participant Sports

Golfing Two championship courses attract golfers from around the world. **The Royal Thai Navy Golf Course** (Phiu Ta Luang Golf Course, Sattahip, Chonburi, tel. 02/466–1180, ext. Sattahip 2217), located 30 km (18 mi) from Pattaya, is Thailand's longest course at 6,800 yards and is considered one of the country's most difficult with rolling hills and dense vegetation. The other course is at the **Siam Country Club** (Pattaya, Chonburi, tel. 038/418–002), situated close to Pattaya and offering a challenging course with awkward water traps and wooded hills.

Water Sports All kinds of water sports are available, including windsurfing (B200 per hour), waterskiing (B1,000 per hour), and sailing on a 16-foot Hobie Catamaran (B500 per hour). Private entrepreneurs offer these activities all along the beach, but the best area is around the **Sailing Club** on Beach Road. Water scooters (B250 per hour) and parasailing (B250 for 10 minutes) are also offered, but these sports are dangerous and shouldn't be tried for the first time here. Be on the lookout for unscrupulous operators who rent a defective machine and hold the customer responsible for its repair or loss. Parasailing boat operators tend to be inexperienced, making sharp turns or sudden stops that bring the parachutist down too fast.

Diving and Snorkeling The clear waters and sea life of the coral reefs around Pattaya's offshore islands are ideal for snorkeling and scuba diving, and the beaches are less crowded than in Pattaya. These islands may be reached in approximately one hour aboard converted fishing trawlers. **Ko Larn** is the nearest and most popular of the three nearby islands. At the Sailing Club you can catch the boat, which departs at 9:30 AM and 11 AM and returns at 4:30 PM. The fare is B120. The southern bay has restaurants and quiet beaches. Farther offshore and without facilities are **Ko Rin** and **Ko Phai;** don't forget to take along your lunch. If you can, charter a boat for the day (approximately B2,000). Boats leave from the old fishing pier and the Sailing Club.

Several operators offer boats and equipment for snorkeling and scuba diving. For your well-being, select a licensed dive shop, such as the **Seafari Sports Center** (South Pattaya Beach Rd., tel. 038/429–060).

Dining

Every type of cuisine seems to be available in Pattaya. Visitors may find it harder to find good Thai restaurants here than other types of eateries, though several rather earthy Thai restaurants are located in the center of town, back from the tourist strip. With the Gulf of Siam at Pattaya's doorstep, seafood is the local specialty.

Expensive **Buccaneer Terrace.** The view of the bay from this rooftop restaurant in the Nipa Lodge Hotel is its prime attraction, although it also offers a good choice of fresh seafood and grilled steaks. *Beach Rd., Pattaya, tel. 038/428–195. Reservations accepted. Dress: casual but neat. AE, DC, MC, V.*

Dolf Riks. The menu here reflects Dolf's many years in Indonesia before settling in Pattaya. A very reasonable *rijsttafel* (a Dutch Indonesian meal consisting of many dishes, including chicken with jackfruit, beef and grated coconut, spicy vegetables and rice) improved by Thai spices is the specialty, but the European dishes are superior, as is the seafood casserole. Only good-quality ingredients are used. The bar is popular with expatriates and the few tourists who find this oasis. *463/28 Sri Nakorn Centre, N. Pattaya, tel. 038/428–269. Reservations accepted. Dress: casual but neat. AE, DC, MC, V. Expensive.*

Peppermill Restaurant. Tucked away next to P.K. Villa, this distinctly French restaurant takes a classical approach to dining, with an emphasis on flambéed dishes. More creative dishes such as fresh crab in a white-wine sauce and poached fillet of sole with a lobster tail are also offered. Dinner is a special occasion, here, particularly if complemented by a good bottle of wine from the respectable cellar. *16 Beach Rd., tel. 038/428–248. Reservations accepted. Dress: casual but neat. AE, DC, MC, V. Dinner only.*

Moderate **Nang Nual.** Next to the transvestite Simon Cabaret night spot, this restaurant is one of Pattaya's better places for seafood, cooked Thai-style or simply grilled. The huge steaks are an expensive treat. Similar dishes are found at Nang Nual's Jontien Beach branch, located near the Sigma Resort. *214–10 South Pattaya Beach Rd., Pattaya, tel. 038/428–478. No reservations. Dress: casual. AE, MC, V.*

Pinocchio. This good Italian restaurant serves homemade pasta and fish dishes. The neat dining room, with pale pink tablecloths, has the ambience of a small European restaurant rather than that of a Thai eatery. *215/7 Pattaya 2 Rd., Pattaya, tel. 038/426–269. Dress: casual. No credit cards.*

Tak Nak Nam. In a Thai pavilion at the edge of a small lake, this floating restaurant has an extensive menu of Chinese and Thai dishes. Live classical Thai and folk music is played while you dine on such specialties as steamed crab in coconut milk or blackened chicken with Chinese herbs. *252 Pattaya Central Rd., next to the Pattaya Resort Hotel, tel. 038/429–059. Reservations accepted. Dress: casual. MC, V.*

Lodging

The Pattaya area has more than 500 hotels. With the exception of the Royal Cliff Hotel, most deluxe hotels line South Pattaya Beach Road, with their choice guest rooms overlooking the bay. Less expensive hotels are generally a block or two from the shore. Hotel tariffs fluctuate widely, depending on the season, the day of the week, and on holiday periods, when they can more than double. The congestion of hotels on Pattaya's beachfront has spawned a rapid development of hotels and condominiums all along Jontien Beach, a B150 taxi ride to the south.

Very Expensive **Royal Cliff Beach Hotel.** Pattaya's most lavish accommodation, this hotel is 1½ km (1 mi) south of Pattaya on a bluff jutting into the Gulf of Siam. The self-contained resort has three wings. The least expensive rooms are those in the main building facing the parking lot. Rooms in the Royal Wing are double the price of a standard deluxe room in the main building; for all of these 84 one-bedroom suites there is butler service, breakfast is served in the room, and a deck chair is reserved for you at the pool. The Royal Cliff Terrace has two-bedroom and honeymoon suites with four-poster beds. The swimming pool sits on top of a cliff and overlooks the sea. *Jontien Beach, Pattaya, Chonburi, tel. 038/421–421. Bangkok reservations: tel. 02/282–0999. 700 rooms and 100 suites. Facilities: 4 restaurants, 3 outdoor pools, 2 private beaches, 2 floodlighted tennis courts, 2 squash courts, minigolf course, jogging track, sauna, water sports, pastry shop, boutique shops. AE, DC, MC, V.*

Expensive **Dusit Resort Hotel.** On a promontory at the northern end of
★ Pattaya Beach, this large hotel opened in 1989 and offers superb sea views. The spacious rooms feature large bathrooms, balconies, oversize beds, sitting areas, and pastel furnishings. The Landmark Rooms are even more spacious and make extensive use of wood trim. At the Peak restaurant, contemporary French cuisine is served against the backdrop of Pattaya Bay and the gulf. For daytime pleasure, guests can use the two swimming pools or visit the two small beach areas. While the Dusit is a retreat from the Pattaya tourists, it is also only a B5 songthaew ride along Pattaya Beach Road to where all the action is. *240/2 Pattaya Beach Rd., Pattaya, Chonburi 20260, tel. 038/425–611. Bangkok reservations: tel. 02/236–0450. 500 rooms and 28 suites. Facilities: 4 restaurants, 2 outdoor pools, 3 floodlighted tennis courts, 2 squash courts, fitness center, sauna, water sports, billiards and snooker room, table tennis, boutique shops. AE, DC, MC, V.*

Montien. Though not plush, this hotel has a central location and design that takes advantage of the cool sea breezes. With the hotel's generous off-season discounts, a room with a sea view can be one of the best values in town. The air-conditioned section of the newly renovated Garden Restaurant has a dance floor and stage for entertainment. *Pattaya Beach Rd., Pattaya, Chonburi 20260, tel. 038/418–155. Bangkok reservations: tel. 02/233–7060. 320 rooms. Facilities: 2 restaurants, 24-hr coffee shop, outdoor pool with snack bar, 2 floodlighted tennis courts, cocktail lounge with live music, meeting rooms. AE, DC, MC, V.*

The Royal Cruise Hotel. Easily recognized by its shiplike exterior, this new hotel employs a nautical motif throughout, with anchor designs on the carpets and guest rooms called cabins. Regular guest rooms have an angled view of the bay, while the suites have a frontal view. A decor of pastels and teak give the hotel a comfortable feeling. For a romantic evening, sample the ninth-floor restaurant with its sweeping views of the bay and French-style cuisine. *499 North Pattaya Beach Rd., Pattaya, Chonburi 20260, tel. 038/424–242. Bangkok reservations: tel. 02/233–5970. 190 rooms and 10 suites. Facilities: restaurant, coffee shop, outdoor pool with poolside bar, health center, sauna, business center, travel desk. AE, DC, MC, V.*

Inexpensive **Diamond Beach Hotel.** In the heart of Pattaya's nightlife section amid discos and cafés, this hotel is a bastion of sanity. Rooms are clean, and security guards make female guests feel safe. The staff, however, is not particularly friendly or helpful—perhaps that's why you can often find a room here when other hotels are full. *373/8 Pattaya Beach Rd., Pattaya, Chonburi 20260, tel. 038/418–071. 126 rooms. Facilities: restaurant, travel desk, massage room. No credit cards.*

Palm Lodge. This no-frills hotel has the benefit of being centrally located, quiet, and inexpensive. Guest rooms are sparsely furnished and don't have carpeting, bathrooms are basic, and the outdoor pool is small. The staff is reliable, however. *Beach Rd., Pattaya, Chonburi 20260, tel. 038/428–780. 80 rooms. Facilities: coffee shop, outdoor pool, laundry services. MC, V.*

Budget **The Nag's Head.** Owned by an Englishman, this small hotel opened in 1989 and offers some of the cleanest, most inexpensive air-conditioned rooms with private baths in Pattaya. Its location on a busy road is not the best, but the friendly atmosphere makes this the top choice in the budget category. On the ground floor is an open-front bar and a restaurant inside that serves British fare. *179 Pattaya 2 Rd., Pattaya, Chonburi 20260, tel. 038/418–264. 15 rooms. Facilities: restaurant, bar. No credit cards.*

Nightlife

Entertainment in Pattaya centers around the bars, bar-cafés, discos, and nightclubs. You can choose from hundreds of them, but one doesn't differ much from the next. One popular night spot is the **Pattaya Palladium** (tel. 038/424–922), which bills itself as the largest disco in Southeast Asia. The **Marina Disco** in the Regent Marina Hotel (S. Pattaya Rd., tel. 038/429–568) has a laser light show, live entertainment, and three DJs who keep the activity going until the wee hours of the morning. Bars and clubs stay open past midnight, and some are open much later. Discos usually have a cover charge of B100 and drinks cost about B50. Drinks for any hostess who joins you are B100.

Excursion to Ko Samet and Chantaburi

Pattaya is often used as a base for trips farther south to the beach resort of Ko Samet or even to the mining district of Chantaburi. You can visit either of these destinations in a day, but not both.

Getting There Travel companies will arrange transportation to Ko Samet. Try the **Malibu Travel Centre** (Post Office La., Pattaya, tel. 038/423–180), which has daily 8 AM departures for B120. You can also travel by local bus or by car to Ban Phe and transfer onto the ferry. Buses go to Rayong, where you pick up the minibus (departs from behind the Clock Tower) to Ban Phe. The total journey takes about two hours.

Exploring If you travel by car, take the main highway (H3) south. A right turn off H3 at the 165-km marker will lead you to the village of **Bang Saray,** 20 km (12 mi) from Pattaya. The village consists of jetties, a fishing fleet, a small temple, and two narrow streets running parallel to the bay. Fully equipped game-fishing craft are tied up to the jetty, and photos to prove fishermen's stories are posted in the area's two hotel bars, Fisherman's Lodge and

Fisherman's Inn. It costs about B2,500 to charter one of the faster fishing boats for the day. If you just want to soak up the scene, stop next to the main jetty at the Ruam Talay Restaurant, where most people congregate when they're not at the beach. Windsurfers are available for rent at the beach, just north of the bay at the Sea Sand Club.

Back on H3, drive through Sattahip, a Thai naval base, or you can avoid this busy town by taking bypass H332. The road passes through countryside full of coconut groves and tapioca plantations. **Rayong**, 15 km (9 mi) from Sattahip, is a booming market town, famous for its seafood and *nam plaa*, the fermented fish sauce Thais use as a salt substitute. **Ban Phe** is 20 km (12 mi) farther.

Two ferries from Ban Phe make the 30-minute crossing to **Ko Samet** (fare: B20): One goes to Na Duan on the north shore, the other to An Wong Duan on the east shore. All of the island's beaches are an easy walk from these villages. Ko Samet is known for its beaches. The other name for Ko Samet is Ko Kaeo Phitsadan (meaning "sand like crushed crystal"), and its fine sand is in great demand by glassmakers. The shape of the island is like an 8-km- (5-mi-) long screw. The island's wide head, which faces the mainland, quickly narrows so that the strip of land penetrating south is no wider than a mile. Tucked into each curve of the shore is a beach, and each beach is different.

Ko Samet doesn't have any big, luxury hotels, just numerous bungalows and cottages, some with and some without electricity. Make sure that your bungalow has mosquito netting: Ko Samet's mosquitoes are malarial. After dusk, cover yourself up or use repellent. Malaria is not very easy to catch, but if you do start showing symptoms, make your way to the Rayong Hospital, which has a malaria clinic.

East of Rayong near the Kampuchea border is Chantaburi, 180 km (108 mi) from Pattaya. Buses from both Rayong and Ban Phe make the 90-minute journey. Much of the jewelry that you find sold in Pattaya contains gemstones from the open-pit mines around this ancient town. Star sapphires and rubies are the two most popular stones. You can take a tour of the mining area and see the 9-m- (30-ft-) deep holes where prospectors dig in hopes of finding priceless gems.

Chantaburi is divided in two by its river, and it is surrounded by lush rain forests. The town is home to Thailand's largest Christian house of worship, the Church of the Immaculate Conception, built by Catholic Vietnamese who fled persecution by the Emperor Gia Long in the mid-1880s.

Hua Hin and Cha' Am

Hua Hin's glory days were in the 1920s, when the royal family built a palace there in which to spend its summers. The royal entourage would travel the 198 km (123 mi) from Bangkok on special trains, and high society followed. After World War II, the resort lost favor to Pattaya, and Hua Hin became a quiet town once again. Pattaya's seedy reputation has caused Thais and foreign visitors to reconsider Hua Hin and its neighbor Cha' Am as beach resorts close to the capital. In the last several years, the area has enjoyed a boom in the construction of resort hotels and condominiums.

Cha' Am and Hua Hin are low-key destinations. Nightlife is restricted mostly to the hotels. During the day, Hua Hin is a busy market town, but most tourists are at the beach, only coming into town in the early evening to wander through the bazaars before dinner. There is no beachfront road to attract boisterous crowds; so stretches of beach remain deserted. Beaches have gently sloping drop-offs, and the waters are usually calm. The only drawback is the occasional invasion of jellyfish—check for them before you plunge in.

Arriving and Departing

By Car A few hotels, such as the Regent and Dusit Thani, run minibuses between their Bangkok and Cha' Am/Hua Hin properties for a flat fee of B200. Nonguests may use these. Otherwise, you can hire a car and driver for approximately B1,750 or B2,500 to or from the airport.

By Train The train from the Bangkok Noi station in Thonburi takes four long hours to reach Hua Hin's delightful wooden train station (Damnernkasem Rd., tel. 032/511–073).

By Bus Buses, air-conditioned and nonair-conditioned, depart from the Southern Bus Terminal in Bangkok every half hour during the day. Express air-conditioned buses take three hours to reach Hua Hin's terminal (Srasong Rd., tel. 032/511–654).

By Ferry The *Thepsirinta* hydrofoil that runs between Bangkok and Pattaya also includes Cha' Am, some days with a stop in Pattaya and some days direct. Contact Thai Intertransport (2074/32–38 Thai Intertransport Bldg., next to the Meanam Hotel, New Rd., Yanawa, Bangkok 10200, tel. 02/291–9613; in Cha' Am, tel. 032/471–145) for scheduled departures.

Getting Around

Taxis are available, but bicycle *samlors* (small tricycle cabs) are more convenient for short distances. You can walk to most of the sights in town, but if you are staying at a resort hotel in Cha' Am, use the hotel shuttle bus or take a taxi. Tours to nearby attractions are arranged through your hotel. Local buses frequently travel along the main highway, making it easy to travel between Cha' Am and Hua Hin, as well as points south of Hua Hin.

Important Addresses and Numbers

Tourist Information The **Hua Hin Tourist Information Center** is near the railway station. *114 Phetkasem Rd., tel. 032/512–120. Open daily 8:30–4:30.*

Emergencies The town doesn't have any Tourist Police; in an emergency, contact the local police in Hua Hin (tel. 032/511–027) or in Cha' Am (tel. 032/471–321). The local hospital is in **Hua Hin** (Phetkasem Rd., tel. 032/511–743).

Exploring Hua Hin and Cha' Am

On the east side of the highway at the northern boundary of Hua Hin is the royal summer palace. Every April, the king and queen spend a month here, during which they celebrate the anniversary of their royal wedding. The palace was completed in

1928 by King Rama VII, who named it Klai Kangwol ("far from worries"). Four years later, while he was staying at Klai Kangwol, the army seized power in Bangkok, demanding that he relinquish absolute power for a constitutional monarchy. He agreed, and the generals later apologized for their lack of courtesy.

The highway to the southern provinces passes through the center of Hua Hin. In fact, it's the town's main street, with shops and cafés lining the sidewalk; a congested street of market stalls and buses runs parallel to the main street. Toward the southern end of town is the quaint wooden railway station. Across the tracks is the respected **Royal Railway Golf Course;** nonmembers can play the par-72 course. You can rent clubs, and a coffee lounge offers refreshments. In the opposite direction, toward the beach, is the local tourist office, which has a friendly staff, but limited information.

Across the main road from the tourist office is Damnernkasem Road, which leads to the public beach. Lining both sides of the street are shops for tourists and moderately priced hotels. Near the end of the street on the right-hand side, you will see the **Sofitel Central Hua Hin Resort,** formerly the Royal Hua Hin Railway Hotel, which hosted royalty and Thailand's elite during the town's glory days. The magnificent Victorian-style colonial building was portrayed as the French Embassy in Phnom Penh in the film *The Killing Fields*. Be sure to wander through the property's well-tended gardens and then along the verandas of the hotel.

Fifty yards farther down the road is the public beach. On your way to the beach, keep your eyes open for **Nab Chai Hat Lane,** just before the Sofitel, where Damnernkasem Road becomes closed to traffic. Several small restaurants are located here, which are excellent places to keep in mind for dinner. Most have their offerings displayed on slabs of ice. You choose the fish, negotiate a fair price, and then take a table and order any other dishes and drinks you want. Farther down Nab Chai Hat, past numerous inexpensive guest houses, is **Fisherman's Wharf.** It's alive with activity in the morning when the catch comes in, but is less interesting in the afternoon.

Retracing your steps to Damnernkasem Road, take a left and walk past the souvenir stalls to the public beach. If you look south along the coast you'll see a small hill, **Khao Takiab,** and a small island, **Koh Singto.** You can reach the headland by taking a songthaew from across the road from the tourist office or from the main bus station, but the fun way to get there is to hire a pony and trot along the beach. The 7-km (4-mi) stretch leads past the Sofitel, the Royal Garden Hotel, the Sai Lom Hotel, and past villas until the beach becomes virtually deserted. You will eventually reach the beach of Khoa Takiab (the village is a little way inland), where, unfortunately, three tall condominiums are under construction. At the end of the beach where restaurant stalls abound, dismount for the steep climb past a large statue of the Lord Buddha up to the small Buddhist monastery at the summit—the views are worth the climb. Then if you can, rent a fishing boat at the base of Khao Takiab to cross over to Koh Singto, where you are guaranteed a catch within an hour.

About 40 km (25 mi) south of Hua Hin is the **Sam Roi Yod National Park,** with rice fields, sugar palms, pineapple plantations, and crab farms. The charming fishing village of **Wang Daeng** is typical of coastal Thailand 20 years ago. Farther south, the countryside is even more magnificent, with jungle-clad hills and a curving shoreline. Be sure to travel as far as the fishing village of **Ao Noi** and the city of **Prachuab,** about 90 km (56 mi) south of Hua Hin. For staggering panoramic views, climb the hills at the back of the bay.

Dining and Lodging

The restaurants along Nab Chai Hat in Hua Hin offer a warm ambience and good value, especially for fresh seafood. For Western food, it's best to eat at one of the major hotels. Hotels are completely booked during Thai holiday weekends; so reservations should be made in advance. At other times, you shouldn't have any problems making reservations. During peak season—October through mid-March—the prices are nearly double those in the off-season.

Dining **Market Seafood Restaurant.** The nautical decor sets the tone for the Royal Garden Resort's excellently prepared gulf seafood—clams, lobsters, mussels, sea-tiger prawns, and crabs. Depending on your taste, these can be cooked with Thai spices (such as lobster with garlic and peppers) or simply grilled. *107/1 Phetkasem Rd., tel. 032/511–881. Reservations accepted. Dress: casual but neat. AE, DC, MC, V. Expensive.*

Sang Thai. For interesting seafood dishes—from grilled prawns with bean noodles to fried grouper with chili and tamarind juice—this open-air restaurant down by Fisherman's Wharf has been consistently popular with Thais. Certainly, the extensive menu is appealing, but you need to close your eyes to the ramshackle surroundings and floating debris in the water. Don't miss the *kang* (mantis prawns). *Naresdamri Rd., tel. 032/512–144. No reservations. Dress: casual. DC, MC, V. Moderate.*

Lodging **Sofitel Hua Hin Resort.** Even if you don't stay here, visit to experience the Old World charm of this tastefully renovated hotel. Wide verandas fan out in an arc, following the lines of the wooden building, which opens onto gardens leading down to the beach. The lounges around the reception area are open to the sea breezes, and the airiness revives memories of Somerset Maugham. The best guest rooms are those on the second floor with sea views. Less attractive are the additional units in an annex across the street. *1 Damnernkasem Rd., Hua Hin 77110, tel. 032/512–021; fax 032/511–014. Bangkok reservations: tel. 02/233–0974. 154 rooms. Facilities: 2 restaurants, coffee shop, bar and nightclub, outdoor pool, tennis courts, water sports, conference facilities. AE, DC, MC, V. Very Expensive.*

Royal Garden Resort. Adjacent to the Sofitel, this hotel offers accommodations and service equal to those of its neighbor. Because it doesn't have the colonial ambience, however, the prices are a few hundred baht less. The hotel tends to draw a younger set, attracted by the nightclub and the proximity to the beach. Guest rooms are decorated with modern, unimaginative furniture. The hotel's Market Seafood Restaurant is less elegant than Sofitel's Salathai, but serves better food. The Jungle is Hua Hin's hottest disco. *107/1 Phetkasem Rd., Hua Hin 77110, tel. 032/511–881; fax 032/512–422. Bangkok reservations: tel. 02/255–8822. 215 rooms. Facilities: 2 restaurants, coffee shop, cocktail lounge, evening entertainment, outdoor pool, tennis* *courts, water sports, children's playground. AE, DC, MC, V. Very Expensive.*

★ **Dusit Resort & Polo Club.** Although this resort opened in early 1991, the polo grounds and riding stables are still to be added. Perhaps not so many guests will be playing polo, but the game's availability establishes the tone—smart, exclusive, and luxurious. The spacious lobby serves as a lounge for afternoon tea and evening cocktails to the soft tunes of the house musicians. To the side of the lobby overlooking the pool area is the polo bar, designed to give the feeling of a London club. Beyond the ornamental lily pond out front is the swimming pool with bubbling fountains, and beyond that is the beach. Facing the lily pond is the Palm Court, the main dining room serving Thai, Chinese, and European fare. Off to the left is the San Marco, an alfresco Italian restaurant. To the right is the Benjarong, featuring Royal Thai cuisine in a traditional Thai-style pavilion. All the guest rooms have private balconies and a pool or direct sea view. The rooms are furnished in pastels. If you need extra space, select one of the "Landmark" rooms that have separate living rooms and indulgent bathrooms. *1349 Petchkasem Rd., Cha' Am, Petchburi 76120, tel. 032/520–009, fax 032/520–010. Bangkok reservations, tel. 02/238–4790. 308 rooms and suites. Facilities: 4 restaurants, 2 bars, pool, children's pool, riding stables, polo ground, watersports, boat rentals including speedboats for waterskiing and parasailing, fitness center, 2 squash courts, private in-room safes, shuttle service to Hua Hin, car service to Bangkok, and banquet facilities. AE, DC, MC, V. Expensive–Very Expensive.*

★ **Regent Cha' Am.** A modern beach resort, this hotel has everything from water sports to gourmet dining to shopping arcades. The Lom Fang restaurant, overlooking the lake at the back of the hotel, serves excellent fish with a spiced-curry-and-lime sauce. The more formal restaurant, the Tapien Thong Grill Room, offers seafood and steak. Some guest rooms are located in bungalows, a number of which face the beach (no. 309 looks onto the sea and is away from the main building), while others are housed in one of two 12-story buildings set back from the beach. Gardens separate the bungalows, the main building, two large outdoor pools, and two smaller outdoor pools. The gold-sand beach is well patrolled for privacy. In the evening, a small group sings Western songs in Thai. The hotel has its own car service from Bangkok. *849/21 Cha' Am Beach, Petchburi, tel. 032/471–480; fax 032/471–492. Bangkok reservations, tel. 02/251–0305; fax 02/253–5143. 400 rooms. Facilities: 3 restaurants, coffee shop, 2 large and 2 small outdoor pools, water sports, nightly entertainment. AE, DC, MC, V. Expensive–Very Expensive.*

The Pran Buri Beach Resort. This isolated holiday complex south of Hua Hin offers a collection of small bungalow units along the shore. The first row of bungalows facing the beach is obviously the best. Though simply furnished, guest rooms have their own terraces and come with a minibar, telephone, and TV with in-house VCR. The main lodge contains the bar/lounge and dining room, where Thai, Chinese, and Western food is served. The atmosphere is laid-back, casual, and fun. *9 Parknampran Beach, Prachuapkhirikhan 77220, tel. 032/621–701. Bangkok reservations: tel. 02/233–3871; fax 02/235–0049. 60 rooms. Facilities: outdoor pool, 2 tennis courts, fitness center, sailboats, conference center. AE, DC, MC, V. Expensive.*

Hua Hin Raluek. Centrally located on the main tourist street, this hotel has bungalow cottages in its courtyard. Rooms have huge double beds and not much else, but the price is right. The terrace restaurant facing the street stays open late and is a popular spot from which to watch the parade of vacationers walking past. *16 Damnernkasem Rd., Hua Hin 77110, tel. 032/ 511–755. 61 rooms. Facilities: restaurant/coffee shop. MC, V. Inexpensive–Moderate.*

Thanan-Chai Hotel. Located on the north side of Hua Hin, this hotel supplies the basic amenities of clean guest rooms, friendly service, and a coffee lounge that serves breakfast and light fare throughout the day. Its quiet location, friendly staff, and modest price are its assets, but you do have to walk to the beach. *11 Damrongraj Rd., Hua Hin 77110, tel. 032/511–940. 41 rooms. Facilities: coffee shop. MC, V. Inexpensive–Moderate.*

Index

Personal Itinerary

Departure	*Date*	
	Time	
Transportation		
Arrival	*Date*	*Time*
Departure	*Date*	*Time*
Transportation		
Accommodations		
Arrival	*Date*	*Time*
Departure	*Date*	*Time*
Transportation		
Accommodations		
Arrival	*Date*	*Time*
Departure	*Date*	*Time*
Transportation		
Accommodations		

Personal Itinerary

Arrival *Date*   *Time*

Departure *Date*   *Time*

Transportation

Accommodations

Arrival *Date*   *Time*

Departure *Date*   *Time*

Transportation

Accommodations

Arrival *Date*   *Time*

Departure *Date*   *Time*

Transportation

Accommodations

Arrival *Date*   *Time*

Departure *Date*   *Time*

Transportation

Accommodations

Personal Itinerary

Arrival	*Date*	*Time*
Departure	*Date*	*Time*
Transportation		
Accommodations		

Arrival	*Date*	*Time*
Departure	*Date*	*Time*
Transportation		
Accommodations		

Arrival	*Date*	*Time*
Departure	*Date*	*Time*
Transportation		
Accommodations		

Arrival	*Date*	*Time*
Departure	*Date*	*Time*
Transportation		
Accommodations		

Personal Itinerary

Arrival *Date*   *Time*

Departure *Date*   *Time*

Transportation

Accommodations

Arrival *Date*   *Time*

Departure *Date*   *Time*

Transportation

Accommodations

Arrival *Date*   *Time*

Departure *Date*   *Time*

Transportation

Accommodations

Arrival *Date*   *Time*

Departure *Date*   *Time*

Transportation

Accommodations

Addresses

Name

Address

Telephone

Name

Address

Telephone

Name

Address

Telephone

Name

Address

Telephone

Name

Address

Telephone

Name

Address

Telephone

Name

Address

Telephone

Name

Address

Telephone

Name

Address

Telephone

Name

Address

Telephone

Name

Address

Telephone

Name

Address

Telephone

Name

Address

Telephone

Name

Address

Telephone

Name

Address

Telephone

Name

Address

Telephone

Addresses

Name

Name

Address

Address

Telephone

Telephone

Name

Name

Address

Address

Telephone

Telephone

Name

Name

Address

Address

Telephone

Telephone

Name

Name

Address

Address

Telephone

Telephone

Name

Name

Address

Address

Telephone

Telephone

Name

Name

Address

Address

Telephone

Telephone

Name

Name

Address

Address

Telephone

Telephone

Name

Name

Address

Address

Telephone

Telephone

Fodor's Travel Guides

U.S. Guides

Foreign Guides

Wall Street Journal Guides to Business Travel

Special-Interest Guides